Lisunov L

The Soviet DC-3

Yefim Gordon, Sergey Komissarov
and Dmitriy Komissarov

MIDLAND
An imprint of
Ian Allan Publishing

Lisunov Li-2: The Soviet DC-3

ISBN (10) 1 85780 228 4
ISBN (13) 978 1 85780 228 3

Published by Midland Publishing
4 Watling Drive, Hinckley, LE10 3EY, England
Tel: 01455 254 490 Fax: 01455 254 495
E-mail: midlandbooks@compuserve.com

Midland Publishing is an imprint of
Ian Allan Publishing Ltd

Worldwide distribution (except North America):
Midland Counties Publications
4 Watling Drive, Hinckley, LE10 3EY, England
Telephone: 01455 254 450 Fax: 01455 233 737
E-mail: midlandbooks@compuserve.com
www.midlandcountiessuperstore.com

North American trade distribution:
Specialty Press Publishers & Wholesalers Inc.
39966 Grand Avenue, North Branch, MN 55056, USA
Tel: 651 277 1400 Fax: 651 277 1203
Toll free telephone: 800 895 4585
www.specialtypress.com

Design concept and layout by
Polygon Press Ltd (Moscow, Russia)
Colour artwork by the late Sergey Yershov

This book is illustrated with photos by Yefim Gordon, Dmitriy Komissarov, Sergey Komissarov, Martin Novak, Adrian Curley, ITAR-TASS, Wojskowa Agencja Fotograficzna, as well as from the archives of Yefim Gordon, Sergey and Dmitriy Komissarov, Wacław Hołys, AVICO Press, and the Russian Aviation Research Trust

Printed in England by
Ian Allan Printing Ltd
Riverdene Business Park, Molesey Road,
Hersham, Surrey, KT12 4RG

Visit the Ian Allan Publishing website at:
www.ianallanpublishing.com

Contents

Title page: A wartime shot of a PS-84 of Aeroflot's Moscow Special Mission Air Group. It is armed with a single ShKAS machine gun in an MV-3 dorsal turret. Note the propeller spinners and the smooth bottoms of the engine nacelles broken only by the carburettor inlet scoops, revealing that this is an early-production machine.
This page: A post-war shot of a late-production Li-2T (CCCP-06134); note the chin-mounted oil coolers and the dorsal carburettor intake scoops.

Front cover: The ill-fated Li-2T 01300 ФЛА РФ (that is, 01300 FLA RF, c/n 23441605) flies above the Russian countryside.
Rear cover, top: A Li-2T at the Central Russian Air Force Museum in Monino; bottom: This Li-2 with overpainted windows is part of the Great Patriotic War Memorial in Kiev.

Introduction

The Douglas DC-3 is an aircraft enjoying an unparalleled renown in many countries. The Soviet Union was no exception to this.

In the early 1930s the Douglas Aircraft Company, which until then had specialised in military aircraft, initiated development of a machine to meet the specification issued by Transcontinental & Western Air (TWA, later Trans World Airlines) for a twin-engined passenger aircraft. The objective was to match or excel the performance of the Boeing 247 airliner operated by the TWA's competitor United Airlines. Powered by two 710-hp Wright SGR-1820F3 Cyclone radials, the DC-1 (Douglas, Commercial, First) prototype, which became progenitor of the famous family of Douglas airliners and transports, took to the air at Santa Monica, California, in July 1933. In 1934 and 1935 this aircraft set two transcontinental aircraft speed records.

Although only one DC-1 was ever built and delivered, it served as a basis for developing the improved DC-2 with higher seating capacity and uprated 835-hp SGR-1820FS2 engines which first flew on 11th May 1934 and entered series production in mid-1934 – again with TWA as the launch customer. These machines were to quickly become popular thanks to high performance, reliability and economic efficiency. The DC-2 was the first Douglas airliner to be exported (to Czechoslovakia, Finland and the Netherlands).

December 1935 saw the appearance of the DC-3 on which the oval-section fuselage of the DC-1/DC-2 permitting two-abreast seating only gave place to a new, more capacious circular-section fuselage and three-abreast seating. Additionally, the aircraft had new outer wings with increased leading-edge sweepback and zero trailing-edge sweep and a larger, recontoured tail unit. The first version of the DC-3, known as the DST (Douglas Skysleeper Transport), entered flight test on 17th December 1935 (incidentally, the 32nd anniversary of the Wright brothers' historic flight!); it was equipped with seats that could be transformed into sleeping berths for overnight flights. The DST, which entered service with American Airlines in June 1936, was soon followed by a day (non-sleeper) version with conventional seats which was introduced by the same airline in August 1936. It was this latter version that became the most widely used passenger airliner of the 1930s and 1940s. The first DC-3s were still Wright Cyclone-powered (the 1,200-hp version), but already the second customer for the type, United Airlines, specified identically rated Pratt & Whitney R-1830 Twin Wasp radials with differently shaped cowlings.

The popularity of the DC-3 grew quickly. The aircraft came to be exported in fairly large numbers. The US Department of Defense, which already operated various versions of the DC-2 (known as the C-32, C-33, C-34, C-38, C-39, C-41 and C-42 by the US Army Air Corps and as the R2D by the US Navy), also displayed a keen interest in the DC-3. In September 1940 the DoD issued an order for more than 500 of these machines. These were the first C-47s for the USAAC, which dubbed it Skytrain or Skytrooper; the type was also known as the R4D in US Navy service and, later, as the Dakota in the Royal Air Force when deliveries to Great Britain began.

NC223Y, a Douglas DC-2-112 of Transcontinental & Western Air (TWA). Note the characteristic landing lights in the nose.

Above: Swissair DC-2-115B HB-ITI flying over the Swiss Alps shows its narrow fuselage and tail shape

The DC-3's simple and robust design, reliability and low cost were the factors that accounted for its exceptionally long service career. These aircraft flew in nearly all corners of the world and were not in a hurry to cede their place to new, considerably more advanced airliners.

The longevity of the Dakota became a legend in the history of world aviation. Many DC-3s and C-47s continue flying to this day as joyriding aircraft or humble utility workers; some of them have been retrofitted with turboprop engines (such as the Basler Turbo Dak). Soviet aircraft constructors, too, made their contribution to the glorious history of this aircraft. Unfortunately, in many books devoted to the DC-3 and the C-47, the Soviet licence-built derivative, the PS-84/Li-2, which was built in more than 5,000 copies, is either ignored outright ('pretend it never existed') or just briefly mentioned. In this book the authors consider it their task to fill this gap for the English-speaking reader.

In addition, the C-47 probably had more nicknames over the years than any other contemporary aircraft; these included such appellations as Dak, Tabby, Gooney Bird, Spooky, and Puff the Magic Dragon!

During the Second World War these aircraft were used by the Allies on all fronts with great success, but, as soon as the hostilities ceased, production of the military C-47 was terminated. The commercial DC-3, on the other hand, remained in production until March 1947. Later, the C-47 saw service in many other armed conflicts, including the Vietnam War.

In all, three plants of the Douglas Company (at Santa Monica, Long Beach and Oklahoma City) built 10,655 machines of the DC-3/C-47 family. Thousands of them, including numerous aircraft that had previously been operated by what was now the US Air Force, were sold and resold to the airlines of different countries.

Acknowledgements

The authors wish to thank the editorial team of the *More than Half a Century of Soviet Transports* reference book (Peter Hillman, Stuart Jessop, Adrian Morgan, Tony Morris, Guus Ottenhof and Michael Roch) whose data on Li-2 fleets was a great help. Thanks also go to Konstantin Udalov of AVICO-Press and Nigel Eastaway of the Russian Aviation Research Trust who provided some valuable photos.

DC-3 NC14833, another TWA aircraft, shows off its fatter fuselage, bigger tail and new wings.

Chapter 1

The DC-3 Turns Soviet

The year of 1932 saw the completion of a major reshuffle and consolidation of Soviet civil aviation. This resulted in the emergence of Aeroflot as a state-owned airline combining passenger and cargo transportation with other civil aviation activities, such as crop dusting, aerial photography, forestry patrol and so on. Between 1933 and 1935 the volume of passenger traffic increased almost fourfold. A growing number of aircraft were needed. Moreover, people in the Soviet Union perceived the need to improve airline service standards. The main types operated on Aeroflot's routes and in special civil aviation squadrons (air detachments) were the single-engined Kalinin K-5 and the twin- or three-engined Tupolev ANT-9 (alias PS-9); as per 1st October 1935 there were 85 K-5s and 48 ANT-9s in service. Both types were rapidly becoming obsolete, and the new ANT-35 (PS-35) and ZIG-1 (PS-89) passenger aircraft (designed respectively by Andrey N. Tupolev, the most renowned Soviet aircraft designer, and André Laville, a French engineer working in the USSR) provoked no particular enthusiasm on the part of the Civil Air Fleet (GVF – *Grazh**dahn**skiy voz**doosh**nyy flot*).

At that time Soviet aviation specialists began to show great interest for the achievements of the US aircraft industry in the field of all-metal aircraft construction. Pursuant to a directive issued by the Soviet Council of People's Commissars (that is, government) on 13th December 1934, which was followed up on 28th January 1935 by directive No.61 of the Labour and Defence Council (STO – *So**vet** po tru**doo** i obo**ron**e*), a delegation was dispatched to the USA for purchasing a Martin B-10 bomber and a Douglas DC-2 airliner. The delegation was headed by Andrey N. Tupolev. It included specialists from the Chief Directorate of Aircraft Industry (GUAP – ***Glahv**noye oopravl**en**iye aviatsi**on**noy promy**sh**lennosti*) and the Air Force Directorate (UVVS – *Oopravl**en**iye Vo**yen**no-voz**doosh**nykh seel*), including some close collaborators of Tupolev such as Aleksandr A. Arkhangel'skiy, B. M. Kondorskiy, Vladimir M. Myasishchev *et al*. When reviewing the draft list of participants, Tupolev struck only one name from the list – that of Iosif G. Neman (a designer from Khar'kov who was later responsible for the R-10 reconnaissance aircraft). Even so, at the insistence of the STO secretariat Neman was reinstated as a member of the delegation.

As a result of this mission, in the same year of 1935 the Soviet-US foreign trade company Amtorg Trading Corporation purchased a Douglas DC-2-152 registered NC14949 (construction number 1413), as well as a Northrop 2E single-engined reconnaissance/attack aircraft. The airliner was placed on the Soviet register as URSS-M25 (in those days Soviet aircraft flying international services had the French acronym URSS (*Union des Républiques Sovietiques Socialistes*) as the country prefix). At the initiative of Yakov I. Alksnis, the then Chief of the UVVS, it was envisaged that upon arrival of the aircraft in the USSR Soviet aviation specialists would have an opportunity to study the design features,

Members of the Soviet trade delegation pose beside DC-2-152 URSS-M25, the sole example of the type to be commercially operated in the Soviet Union.

Above: The fuselage of a DC-3 destined for the Soviet Union in the assembly shop at Santa Monica. Note the wing spar attachment fittings, the emergency exits and the baggage hatch.

production technology and equipment of these aircraft thoroughly.

It was the DC-2 that was deemed by the specialists of the Central Aero- & Hydrodynamics Institute named after Nikolay Ye. Zhukovskiy (TsAGI – *Tsen***trahl'***nyy* ***a****ero- i* ***ghid****rodina***mich***eskiy insti***toot**) to be particularly interesting as regards design and production features and the equipment used. As for the Northrop 2E, only the very rational cockpit heating and ventilation system attracted the Soviet engineers' attention; it was proposed that this system be introduced on new Soviet aircraft. On 2nd October 1935, in connection with the delivery of the DC-2 powered by two Wright Cyclone engines, GUAP chief G. N. Korolyov issued order No.58/319 which called for preparing a presentation schedule for this aircraft for examination by industry and UVVS specialists. This was a demonstration tour which would take

Above: URSS-M135, an early-production Wright Cyclone-powered DC-3-196 or DC-3-227, shows the early cowling design (with the cooling air inlet flattened at the top) and the landing lights in the wing leading edge. Note the large exposed DF loop aerial.

Sister ship URSS-M132 displays a different style of registration. Aeroflot's DC-3s had an extremely restrained finish.

Top and above: DC-3-196A URSS-M138 shows the starboard-side entry door (in keeping with Soviet requirements) and the different shades of metal skin on the fuselage and the fin. Note the placement of Aeroflot's winged hammer and sickle logo on the rudder and the faired DF loop aerial on the flightdeck roof.

the aircraft from Moscow to Khar'kov, Voronezh, Taganrog, Gor'kiy (now renamed back to Nizhniy Novgorod) and back to Moscow. There, after an examination by TsAGI the aircraft was to be disassembled so as to enable designers and production engineers from Moscow aircraft plants to get a closer acquaintance with the design details. There is evidence confirming that all these measures were put into effect.

Later the DC-2 was transferred for close examination to the Air Force Research Institute (NII VVS – *Na**ooch**no-is**sled**ovatel'skiy insti**toot** Vo**yen**no-voz**doosh**nykh seel*). Examination of the DC-2 in hardware form was immensely useful for Soviet aircraft industry specialists. Directive No.OK-3 issued by the Labour and Defence Council on 8th January 1936 and called 'On the work of the Soviet aircraft industry in 1935' posed a task: to ensure that *'...by the beginning of 1937 the quality of production aircraft and engines be at least on a par with the best European and American types (the US-produced Douglas DC-2 powered by Wright Cyclone engines shall be regarded as a standard for comparison)'.*

However, as already mentioned, shortly thereafter the Douglas Aircraft Company brought out the much-improved DC-3 airliner, which made its maiden flight on 17th December 1935. Therefore the Labour and Defence Council took a decision to purchase a specimen of this of high-speed airliner in the USA as well; an STO directive to this effect (No.OK-69) was issued on 21st March 1936.

Somewhat later, on 11th April 1936, the STO issued yet another directive, No.OK-86, which called for the purchase of manufacturing licences and technical assistance for American and British aircraft, including the DC-3. For the completion of negotiations and conclusion of agreements with US and British companies it was decided to send a commission comprising representatives from GUAP, UVVS and TsAGI to these countries. N. M. Kharlamov, a GUAP representative, was appointed chairman of the commission. Its other members were Zverev (Plant No.126), Belenkovich (director of Plant No.1), Lyup (Plant No.1) and Rogov, all likewise representing the aircraft industry, Pavel O. Sukhoi from TsAGI, and finally N. I. Bazenkov, Zagainov and B. T. Goroshenko from the Air Force Directorate.

The agreement on the purchase of manufacturing rights for the DC-3 was signed on

This photo of NC14988, the DC-3 (to be precise, the DST-144 Douglas Skysleeper Transport) prototype in the livery of American Airlines, was supplied by Douglas with the manufacturing documents. Hence it figured in the early Soviet technical manuals for the PS-84 (with the markings retouched away, of course).

The cabin of a DC-3 was well-appointed by the day's standards, with individual reading lights, individual ventilation and window curtains. This photo was also supplied by Douglas and included in the early Soviet manuals.

15th July 1936. Under the terms of an understanding reached with Douglas, 34 Soviet specialists were sent to its Santa Monica plant at different times for the purpose of obtaining a closer acquaintance with the aircraft's design and production methods. Since no decision had been taken before the departure of the specialists as to which Soviet aircraft factory would be entrusted with the licence production, specialists from different plants were sent to the USA.

The first group, which departed on 4th September 1936, included Boris P. Lisunov and military engineer-technician Anatoliy A. Sen'kov, both coming from Aircraft Plant No.39, then located in Moscow. Later Sen'kov was appointed chief designer of Plant No.84 in Khimki, a northern suburb of Moscow, while Lisunov became chief engineer of the same plant. On 28th September 1936 I. R. Chertov, a representative of Plant No.22 (then likewise located in Moscow), also left for the USA; he later became chief production engineer of Plant No.84. On 3rd April 1937 Ye. A. Kostenko, an engineer from Plant No.84, was sent to the USA; later he was appointed chief production engineer of Plant No.156 (the fighter design bureau headed by Artyom I. Mikoyan). On 31st December 1937 I. P. Moso-lov, another representative from Plant No.84, flew on a mission to the USA; later he was appointed the plant's deputy chief designer. Thus, in 1936 many prominent Soviet aviation specialists visited the States; they included Vladimir M. Myasishchev, I. P. Tolstykh, Mikhail I. Gurevich (Mikoyan's closest aide), S. M. Belyaikin, P. A. Voronin, V. I. Zhooravlyov, N. A. Zak and others.

On 26th December 1936 the Labour and Defence Council issued directive No.OK-253 'On the production of aircraft under licence', under the terms of which the DC-3 was to be produced, in accordance with a proposal made by GUAP, at Plant No.84 in Khimki in two versions: an airliner and a transport.

On 10th January 1937 Order No.02 was issued by the First Chief Directorate of the People's Commissariat of Defence Industry which called for the beginning of series production of the DC-3-196 (an export version developed by the Douglas Company) at Plant No.84. That year, immediately after his return from Santa Monica, Vladimir M. Myasishchev was appointed chief designer of the plant, and Team 6 which had worked under his guidance at TsAGI's Experimental Aircraft Construction Committee (KOSOS TsAGI – *Komi**tet** po **op**ytnomu samo**lyo**tostro**yen**iyu Tsen**trahl'**novo **a**ero- i **ghid**rodina**mich**eskovo insti**too**ta*) in Moscow was transferred to Khimki and reorganised as a special design bureau located at Plant No.84. Grouped around Myasishchev was a potent team of engineers and designers: A. I. Gordinskiy, M. A. Mostovoy, A. A. Sen'kov, B. P. Kashcheyev, Rachitskiy, Bardyshev. Additionally, I. P. Tolstykh and I. P. Mosolov were appointed Myasishchev's deputies.

The abovementioned STO directive of December 1936 also envisaged the development of a military version of the licence-built DC-3. This task was entrusted to the plant's director Moorashov and the plant's chief designer Myasishchev.

To speed up the commencement of licence production at the Khimki plant, GUAP issued order No.292 dated 16th September 1937 which required the 1st State Project Institute to send a team to the production plant for then purpose of rendering technical assistance in mastering the production methods obtained together with the manufacturing licence. In addition, Order No.400 issued by the First Chief Directorate on 22nd December 1937 proposed setting up a commission for studying the questions of strength of the licence-built aircraft and for assessing whether its structural strength met the Soviet strength norms that were valid in 1937. The work performed by TsAGI jointly with the commission, led to the conclusion that some it local structural re-inforcement was necessary; this resulted in an increase of the aircraft's all-up weight.

According to Russian sources, 18 DC-3s were purchased in the USA. To ensure implementation of the licensing agreement and the order, and to effect the conversion of the DC-3's production drawings from Imperial units to metric units, a special commission

Above: A Douglas-supplied photo of the DC-3's flightdeck glazing. Note the sliding windshield sections added outboard of the original DC-2 windshield. The forward baggage loading door is just visible.

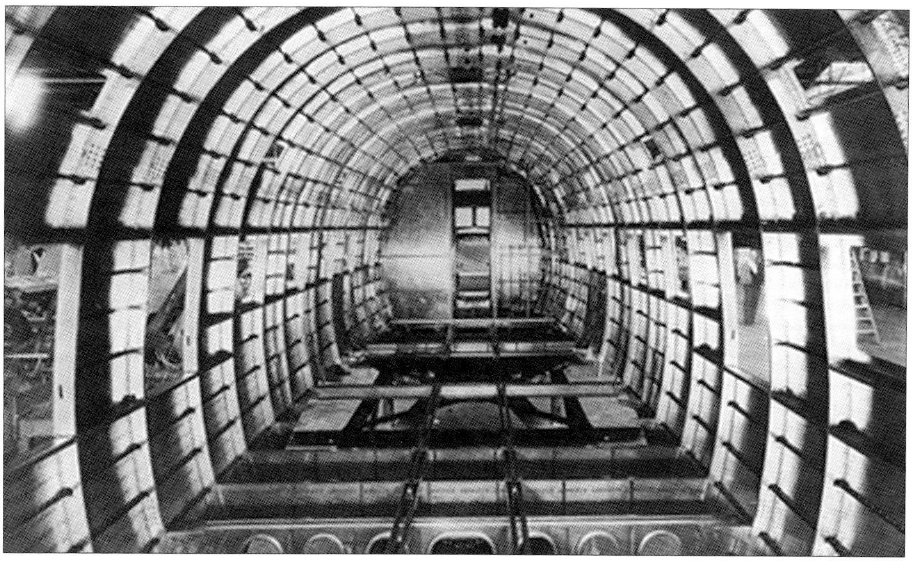

A photo from an early Soviet manual showing the fuselage structure of a DST, looking toward the nose. The empty space in the middle (with no transverse floor beams) is where the wing centre section fits in.

More Douglas photos which figured in early Soviet manuals (in retouched form).
Left: The starboard Schrenck flap of a DC-3 in fully open position, showing the actuating rams. Part of the wings' internal structure is visible

Below left: The wide-chord NACA cowling of the starboard Wright SGR-1820-F3 Cyclone engine. Note the ventrally mounted carburettor air intake, a feature that was repeated on early production PS-84s, and the exposed exhaust pipe.

Bottom left: One of the main fuel tanks located between the wing spars. The tanks are of welded metal construction.

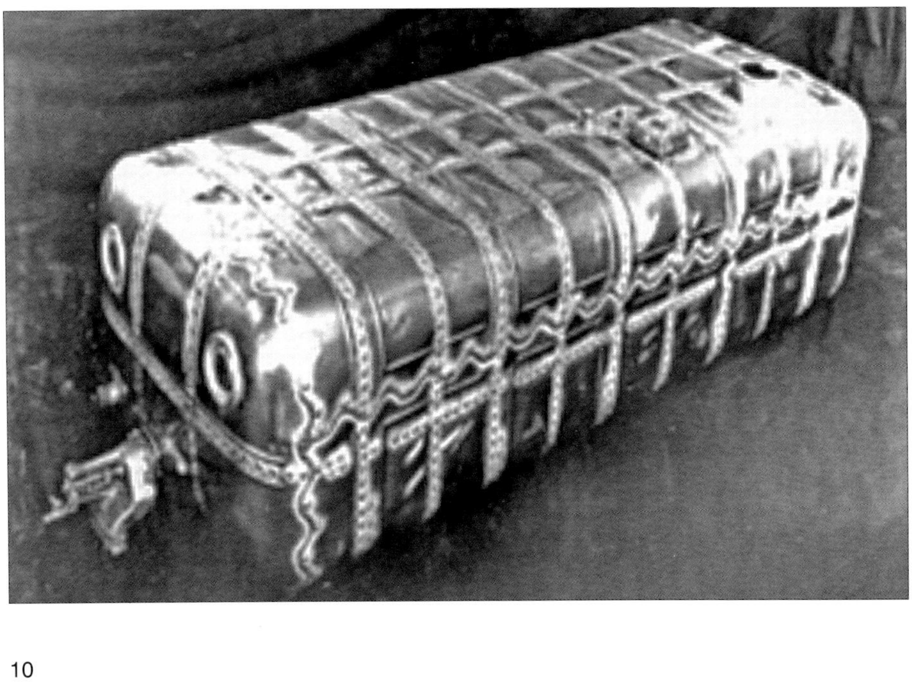

was sent to the United States. Albeit with much delay, it secured the shipment of the sample aircraft to the USSR. Furthermore, a set of production drawings (marked in inches) was sent from the USA to the USSR, as well as ten sets of blueprints and two sets of drawings on tracing paper (marked in millimetres) with a Russian-language text. The DC-3s were purchased and shipped to the Soviet Union via two fictitious airlines, North Eastern and Excello, set up by Amtorg. It was to these companies that the Douglas Company purported to have delivered the mentioned 18 aircraft between November 1936 and March 1939. The first of these was DC-3 c/n 1588, which was shipped to the French port of Cherbourg on 30th November 1936. It was followed by a batch of 11 aircraft in the period between May and August 1938, supplemented later by the remaining six DC-3s, the last of which was delivered in disassembled condition, allegedly as a set of spare parts. The fictitious firms remained in existence just as long as was necessary for the delivery of all the aircraft to the USSR.

According to research conducted by the Swedish historian Lennart Andersson, the Soviet Union purchased 21 aircraft which were delivered between November 1936 and March 1939 via the trading companies Amtorg, Mongolian Transport Co. and Northeast (*sic*). The first of them (DC-3-196 c/n 1589) was delivered via Amtorg, the second (DC-3-227 c/n 1974) that followed in August 1937 was purchased via the Mongolian Transport Co. A further two DC-3-227s, c/ns 1987 and 1988, were dispatched in September of that year, again via the Mongolian Transport Co. The following three machines, DC-3-196As this time (c/ns 2031 through 2033), were received by the USSR via the Northeast company in August 1938. In the same month two more aircraft (c/ns 2034 and 2035), reported as DC-3-195s in some sources but as DC-3-196As in others, were sent to Plant No.84 in disassembled condition (as knock-down kits) and without engines. Six more DC-3-196As (c/ns 2042 through 2047) were received by the Soviet Union in June-September 1938 via Northeast.

The final shipment of six DC-3-196Bs (c/ns 2112 through 2117) was dispatched in March and April of 1939.

Most probably, the differences between the two accounts of the events do not merit any particular attention. What really matters is that without obtaining the US-built aircraft in hardware form the Soviet aircraft industry would have faced far more serious difficulties in mastering the new production methods and would hardly have been able to achieve considerable success in getting licence production under way within a relatively short space of time.

The launch of series production in Khimki was preceded by a huge amount of work aimed at preparing the appropriate technical documentation on the aircraft. Plant No.84 set about reworking the technical drawings supplied by Douglas in conformity with the standards adopted in the USSR. In addition, the aircraft's equipment was revised to incorporate Soviet-produced items. This work was effected under the brilliant guidance of Vladimir M. Myasishchev. The complexity of this work is testified to by the fact that the Mitsubishi and Fokker companies, which had bought similar licences in the USA, did not succeed in reworking the technical drawings and had to assemble the aircraft from imported parts.

Getting series production of the DC-3 under way in the USSR entailed a fair share of difficulties, the biggest of which was concerned with the introduction of the loft floor and template method. The first attempt to introduce the new production method in the USSR had been undertaken as early as 1936 during the construction of Tupolev's ill-starred ANT-43 airliner prototype in TsAGI's Landplane, Seaplane and Experimental Aircraft Construction Department (AGOS – *Avi**ah**tsiya, **ghid**roavi**ah**tsiya i **op**ytnoye stro**it**el'stvo*) which was then, to all intents and purposes, Tupolev's design bureau. However, in the course of the ANT-43's construction the designers introduced many changes and production engineers started using the time-honoured 'trim to fit' method on many parts. As a result, doubts arose as to the aircraft's structural integrity, and TsAGI did not

More detail views from the same manual.
Top right and centre right: Two views of the DC-3's main landing gear units, showing the 'knee-action' twin main struts whose lower sections incorporate shock absorbers. Note the single tubular drag struts attached to the rear forks, a feature retained on early batches of the PS-84.

Right: The port main gear unit of a Pratt & Whitney R-1830 Twin Wasp-powered DC-3 (note the different exhaust pipe) in retracted position, showing the folded oleo struts; the wheels remain semi-exposed. no doors being provided. Note the inner/outer wing joint just outboard of the nacelle.

Above: The non-retractable tailwheel.

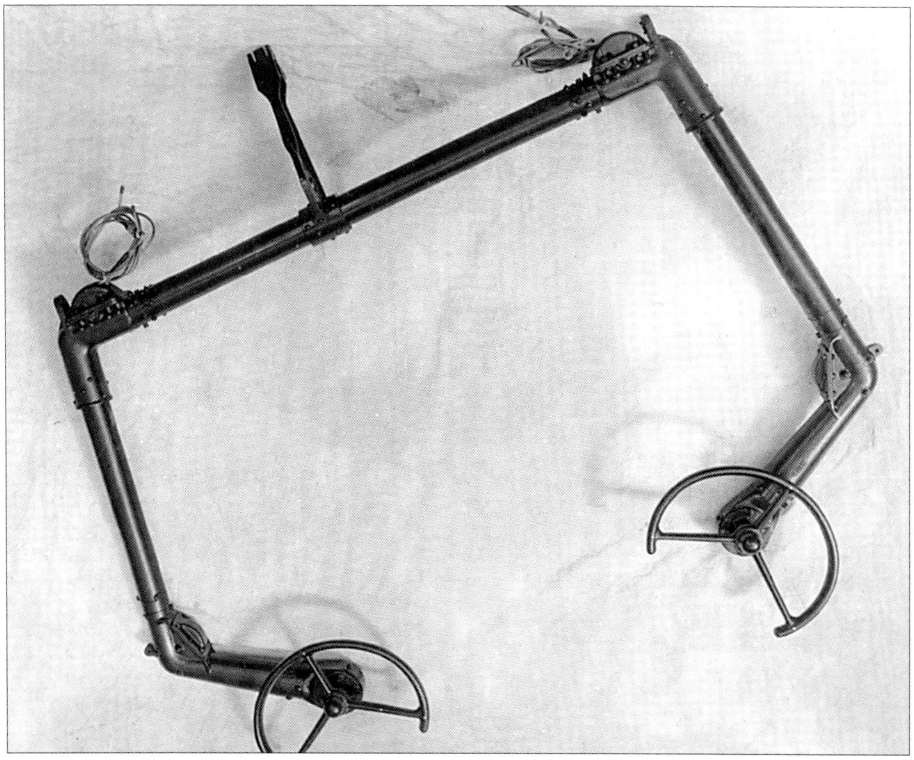

The control columns of the DC-3 were offset to the flightdeck walls and attached to a common tubular axle with cables and rollers for the aileron control wheels. Note the shape of the control wheels.

allow the aircraft to be flight-tested. To avoid similar mistakes, Myasishchev forbade the introduction of any improvements in production methods as far as the assembly of the DC-3 was concerned.

In 1938 Anatoliy A. Sen'kov was appointed chief designer of Plant No.84, while Myasishchev was accused of subversion and espionage and arrested. The NKVD (People's Commissariat of Internal Affairs/ security service) investigators blamed him for the crash of the ANT-41 torpedo-bomber prototype which had been developed by Myasishchev during his work at KOSOS TsAGI. Myasishchev's aforementioned trip to the USA now became 'evidence' against him. The NKVD's point was that he had travelled to the States all alone via London and Southampton, crossing the Atlantic aboard an ocean steamer and then travelling from New York across the entire USA to Santa Monica. In the opinion of the investigators, in the course of such a long journey he would inevitably be recruited by a foreign intelligence service.

At that time Afanasiy M. Yaroonin held the post of director of Plant No.84, while Boris P. Lisunov was, as mentioned earlier, the plant's chief engineer, with N. V. Lysenko as chief production engineer.

Construction of the first Soviet version of the DC-3, powered by Shvetsov M-62IR engines (a derivative of the M-25, which was a licence-built copy of the Wright SGR-1820-F that powered the DC-2) was completed by the 21st anniversary of the revolution – that is, 7th November 1938. The machine was assembled entirely from an imported set of parts and subassemblies. In the plant's documents the aircraft was designated DC-3 2M-62IR – a typically Soviet way of designating aircraft which, after the fashion adopted at that time, included the mention of the engines. After manufacturer's tests, which did not last long, the aircraft was transferred to NII GVF (Naoochno-issledovatel'skiy institoot Grazhdahnskovo vozdooshnovo flota – Civil Air Fleet Research Institute). There, between 3rd September and 17th December 1939, it successfully passed state acceptance trials and was recommended for series production. At that time the aircraft was redesignated PS-84 (*passa***zheer***skiy samo***lyot** [*proiz***vod***stva za***vod***a* **nom***er*] **vo***sem'desyat che***tyr***e* – passenger aircraft produced by Plant No.84, as simple as that). In those years such designations were not uncommon in the Soviet Union; Tupolev's designs normally had sequential numbers allocated by the manufacturer (say, ANT-35, alias PS-35) but, for instance, the huge ANT-20*bis* airliner manufactured by Plant No.124 in Kazan' was also known as the PS-124. In the USA the 'Soviet Douglas' received, much later, the NATO reporting name *Cab*.

The PS-84 cannot be called a faithful copy of the US aircraft. Suffice it to say that it was built almost entirely of Soviet materials. The aircraft was powered by Soviet engines driving locally designed variable-pitch propellers and was fitted with wheels of Soviet design. Unfortunately, the manufacturing quality also proved to be notoriously 'Soviet' – but that became apparent later. In its characteristics the PS-84 was somewhat inferior to its US progenitor, but more about this in an appropriate chapter.

In concluding this chapter it is worth mentioning that the US-built DC-3s that had been purchased were operated on Aeroflot's international routes from late June 1937 onwards. Known registrations of these machines are URSS-M132 and URSS-M135 through URSS-M138; the strange letter-only registrations URSS-A, URSS-B, URSS-C, URSS-D, URSS-G, URSS-H, URSS-K and URSS-N have also been reported.

Chapter 2

Version Variety

PS-84 2M-62IR Transport and Airliner

Series production of the DC-3 powered by Soviet M-62IR engines was launched at Plant No.84 in 1939. It was planned to manufacture 50 machines that year; actually, however, only six were delivered, all of them in the airliner version. With the exception of the first machine to be assembled in Khimki, all DC-3s manufactured by the plant were built virtually entirely of Soviet materials and parts.

The difficulties in getting DC-3 manufacture under way were due to the fact that Plant No.84 had been transferred from the Chief Administration of the Civil Air Fleet (GU GVF – ***Glahv**noye ooprav**len**iye Grazh**dahn**skovo voz**doosh**novo **flot**a*) as late as 1935. Previously it had been a GVF aircraft repair facility, its engineering staff and workers were not sufficiently skilled, and its machine-tool stock was outdated. When the plant was tasked with the construction of several prototype aircraft developed by Nikolay N. Polikarpov and, somewhat later, by V. I. Levkov and Viktor F. Bolkhovitinov, the situation began improving gradually, but not to the extent that would make it possible to master large-scale production of a new transport and passenger aircraft quickly. It took an awful lot of effort to organise the infrastructure of the plant's housing estate and of the plant itself; this included tackling the problems of electric power supply, housing and amenities for the plant's personnel, and of improving transport links with Moscow. All this made it possible to employ an additional workforce of more than a thousand persons.

Urgent measures were taken to raise the standard of the plant's machine tools and equipment. Steps were taken to ensure a steady supply of materials and components. Co-operation was established with eleven subcontractor organisations. In this situation the plant's management proved equal to the task; the industry's commanding organisations, on their part, aided the plant in an efficient way. All this produced the first results already in 1940; thus, on the eve of the Great Patriotic War the plant was already functioning normally.

A. M. Yaroonin, who was appointed director of the plant, did an enormous job getting licence production of the DC-3 under way. It fell to his lot to turn this enterprise, which was a minor factory at the time when the manufacture of the aircraft started, into a sufficiently potent production plant. He had also to shoulder the burden of organising the subsequent evacuation of the plant to the rear after the outbreak of the war.

Deputy chief designer Mosolov also played a certain positive role in mastering the production of the aircraft. One can hardly overestimate the role of the plant's chief production engineer Chertov and his deputy Lysenko, chief of the assembly workshop Yes'kov and the chief of the loft floor and template shop; it was these persons who shouldered the bulk of the work associated with the mastering of American production methods and the introduction, for the first time in the USSR, of the loft floor and template method. The plant's chief engineer was responsible for tackling the complicated task of mastering the new machine tools that were coming to the plant in large numbers, and putting into operation the complicated forging and stamping equipment, as well as manufacturing and adjusting the assembly jigs. Difficulties in tackling this task were among the main reasons for a delay in getting the series manufacture of the DC-3 under way in 1939-1940.

As already mentioned in Chapter 1, shortly after production entry the Soviet version of the DC-3 received the designation PS-84 2M-62IR. It was not an exact copy of the DC-3; the aircraft was reworked to suit the Soviet strength norms, all dimensions were converted to metric units with due regard to these norms applicable to materials and components. Production machines were built almost entirely of Soviet materials. In compliance with then-current Soviet standards the entry door was located to starboard, not to port as on most DC-3s, and opened inward and aft rather that outward and forward; this was one of the PS-84's external identification features. The passenger cabin had an internal passageway connecting it with the baggage compartment. Wright Cyclone-powered DC-3s were few, as most production examples (and the military C-47) were powered by Pratt & Whitney R-1830 Twin Wasps in recontoured nacelles. In contrast, the Soviet version was powered by M-62IR engines driving VISh-21 variable-pitch propellers (*vint izme**nya**yemovo **sha**ga*) of Soviet manufacture and enclosed by cowlings of the original 'Cyclone' shape. The PS-84 also had Soviet-produced undercarriage wheels.

Initially the PS-84's passenger cabin was outfitted with 14 seats (seven rows of two), later the number of seats was increased to 21 (seven rows of three). Airline pilots who had a chance to fly the PS-84 spoke highly of the machine. This aircraft was capable of flying with one engine inoperative. The flightdeck

Passengers and Aeroflot personnel crowd around a PS-84 registered СССР-Л420... (that is, SSSR-L420...; the last digit is not visible because of the open door).

windshield was provided with a de-icing device; at the customer's request the wings and tail surfaces could also be provided with de-icers. The passenger cabin had ventilation and heating, individual reading lights and overhead bins for small luggage, which, by the standards of the day, represented a fairly high degree of comfort for Soviet passengers. In 1940 the PS-84 entered service on Aeroflot's routes.

In 1940 the Second World War was already raging in Europe; in these conditions, on 26th July 1940, the Soviet Union's State Defence Committee (GKO – *Gosoo***dar***stvennyy komi***tet** *obo***rony**) issued Directive No.335 'On increasing the output of aircraft and engines in the period from August to December 1940'. In accordance with this directive Plant No.84 was to build 52 DC-3 2M-62IR aircraft. In addition, Plant No.124 in Kazan' was to build a further 23 machines by the end of the year. All aircraft were to be produced in the passenger version only.

However, since Plant No.124 was commencing production of the Petlyakov TB-7 bomber, the plant's director Mikhail M. Kaganovich (the former People's Commissar of Aircraft Industry) requested that the DC-3 programme be reduced to ten examples. People's Commissar of Defence Kliment Ye. Voroshilov categorically objected to that. Eventually the Kazan' plant manufactured just these ten machines, whereupon its involvement with the type ended. By the end of 1940 the main production Plant No.84 had built a further 57 PS-84s (some sources say 64).

In May 1941 an attempt was made to fit the aircraft with a liquid de-icing system designed by engineer Feigelson at NII GVF. An antifreeze liquid transpired through a leather strip bonded to the leading edges of the wings and tail surfaces. The system proved to be unreliable: it was difficult to achieve reliable bonding, the leather parted company with the metal structure, became stiff in cold weather and overly dry in hot weather. This de-icing system was not adopted for production machines.

On 22nd June 1941 Germany invaded the USSR. Like many other Soviet factories, pursuant to a GKO decision issued on 15th October 1941 Plant No.84 was to be evacuated to the East, into Siberia. As early as 14th October the plant began to curtail production and on 18th October production stopped completely in connection with the evacuation. The last trainloads were sent from Khimki on 12th November 1941. In 1941, by the time the evacuation started, the plant had built 237 examples of the PS-84, and, importantly, they were all built in the passenger version! The People's Commissariat of Defence had not raised the issue of producing this aircraft in other versions.

However, when the trains carrying the plant's equipment were on their way to Siberia, Usman Yusupov, the Secretary of the Central Committee of the Communist (Bolshevik) Party of Uzbekistan, made a telephone call to Stalin and asked him that evacuated enterprises be sent also to Uzbekistan. This request was granted, and in accordance with a decision adopted by the GKO the trains carrying the equipment of Plant No.84 were assigned a new destination – Tashkent, the capital of the Uzbek Soviet Socialist Republic.

Plant No.84 was deployed at Tashkent-Vostochnyy (Tashkent-East) airfield, the site of Aircraft Plant No.34 then under construction. For all practical purposes Plant No.34 was non-existent, as it never built a single aircraft. Manufacture of the PS-84 resumed in difficult conditions on 7th January 1942 and the first eight Tashkent-built machines were completed before the end of the month. Measures were taken to speed up the deployment of the manufacturing facilities. In February the plant had already doubled the output as compared to January, assembling 16 aircraft, and from March onwards the production rate reached one machine per day.

Since Sen'kov, in addition to being the plant's chief designer, also held the post of Design Bureau chief at TsAGI, the leaders of the People's Commissariat of Aircraft Industry (NKAP – *Na***rod***nyy komissari***aht** *aviatsi***on***noy pro***myshl***ennosti*) put him in charge of evacuation of a part of TsAGI which moved to Kazan'; As a result, he did not go to Tashkent. His deputy I. P. Mosolov became the new chief designer of Plant No.84. Having achieved the required production tempo, the plant's management and personnel began to pay attention to improving the manufacturing quality and to raising the combat and operating performance of the PS-84 2M-62IR.

The First Military Version of the PS-84 (Project)

As soon as the first DC-3 made its appearance in the USSR, an attempt was made to adapt the type for military duties. In late 1936 the famous aircraft designer Nikolay N. Polikarpov (known as 'The King of Fighters') and Boris G. Shpital'nyy, the chief designer of an aircraft weapons design bureau, sent a proposal to Mikhail M. Kaganovich, who was then Deputy People's Commissar of the Defence Industry. The proposal envisaged an armed version of the DC-3/PS-84. The machine was to be fitted with five cannons: two 37-mm (1.45 calibre) Shpital'nyy 11P-37 cannons (then under development) and three 20-mm (.78 calibre) Shpital'nyy/Vladimirov ShVAK cannons, supplemented by three 7.62-mm (.30 calibre) Shpital'nyy/Komaritskiy ShKAS machine guns. In overload configuration the aircraft could also take a 500-kg (1,102-lb) bomb load. The result was a veritable 'flying fortress', though not of the same kind as the later AC-47 'Spooky' gunship.

Kaganovich tasked Vladimir M. Myasishchev with the implementation of the proposal. In 1937 Myasishchev got down to practical work on the project, but for purely political reason Shpital'nyy refrained from cooperating with him – that was the time when political repression was at its highest, and Myasishchev was already proclaimed an 'enemy of the people'. The project never materialised.

DC-3 (PS-84) Re-Engining Projects

As early as September 1939 chief designer of Plant No.84 A. A. Sen'kov wrote to M. M. Kaganovich (who had by then become People's Commissar of the Aircraft Industry), stating his considerations as to the further improvement of the DC-3. Giving reasons for his proposals, he pointed out that that the DC-3, while being one of the best passenger machines with regard to comfort and extremely suitable for production in its design, would nevertheless fall behind the more modern passenger aircraft in its basic performance characteristics: speed, service ceiling and range. Sen'kov held the opinion that the best way to upgrade the aircraft was the introduction of more powerful engines. Several versions of a new powerplant for the PS-84 were developed under the direction of Sen'kov; initially these were based on the use of more powerful US engines, later only Soviet engines were envisaged. The most important of these versions are listed below.

1. The first of the versions proposed was a version of the licence-built DC-3 re-engined with the more powerful Wright R-2600 Double Cyclone 14-cylinder two-row radials with a nominal rating of 1,200 hp at the rated altitude of 1,650 m (5,414 ft), with a re-stressed airframe and a maximum speed raised to 400 km/h (249 mph). Kaganovich supported this initiative, but the project was not implemented because these engines were unavailable in the USSR.

2. The Shvetsov M-63 nine-cylinder radial (a refined version of the M-62) and the 1,100-hp Tumanskiy M-88 14-cylinder radial (a derivative of the Gnome-Rhône 14K built under French licence in the USSR) were the most convenient engines for the installation in the DC-3, involving a minimum of alterations which would, in the main, be concerned with the control linkages.

3. One more project envisaged the use of the new powerful Soviet engines – the 1,600-hp Shvetsov M-81 14-cylinder radial or the 2,000-hp Urmin M-90 18-cylinder radial – which would ensure a 50- to 60-km/h (31- to 37-mph) increase of the flight speed. For

example, a version of the DC-3 powered by Soviet M-90 engines would be able to attain an estimated maximum speed of no less than 430-450 km/h (267-280 mph) at an all-up weight of 13,500-13,800 kg (29,770-30,430 lb), the range would be increased to 2,000 km (1,243 miles). In case of need the range could be further increased at the expense of reducing the payload or increasing the take-off run by means of additional fuel tanks which could be installed in the outer wing panels. The proposal envisaged series manufacture of the aircraft in airliner, ambulance and transport/ troop-carrier versions.

4. Sen'kov also studied the possibility of installing the Mikulin M-34 and M-35 engines on the DC-3; these Vee-12 water-cooled engines delivered 1,200 hp (in the M-34's late geared fuel-injected versions) and 1,300 hp respectively. The studies showed that, for better integration with the new engine nacelles, the main gear units would have to be redesigned, retracting aft instead of upward and forward. This, in turn, would entail the need to redesign the wing centre section and make it a two-spar, not three-spar, structure. Several other alterations were needed, in particular, the engines' cooling system had to be accommodated somehow. Additional fuel tanks were to be accommodated in the detachable wing outer panels. The CG position would change, which entailed some alterations in the aircraft's layout.

In the first half of December 1939 Sen'kov again submitted his proposals for using the AM-35 (formerly M-35), the 1,500-hp AM-37 and the 1,600-hp AM-38 liquid-cooled engines on the PS-84, the Soviet version of the DC-3. The proposals were supported by the plant's director A. M. Yaroonin and discussed at a conference held by chief of the 1st Main Directorate of NKAP Shishkin. At this conference Sen'kov made a report about the results of the calculations and preliminary design work on modifying the aircraft to accept these engines (in airliner, ambulance, transport/ troop-carrier and night bomber versions). Yaroonin promised to build the first prototype by 1st August 1940 and the second prototype by 1st October 1940. The plant's deputy chief designer Mosolov noted in his statement that more than 65% of the PS-84's existing jigs and tooling could be used in the construction of this aircraft.

The participants of the conference came to the conclusion that the designer's calculations were correct and that it was expedient to build two prototypes powered by AM-35 engines. The scheduled dates for the completion of the prototypes were moved a bit forward. Sen'kov asked for the plant's design bureau staff to be supplemented by some 30 to 40 persons. The conference supported this request. However, the prospects of a war with Germany loomed large, the AM-35 engines were required for the newest Mikoyan/Gurevich I-200 (MiG-1) fighters and the Il'yushin IL-2 attack aircraft. As a result, the work on re-engining the PS-84 with the Mikulin engines was suspended.

5. A version with Klimov M-103, M-103A or M-105 Vee-12 water-cooled engines (rated at 930, 960 and 1,100 hp respectively) was more suitable to the designers because these engines were more compact and could be more easily incorporated into the structure of the aircraft. They did not require a change in the undercarriage retraction arrangement and, in consequence, did not entail a redesign of the wing centre section.

Bomber Version of the DC-3 (Project)

The history of the projected bomber versions emerging in the Soviet Union on the basis of the licence-built DC-3's design and production methods takes its inception in the aforementioned proposal by Nikolay N. Polikarpov and Boris G. Shpital'nyy which they sent to Secretary of the Labour and Defence Council Bazilevich on 17th January 1937. People's Commissar of the Aircraft Industry Mikhail M. Kaganovich, however, considered it impossible to entrust Polikarpov with this work – both for political reasons and because Polikarpov was overburdened with the work on the I-16 fighter, the 'Ivanov' tactical bomber, the VIT 'tank buster' attack aircraft and other designs. Nevertheless, Kliment Ye. Voroshilov considered that the proposal of Polikarpov and Shpital'nyy should be discussed at the nearest meeting of the Defence Committee.

Later a decision was taken calling for the development of a night bomber version of the DC-3; its development became the responsibility of A. A. Sen'kov, chief designer of Plant No.84. The latter, however, was of the opinion that the construction of a bomber on the basis of the licence-built DC-3 was inexpedient. In September 1939, in a letter to Kaganovich, Sen'kov questioned the feasibility of reworking the DC-3 for the purpose of turning it into a bomber. He considered that 'little would be left' of the DC-3 after the reworking. Sen'kov chose a different path and developed a project of a dedicated high-speed bomber powered by two M-63 engines which made wide use of the DC-3's design and production features. The bomber had a tricycle (nosewheel) undercarriage which eased the take-off of a heavily laden machine and enhanced the landing safety. It was planned to use retractable turrets which would ensure good self-defence for the aircraft. A report submitted to Council of People's Commissars Chairman Vyacheslav M. Molotov on 1st October 1939 stated: '*...The DC-3 aircraft, now in production at Plant No.84, can be transformed in a matter of 50 hours into a bomber, for which purpose provisions are made on the aircraft for hatches and fittings for the installation of three machine gun turrets and bomb containers holding a 1,200-kg* [2,650-lb] *bomb load. In a bomber version the DC-3 aircraft with two M-63 engines will have the following performance: a maximum speed of 330-340 km/h* [205-211 mph]*, a landing speed of 100-110 km/h* [62-68 mph]*, a range of 2,000 km* [1,243 miles]'. People's Commissar of the Aircraft Industry Mikhail M. Kaganovich submitted a draft Directive 'On the development and construction of the DC-3 aircraft in a bomber

The first prototype PS-84-K military transport in bomber configuration with eight FAB-100 bombs under the wing centre section. Note the early-style engine cowlings and the aperture in the nosecone.

Above: The second prototype PS-84-K converted as a stand-in for the wrecked first prototype differed from the latter in having revised engine cowlings with perfectly circular inlets and additional flightdeck windows. It is seen here at NII VVS.

Above, left and right, and below left: The cabin of the PS-84-K featured modular units of back-to-back seats for paratroopers; two such six-seat modules are shown on the right. Note how the small entry door in the port side cargo door opens inward and upward.

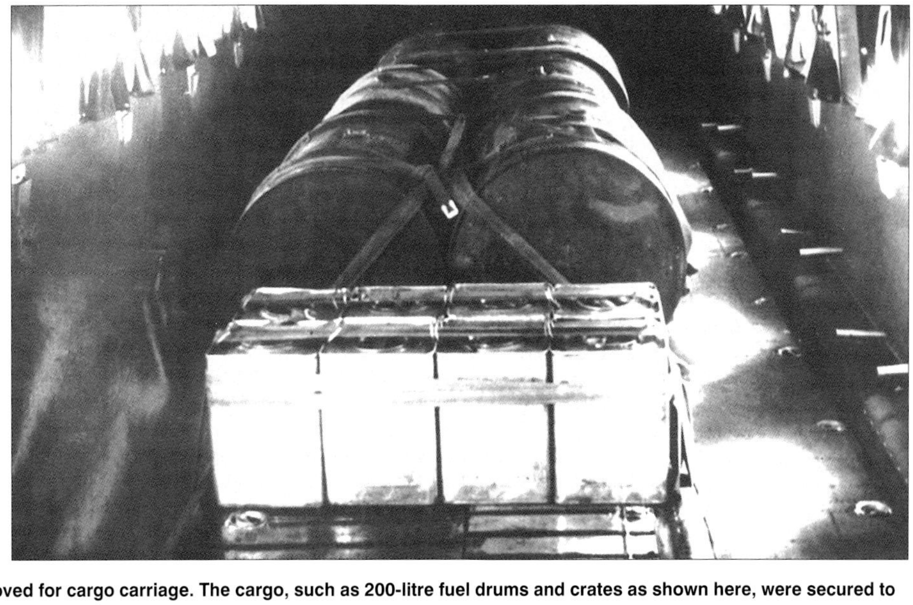

Right: The seats in the PS-84-K's cabin could be removed for cargo carriage. The cargo, such as 200-litre fuel drums and crates as shown here, were secured to tie-down cleats on the floor by straps.

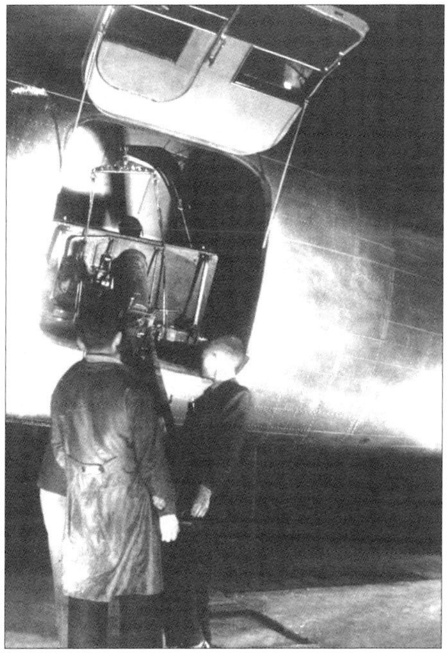

Above: These three photos show how bulky loads, such as a 45-mm P-45 field gun or an M-62I engine, could be loaded into the PS-84-K's cabin by means of the onboard hoist and crane arm. The narrow cargo door severely restricted the size of the items that could be carried. Note the twin retaining arms supporting the door in the open position.

Left and right: Two more views of the PS-84-K's cargo door with the crane arm lowered for lifting a 200-litre fuel drum; note the spreader bar attached to the crane arm. and the forward position of the entry/paradrop door on the cargo door.

version', whereupon People's Commissar of Defence K. Ye. Voroshilov made some corrections to it; the main alteration provided for increasing the bomber's maximum speed to 340-350 km/h (211-218 mph). The aircraft was to be submitted for state acceptance trials by 1st May 1940.

However, at the meeting of the State Defence Committee the majority of those present voted in favour of the opinion that adapting the passenger DC-3 for the bomber role was 'inexpedient'. That put an end, for the time being, to the epic story of an M-63-powered bomber version of the DC-3.

PS-84-K Transport and Troop-Carrier Aircraft and PS-84-I Medevac Aircraft

When the DC-3 entered series production at Plant No.84, Vladimir M. Myasishchev was tasked with developing military versions of this aircraft, but he had other irons in the fire. Hence this development work was conducted by A. A. Sen'kov in early 1939. In June 1939 he submitted to NKAP a project of a standardised troop carrier and medevac version of the PS-84. By introducing special changes into the airframe design (the most significant change being the addition of a cargo door on the port side) and by producing special additional equipment typical of the troop carrier, transport and medevac versions the passenger aircraft could be transformed into any of these versions within a short time. Conversely, from any of the three versions the aircraft could be converted into the airliner version or some other version. It should be

Above left: Three 45-mm P-45 field guns in the cargo cabin of the PS-84-K.
Above right: A 76-mm P-76 field gun in the cargo cabin of the PS-84-K.

Above left: Here, four PDMM paradroppable supply bags are seen suspended on the bomb shackles of the PS-84-K. Note the parachute static lines.
Above right: Another view inside the cabin with a P-76 field gun shows the open entry/troop door on the starboard side.

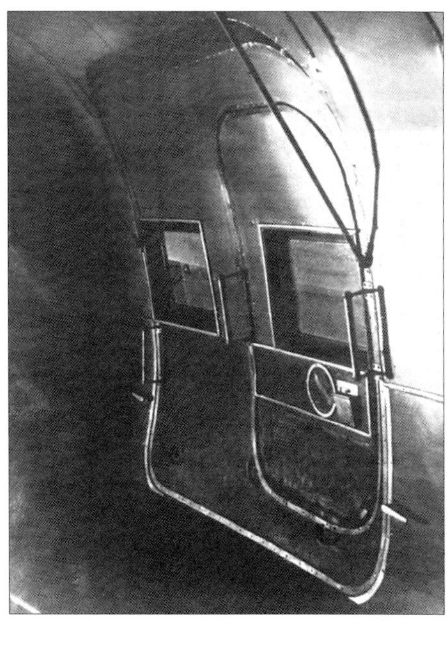

Left: With one of the bags removed, the Der-19 bomb shackles are clearly visible.
Right: The inside of the PS-84-K's cargo door, showing the stowed retaining rods and the internal locking handles.

noted that the Douglas company created a transport version of the DC-3 – the C-47 Skytrain – as late as 1940.

On 29th July the State Defence Committee issued directive No.239 'On the construction of the DC-3 aircraft in medevac, transport and troop carrier versions'. This document tasked chief designer of Plant No.84 A. A. Sen'kov and the plant's director A. M. Yaroonin with developing and building one example of the DC-3 simultaneously in three versions: medevac, transport and troop carrier version; the aircraft was to be submitted for state acceptance trials in December 1939. The directive stipulated the following performance figures: maximum horizontal speed 340 km/h (211 mph), landing speed 100-110 km/h (62-68 mph), range in overload configuration at 0.9 of the maximum speed 2,000 km (1,243 miles). Interestingly, the directive cited the name of chief designer Sen'kov first, and factory director Yaroonin came second; usually it was the director who came first.

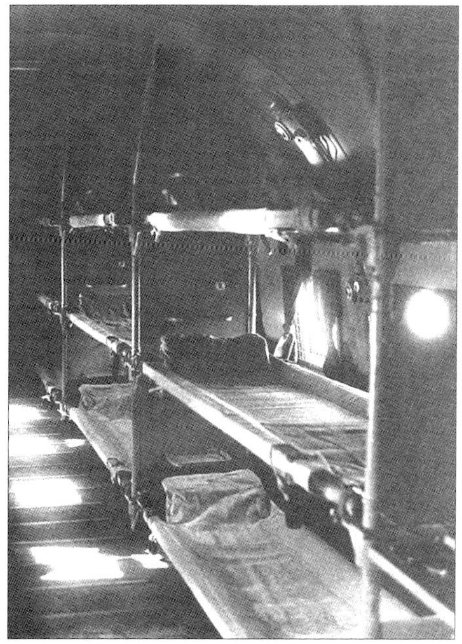

Left and right: The three tiers of stretchers attached to uprights in the cabin of the PS-84-I medevac aircraft. The stretchers of the lower tier are almost lying on the floor.

To fulfil the task thus posed, in November 1939 one of the first production passenger machines was converted into a transport and troop-carrier version designated PS-84-K (*sic* – the documents of the day cited the designation with two hyphens), whereupon it was submitted for manufacturer's tests. On 4th January 1940, as it was being ferried from the factory airfield to NII VVS, the PS-84-K prototype made a crash landing due to adverse weather and had to undergo repairs. A second prototype was urgently built and submitted for the state acceptance trials which were conducted between 1st May and 29th June 1940. The test team included test pilot Predeyin, test navigator Marin-Fyodorov and project engineer Pauzer.

The cargo door featuring the two rearmost cabin windows to port measured 1.65 x 1.52 m (5 ft 5 in x 5 ft 0 in); it opened outward and upward and incorporated a small inward/upward-opening entry/paradropping door into which the forward window was built. The port side door served both for cargo loading/unloading and for the embarkation/disembarkation of troops on the ground. The regular entry door to starboard also opened inward and aft instead of outward and forward. Apart from the cargo door, the PS-84-K differed from the airliner version in having a reinforced cabin floor and being provided with assault and transport equipment. The latter included a hoist of 850 kg (1,870 lb) capacity with an inverted-L shaped crane arm located opposite the cargo door and other devices. The cargo handling equipment ensured the loading and unloading of such items as aircraft engines; P-45 or P-76 field guns with a calibre of 45 mm (1.77 in) and 76 mm (2.99 in) respectively with their ammunition boxes; aviation bombs of all main calibres; fuel tanks, gasoline and oil drums, small arms and ammunition in crates, packages with uniforms, bags and packages with foodstuffs and so on. The normal payload was 1,600 kg (3,530 lb); in a slightly overloaded condition the aircraft could take a 2,000-kg (4,410-lb) payload. Provision was made for the carriage of paradroppable cargo containers weighing up to 2,000 kg on beam-type racks under the wing centre section (gasoline in barrels, packages with all sorts of military cargoes and so on).

In the troop carrier version the PS-84-K could transport 25 paratroopers with full kit. In this version the aircraft was fitted with benches along the centreline; the paratroopers sat back to back, facing the windows. At the moment of the airdrop each row of the paratroopers moved to one of the two inward-opening troop doors. Special hooks were provided in the cabin for attaching the parachute static lines. If the paratroopers were provided with PD-41-1 or PD-6PR parachutes with static lines, the airdrop could be performed from an altitude of 150 m (490 ft) or more at a speed of up to 300 km/h (186 mph) for the PD41-1 or up to 250 km/h (155 mph) for the PD-6PR. The airdropping of paratroopers through the main and the auxiliary doors from an altitude of 500 m (1,640 ft) and at a speed of 140-150 km/h (87-93 mph) took a mere 13-20 seconds. When fully loaded, the aircraft could accommodate up to 30 paratroopers. In the transport version the seats folded up against the cabin walls and were fixed with small belts. Embarkation of the troops through the main entry door on the starboard side of the fuselage took 80 seconds; when both doors were used the time was reduced to 25-30 seconds. The load carried by the PS-84-K over a 500-km (311-mile) radius of action reached 2,400 kg (5,292 lb), which surpassed the payload of the passenger version by 400 kg (880 lb).

In case of need the PS-84-K transport/troop-carrier could be quickly converted into the PS-84-I medevac version (again, the suffix letter was separated by a hyphen). This could be done by the flight engineer in a matter of ten minutes. The conversion involved installing 18 stretchers in the cabin; they were arranged in three tiers (nine on each side of the cabin). The six stretchers of the first tier were placed directly on the floor and attached to it by leather belts. The stretchers of the second tier were mounted on removable uprights, and the stretchers of the third tier on collapsible brackets and hangers attached to the ceiling. In addition, two walking wounded and a medical attendant could be accommodated on tip-up seats. For transporting medical personnel to the frontline area, the aircraft was provided with 27 tip-up seats.

The PS-84-K and PS-84-I were not fitted with defensive armament.

Tests of the PS-84 aircraft in the transport, troop-carrier and medevac versions were completed successfully. The concluding part of the test report prepared by NII VVS read: *'The PS-84-K and -I aircraft [...] has passed the state acceptance tests satisfactorily and is recommended for service introduction with the Air Force'.*

On 17th and 18th July 1940 the second prototype of this version passed service tests in the 201st Airborne Brigade at Rel'bitsy, an airfield in the Leningrad Military District. Yet the PS-84-K/PS-84-I was never placed in series production.

On 22nd April 1941 A. A. Sen'kov sent a letter to Chairman of the Soviet Union's Defence Council K. Ye. Voroshilov with a request that the go-ahead be given to put the military versions of the PS-84 into production. In response to this letter, on 9th May State Defence Committee Secretary Safonov wrote to Chief of the Main Administration of the Red Army Air Force (GU VVS KA) P. F. Zhigarev, requesting that he state, for the benefit of the GKO, the opinion of GU VVS KA regarding the expediency of putting the troop-carrier, transport and medevac versions into production in 1941 instead of the usual passenger version. However, at the same time he, in effect, advocated producing only the airliner version, citing the opinion of NKAP. The 25% increase in man-hours needed for manufacturing the modified aircraft as compared to the basic PS-84 would require 2-2.5 months for the preparation of production and for the learning curve, which would have resulted in the manufacture of only 225-235 transport machines instead of the 300 passenger aircraft stipulated by the Government directive dated 7th December 1940.

In a letter to the new People's Commissar of the Aircraft Industry Aleksey I. Shakhoorin on 17th February 1941, GU VVS KA confirmed the need for building the PS-84 aircraft in 1941 in military versions. Meanwhile, in his reply to GKO Secretary Safonov, Zhigarev wrote: *'In connection with the measures intended to reinforce the airborne troops units of the Red Army Air Force and with a marked shortage of troop-carrier aircraft I consider it necessary that from the second half of 1941 onwards the PS-84 aircraft should be manufactured for the GU VVS KA only in transport, troop-carrier and ambulance versions. In addition, Plant No.84 should be placed under obligation to manufacture a stock of the necessary devices and parts for converting all other PS-84, delivered to other organisations (in addition to GU VVS KA) into these versions'.* However, Plant No.84 refused to manufacture the aircraft in the abovementioned military versions until the issue was settled by NKAP. In his letter dated 28th March 1941, Deputy People's Commissar of the Aircraft Industry P. A. Voronin likewise refused to build the PS-84 in the transport, troop-carrier and ambulance versions, citing the fact that the Government-endorsed plan provided for the construction of these machines only in the passenger version. Zhigarev suggested that this question be submitted for renewed consideration at a meeting of the GKO.

Thus, when the Great Patriotic War broke out, on the one hand, the leadership of the Air Force had not been sufficiently insistent in its demands when the production plan for 1941 was determined. On the other hand, the leaders of NKAP and the State Defence Committee had displayed a myopic approach – all the more so, considering that the PS-84-K had been shown to K. Ye. Voroshilov at Moscow's Central airfield (alias Khodynka) as early as 31st May 1940 and he had given it a high appraisal. As early as 8th September 1937 Voroshilov, in a letter to Molotov, had pointed out the urgent need to provide the regiments and larger units of all types of aviation with transport aircraft in order to endow them with high mobility, citing the experience of the big Army and Air Force exercises, as well as the experience gained in the Spanish Civil War.

PS-84A 2M-71 Transport and Passenger Aircraft (Project)

In September 1940 Chief Designer of Plant No.84 A. A. Sen'kov submitted a project of upgrading the PS-84 by fitting it with powerful Shvetsov M-71 two-row 18-cylinder air-cooled radials rated at 2,000 hp; this version was referred to in documents as PS-84A 2M-71. The airframe structure was to be reinforced in accordance with the strength norms for 1940. The aircraft's useful load was increased to 5,400 kg (11,910 lb). The number of passengers was increased in one version to 26, in another version to 34. The increase in seating capacity was achieved by narrowing the aisle and reducing the size of the baggage compartment and the galley. The cargo that could be carried by the transport version was estimated at 3,000 kg (6,615 lb). Like the PS-84-K, the new version would be able to carry external stores weighing up to 2,000 kg (4,405 lb) on a special beam rack with multiple shackles. 45 paratroopers could be carried; the number of casualties that could be transported in the medevac version was the same as in the PS-84-I version (18). The estimated range of the PS-84A 2M-71 was 1,200 km (746 miles).

The aircraft's aerodynamics and external finish were refined by providing undercarriage fairings (the way Douglas did on the Super DC-3), adding cooling air outlet flaps to the engine cowlings and increasing the surface area with flush riveting. Hence the maximum speed at an altitude of 5,000 m (16,400 ft) was expected to reach 485 km/h (301 mph). The commission headed by B. N. Yur'yev which assessed the PS-84A advanced development project (ADP) estimated the possible maximum speed at 460 km/h (285 mph).

Vasiliy S. Molokov, the director of Aeroflot, approved the project; on 9th December 1940 he sent a letter to K. Ye. Voroshilov in which he requested the inclusion of the PS-84A 2M-71 in the prototype construction plan for 1941. However, the Secretariat of the State Defence Committee advised Voroshilov to reject Molokov's request, primarily on the grounds that that work on the PS-84A 2M-71 would have a detrimental effect on production of the usual PS-84 2M-62IR passenger version.

In his letter to Voroshilov dated 10th December 1940, S. K. Timoshenko also objected to starting the work on the PS-84A, claiming, in addition to the abovementioned arguments, that this would lead to a cessation of the already insufficient deliveries of the PS-84. Meanwhile, the commission headed by B. N. Yur'yev came to the conclusion that it would be expedient to build a prototype of the PS-84A. However, Aleksandr S. Yakovlev (then Deputy People's Commissar of the Aircraft Industry) did not endorse this decision, remarking that *'...the troop-carrier version of the 'Douglas' is very good. A further, more radical modernisation of this aircraft is inexpedient...'*

Shakhoorin, in his letter to Voroshilov sent on 23rd January 1941 (this action was incited by Yakovlev), also objected to including the PS-84A in the development plan for 1941. On the other hand, he agreed with the opinion of the Air Force that there was a need for further modification of the PS-84 by means of adapting it to diesel engines. NII VVS also rejected the PS-84A project as it did not meet the specifications for 1942 (in particular, it lacked the requisite easily removable defensive armament and had insufficient range). Moreover, it was noted that the M-71 engines were in extremely short supply and required high-octane petrol. However, unlike Yakovlev, NII VVS believed that a further, more radical modernisation of the PS-84 *was* expedient. The conclusion signed by Chief of NII VVS A. I. Filin on 18th February 1941 read: *'There is a need for re-working the advanced development project and adapt it to the specifications for 1942 by studying the installation of diesel engines and taking into account the critical remarks...'* One of the main suggestions was that the normal range should be increased to 1,500 km (932 miles), and the range in overload configuration to 2,000 km (1,243 miles). It was also suggested that the time to 4,000 m (13,120 ft) be reduced to 8-9 minutes, and the question of converting the aircraft to a tricycle (nosewheel) undercarriage be studied.

On 28th January 1941 GKO Secretary M. Pugayev wrote to Molokov, advising him that Voroshilov had agreed with Timoshenko and Shakhoorin who categorically objected against the M-71-powered PS-84 version. Thus, Sen'kov's initiative aimed at creating a more efficient troop carrier, ambulance and passenger aircraft for the Soviet Air Force and Aeroflot, was brought to naught. Preference given to the diesel-powered option doomed further modernisation of the PS-84 due to a number of problems which subsequently came to light in connection with the widespread practical introduction of diesel engines in aviation.

Bomber Version of the PS-84A 2M-71 (Project)

It is worth noting that the PS-84A 2M-71 developed under A. A. Sen'kov's guidance also had a projected bomber version, but this version was not officially submitted to NKAP.

Staff Transport Version of the PS-84A 2M-71 (Project)

For the first time in the USSR, a staff transport version of a military transport aircraft was developed on the basis of the stillborn PS-84A 2M-71. It was provided with all necessary equipment for the work of commanders in field conditions. The passenger cabin included a sleeping compartment for four persons, a study and a conference room for 10 persons.

PS-84M 2M-30 Transport and Passenger Aircraft (Project)

Shortly thereafter Sen'kov developed and submitted to NKAP a new advanced development project – the PS-84M aircraft powered by two 1,500-hp Charomskiy M-30 Vee-12 liquid-cooled diesels. Before the war a full-size mock-up of this aircraft was built and endorsed by a mock-up review commission. The work was included into the plan of the plant's work, but then the war broke out, forcing NKAP to give up upgrades of existing aircraft in favour of more urgent work.

Military Transport Version of the PS-84, 1941 Model

The story of the armed military version of the Li-2 merits a more detailed account.

During the first six months of 1941 the Khimki plant produced the PS-84 only in the commercial version. When the war began, NKAP increased the production plan for the plant by 22% and demanded that it should switch to manufacturing this aircraft in the military transport version. In June 1941, transport/troopship-configured aircraft featuring a simplified cabin layout started leaving the plant's shops. In the first ten days of August the plant began producing aircraft with a wide port side cargo door (identical to that of the PS-84-K, except that the inward-opening smaller door was moved aft, incorporating the rearmost window). The cabin floor was not reinforced. The machine could transport 2 to 3 tonnes (4,410-6,613 lb) of cargo. The cargo handling devices developed for the PS-84-K were omitted. From October onwards the plant began outfitting some machines for the transportation of wounded personnel, using the technical drawings of the PS-84-I as a pattern. In this case the cabin accommodated 18 stretcher cases and two seats.

Top and above: This camouflaged PS-84 was one of many Aeroflot examples pressed into military service with the outbreak of the war (known as the '1941 model transport version'). Note the civil registration Л4171 (that is, L4171; the CCCP- prefix is omitted) and the reinforced V-shaped main gear drag struts.

In the meantime, despite putting up stubborn resistance to the Wehrmacht, the Red Army was on the retreat; the Germans had captured many industrial cities in the western parts of the USSR and besieged Leningrad. In the conditions of siege the city's military industry enterprises did not cease the manufacture of weapons and ammunition for a single day, catering not only for the city's defenders but also for the troops that fought back the German onslaught on Moscow. These weapons, as well as the food supplies for the hunger-stricken Leningrad, were transported via the 'air bridge' that had been set up. The crews of the Moscow Special Mission Aviation Group of GVF (MAGON – *Mos**kov**skaya aviatsi**on**naya **groop**pa o**so**bovo nazna**che**niya Grazh**dahn**skovo voz**doosh**novo **flo**ta*), where the best flying personnel of Aeroflot were concentrated at that time, shouldered the greatest burden in this unique airlift operation. The group included those who had mastered their difficult jobs in the demanding conditions of the High North and the Far East, who could fly in daylight conditions and at night in any weather, who could take off from a tiny airstrip and land the aircraft 'wherever ordered'.

Passenger aircraft were defenceless against the well-armed and manoeuvrable German fighters. In August 1941 alone the enemy put 18 transport machines out of action. The PS-84 was an excellent machine, but when it flew front-line missions, its pilots had to perform veritable circus stunts to shake enemy fighters off their tail. It became obvious that the transports had to be fitted with dorsal (turret-mounted) and waist-mounted machine guns. Therefore, a special armament workshop was set up at the aircraft repair facility at Moscow-Vnukovo (later known as Plant No.400). This is how I. Yel'kin, who was then chief of the Vnukovo repair facility, recalls the progress of this work.

'It was our repair facility that outfitted transport aircraft with armament. We did the whole job on our own, without assistance from design bureaux or production plants. Chief designer of the onboard armament system M. Kulik, chief engineer N. Gradusov, engineers I. Yuvenal'yev and M. Arsen'yev, armament designer-technician V. Baranovskiy, as well as the whole staff of the technical department headed by chief of the special workshop V. Chitayev, the teams of tinsmiths and riveters headed by A. Semyonov and V. Vishnyakov, a team of fitters headed by I. Shebanov – all these people did what might seem beyond human capability; in a matter of a few days they performed a unique job.

The well-known passenger aircraft acquired a completely new look. A hemispherical transparent dome appeared above the fuselage of the PS-84; a heavy machine gun protruded from a slit in this dome. Two more machine guns could be fired through openings on the aft fuselage sides.

By mid-September 1941 the unprecedented work on arming the transports was largely completed. The design of the weapons installation developed by the repair facility was adopted as standard. All technical drawings and descriptions of the gun installations were handed over to the aircraft plant, which was to start series production of PS-84s equipped with three permanent machine gun stations.

One day in September 1941 the following report was submitted to GU GVF Chief, Major-General V. S. Molokov, Hero of the Soviet Union: "While on a mission in the Leningrad area, a PS-84 transport piloted by crew commander Pantelli, was attacked by enemy fighters. As Novitskiy, the gunner of our aircraft, returned fire, one Me 109 enemy fighter burst into flames and fell into the forest. Another one was warded off by the machine gun fire of flight engineer Doomnov and left the scene losing altitude; the remaining two of the four fighters stopped their attacks. Our aircraft received a few bullet holes. The crew and passengers are unhurt."

"At last, we have achieved a victory in aerial combat", – said Molokov, not concealing his joy.

"Soon the Vnukovo repair facility will turn out the fifteenth PS-84 fitted with defensive armament", – said the First Deputy Chief of the GU GVF, Regimental Commissar (senior political officer – *authors' note*) *M. Karushev who was present in the study, addressing Molokov.*

"I hope, Mikhail Fyodorovich, – said Molokov with a kind of youthful ardour, – that henceforth all air squadrons assigned for rendering assistance to Leningrad will fly their missions with machine guns on board."

This task was fulfilled.'

Thus, from late July 1941 onwards the PS-84 transports were progressively fitted with armament. At first this was done in a somewhat primitive way directly in the field, in the front-line air units. For example, Mozharovskiy/Venevidov MV-3 'ball turrets' sourced from written-off bombers were mounted dorsally on the PS-84. From the end of July onwards the installation of armament was effected in an organised way at the repair facility at Moscow-Vnukovo, the home base of the Moscow Special Mission Air Group. Chief Designer of the defensive armament system M. M. Kulik designed the VUS-1 installation (***verkh**nyaya oosta**nov**ka strel**kov**aya* – dorsal gun installation) derived from the series-produced MV-3 turret with a 7.62-mm (.30 calibre) ShKAS machine gun for the PS-84. At the same time provision was made for the installation of two 7.62-mm Degtyaryov DA machine guns on ShKU-1 mounts (*shkvorne**va**ya oosta**nov**ka* – pintle [gun] installation) in the baggage compartment; they fired through apertures in the fuselage sides. One machine was thus modified in Vnukovo and underwent flight tests with M. A. Nikiforov as test pilot. In the very first flight, buffeting was experienced – the bulky turret altered the aircraft's aerodynamics. To cure the problem, the shape of the turret had to be altered. On 17th September, after more test flights, the modified turret was adopted as standard. A workshop was set up at the Vnukovo repair facility; all transport aircraft from the GVF and from the Air Force inventory paid a visit to this workshop for outfitting with the new armament. In addition, the modified PS-84s were fitted with armoured crew seat backs and dished seat pans permitting the use of parachutes; previously crews had been forced to lose precious time donning their parachutes before bailing out. Modification of the machines began before the prototype installation had been officially endorsed. In August 1941 alone, the Vnukovo plant outfitted 30 PS-84s in this fashion.

As stated earlier, before the war Plant No.84 and its chief designer A. A. Sen'kov repeatedly raised the issue of putting specialised military versions into production, but the NKAP leaders did not give the go-ahead. Not until the outbreak of the war and the appearance of the first PS-84 that were fitted with armament in field conditions did the plant receive instructions to convert the passenger machine urgently into a military version. From July 1941 onwards Plant No.84 started producing PS-84s modified for paradropping and transport duties, and from September 1941 onwards for casualty evacuation as well. New-build PS-84s started rolling off the lines with defensive armament in place. Initially (from August 1941 onwards) it comprised an MV-3 turret mounting a 7.62-mm ShKAS machine gun with 1,500 rounds of ammunition. Later (from September 1941 onwards) it was augmented by two DA machine guns with 600 rpg at the beam stations, as well as a fixed nose-mounted installation similar to the one used on the Petlyakov Pe-2 dive-bomber, mounting a ShKAS machine gun with 450 rounds.

However, the manufacture of armed machines in Khimki did not last long because of the necessity to evacuate the plant. In October only eleven machines were assembled, whereupon the plant moved to Tashkent. At the new site it proved impossible to assemble any machines until the end of the year; as already mentioned, not before 7th January 1942 was the first Tashkent-built machine assembled from components brought from Khimki, and the total output in January was a mere eight machines. Due to the evacuation of several subcontractor enterprises many components were unavailable, and some stamped parts had to replaced by sections crudely fabricated from sheet metal by hammering. Parts to be manufactured of alloyed steel had to be made of cheaper metal grades instead; copper and bronze were replaced by cast iron; wooden bulkheads and doors were introduced, and plywood was used for the floor. There was a shortage of wheels, propellers, radios, autopilots, gunsights and machine gun mounts; direction finders were mounted on 50% of the aircraft, and some machines even lacked heating.

The interior was considerably simplified: all cabin fittings (beginning with the forward baggage compartment) were deleted, as were the galley, toilet, luggage racks and ventilation. The comfortable seats of the airliner version gave place to tip-up wooden seats for 25 passengers.

By early April, 27 incomplete aircraft were sitting on the factory airfield; they could not be submitted for acceptance to military representatives. Nevertheless, PS-84 production gradually gathered momentum, and in April 1942 Plant No.84 handed over 21 aircraft to the military, followed by 29 in May and 64 in August. Modernisation of the aircraft was conducted under the direction of I. P. Mosolov.

As noted above, early armed PS-84s had the MV-3 dorsal turret, two pintle-mounted DA machine guns in the aft fuselage and a fixed ShKAS in the nose. However, fairly soon the airmen at the front came to the conclusion that the transport's firepower was insufficient for repelling the attacks of German fighters. As early as December 1941 a proposal was made to replace the ShKAS machine gun in the dorsal turret by the 12.7-mm (.50 calibre) Berezin UBT machine guns, while the DA machine guns in the beam positions were to be replaced by the faster-firing ShKAS. By April 1942 a trial installation of the UTK-1 dorsal turret with the UBT machine gun was made on two PS-84s at a GVF repair facility; the UTK-1 was the MV-3 turret modified to accept a heavy machine gun. The tests gave satisfactory results, and plant No 84 in Tashkent began installing UTK-1 turrets on new-build machines. In July 1942 the modernised aircraft manufactured there successfully passed trials at the Aviation Armament Research & Test Range (NIPAV – *Na**ooch**no-ispy**tah**tel'nyy poli**gon** aviatsi**on**novo vo'oru-**zhen**iya*) in Faustovo, Moscow Region. The armament, together with the ammunition complement, weighed 134 kg (295 lb).

Depending on the altitude, the armament ate up 14 to 17 km/h (8.7 to 10.6 mph) of maximum speed, reducing it to 281 km/h (175 mph) at the same all-up weight. The range accordingly fell to 2,350 km (1,460 miles), the rate of climb deteriorated (a climb to 5,000 m/16,400 ft now took as much as 10 minutes longer!) and the service ceiling became 500 m (1,640 ft) lower. Nevertheless, the modified aircraft was recommended for series production. In August 1942 the Commander of the Air Force wrote to People's Commissar of the Aircraft Industry A. I. Shakhoorin that *'...to increase the aircraft's firepower, it is necessary to fit the UTK-1 turret with the UBT machine gun to all production PS-84 aircraft manufactured by Plant No.84 instead of the previously used MV-3 turret with a ShKAS machine gun'.*

The UTK-1 turret was mounted, as a matter of priority, on the Il'yushin IL-4 (DB-3F) long-range bomber. After the outbreak of the war, when the Soviet aircraft industry stepped up bomber production, the supply of new turrets was of course insufficient to cover the needs of transport aircraft as well. In consequence, some time passed before the UTK-1 was available for mounting on the PS-84 (Li-2) aircraft. From 15th September 1942 onwards all PS-84s rolling off the production line were fitted with UTK-1 turrets, and from October onwards the machines manufactured earlier were progressively retrofitted. However, the DA machine guns were still retained at the beam stations; not before March 1943 did they give place to ShKAS machine guns on production PS-84 (Li-2) aircraft with defensive armament. At the front lines the armament was sometimes supplemented by machine guns in the windows of the passenger/cargo cabin; a case is on record when a 20-mm ShVAK cannon was mounted in one of the windows on starboard side of the fuselage.

Li-2 Night Bomber Version

From the spring of 1942 onwards Plant No.84 began to fit production PS-84s with bomb armament. Since the aircraft was too slow and sluggish for daytime employment, the intention was to use it as a night bomber. There was prior experience to fall back on, as the PS-84 had already been fitted with bomb racks earlier directly in first-line units. For example, on 8th March 1942 two PS-84s modified in the field to accept bomb armament took part in the Soviet air raid against the Finnish port of Oulu.

It was Chairman of the State Defence Committee Iosif V. Stalin himself who posed

Crates of ammunition are loaded from a ZiS-5 3-ton lorry into a Black Sea Fleet Air Arm PS-84 transport fitted with an MV-3 dorsal turret (with stabilising fins) and beam machine guns on ShKU-1 mounts. The aircraft wears temporary winter camouflage; the serial '4027 Black'.may be derived from the c/n (1844027).

the task of converting the PS-84 into a night bomber. The first project of adapting the PS-84 for this role was developed by the OKB-43 design bureau under the direction of A. I. Shool'gin. All bombs were to be carried externally under the wing centre section where a transverse beam carrying four Der-19 racks (*derzhatel'* – holder) was mounted, permitting the carriage of weapons weighing up to 500 kg (1,102 lb) – typically four FAB-250 bombs or two FAB-500 bombs. There was no winch for suspending the bombs. Instead of bombs, paradroppable cargo bags and fuel tanks could be carried. The aircraft was provided with an ESBR-3P main electric bomb release unit (*elektrosbrasyvatel'*) and a backup mechanical bomb release unit. The NKPB-3 collimator night bombsight (*nochnoy kollimahtornyy pritsel bombardirovochnyy*) was mounted externally near the starboard side window of the flightdeck. To conduct the aiming, the navigator who now occupied the seat of the co-pilot stuck his head outside, a small collapsible visor providing protection from the slipstream.

On 23rd April 1942 People's Commissar of the Aircraft Industry A. I. Shakhoorin reported in his letter to I. V. Stalin that one PS-84 transport aircraft had been fitted with bomb armament and tested in a regiment of the Long-Range Aviation (ADD – *Aviahtsiya dahl'nevo deystviya*) – the Soviet Air Force's bomber command. The aircraft was equipped with four beam-type racks which enabled external carriage of four FAB-250 bombs or two FAB-500 bombs, or two VAP-500 spray tanks (*vylivnoy aviatsionnyy pribor* – 'aircraft-mounted pouring device') that could contain either toxic agents or self-inflammable liquid phosphorus.

The bomb armament of the PS-84 passed flight tests satisfactorily and was recommended by ADD specialists for installation on production aircraft, whereupon Shakhoorin instructed Plant No.84 to fit the bomb armament to production PS-84s. Thus, the technical drawings from OKB-43 were transferred to the Tashkent aircraft factory, which was to fit the bomb armament to the aircraft under construction, and to the GVF Aircraft Repair Plant No.89, which was to upgrade existing machines. The intention was to retrofit the bomb armament not only to the aircraft belonging to regular Air Force units but also to those operated by the GVF.

The design of the bomb racks developed by OKB-43 proved to be less than perfect; fitting them was a tricky job, and the wiring to the bomb release devices interfered with functioning of the fuel system. Therefore the technical drawings underwent some revision and improvement at Plant No.89. The first two aircraft left the workshops of this enterprise on 23rd May 1942; somewhat later aircraft factory No.81 in Leningrad also started retrofitting in-service PS-84s with the bomb armament.

The production Plant No.84 decided, nevertheless, to stick to the original drawings supplied by OKB-43. Beginning with Batch 32 manufactured in June 1942, the plant began to equip new-build PS-84s with bomb release units and bombsights, including the NKPB-3. The airframe was reinforced in several places. V-shaped main landing gear drag struts made their appearance. They supplanted two earlier types of drag struts: the one for summer use (with wheels) and the one for winter use (with skis). The reinforced undercarriage struts reduced the number of failures of the upper girder during landings accompanied by a turning of the aircraft. The maximum fuel capacity was increased to 3,110 litres (684.2 Imp gal) by installing additional fuel tanks in the cabin (such tanks had been fitted earlier to operational aircraft). After the conversion of the PS-84 into a bomber the machine's all-up weight increased from 10,900 kg (24,030 lb) in the pre-war version to 11,500 kg (25,360 lb). This resulted in a reduction of the maximum speed and the rate of climb. Moreover, a lengthy climb at full throttle in warm weather caused overheating of the engine oil. To cure the problem the existing two main oil coolers were supplemented by a 9-inch oil cooler specially for summer operations. It was mounted without any fairing on the outboard side of the engine cowling. Tests revealed that the additional oil cooler functioned even more efficiently than the main ones, which were mounted vertically inside the engine cowling.

The modified aircraft were fitted with an inert gas system in which cooled and desiccated exhaust gases were directed into the fuel tanks. This significantly reduced the danger of a fire in the event the fuel tanks were pierced by incendiary bullets, thereby enhancing combat survivability. On some aircraft impregnated fibre fuel tanks were fitted instead of metal ones.

However, the first production PS-84s in the night bomber version were not approved by the military representatives because they lacked the Der-19 bomb racks (these were received by the plant with some delay). Not before July 1942 did production PS-84s fully equipped with bombing devices start leaving the assembly shop of the Tashkent plant.

On 28th July 1942 a PS-84 2M-62IR military transport (c/n 1843603 – that is, type 1 built by Plant No.84, Batch 36, third aircraft in the batch) was submitted to NII VVS for State acceptance trials. It featured bomb armament and was modified in accordance with the remarks that had been made in the PS-84-K's (PS-84-I's) state acceptance trials protocol in 1940. The aircraft had defensive armament; it was fitted with an external transverse beam

PS-84 c/n 1843603, the unserialled prototype of the bomber version, during trials at NII VVS in the summer of 1942. The dorsal turret and beam machine gun mounts are visible but the bomb racks are not.

under the wing centro section carrying four racks for the suspension of cargoes or bombs. The cabin was provided with tip-up wooden seats for 25 troops; a cargo door incorporating an additional entry door was fitted for airdropping troops, loading and unloading cargoes. The pilot's and navigator's seats were provided with armoured backs. Each engine was provided with an extra oil cooler, and an inert gas system enhancing the aircraft's combat survivability was installed. Engineer-Lt. Col. V. M. Kokorin was project test engineer, with Major V. N. Lisitsyn as project test pilot and Lt. (sg) A. I. Starykh as navigator.

The concluding part of the test report stated that the aircraft's defensive armament did not, after all, ensure sufficient protection against fighter attack because of the small calibre of the armament and unsatisfactory protection of the lower hemisphere. (Remember that the UTK-1 dorsal turret with the 12.7-mm UBT machine gun was fitted to production aircraft only from mid-September 1942 onwards; PS-84 c/n 1843603 had been manufactured several months earlier.) It was suggested that the ShKAS machine gun in the dorsal turret be replaced by a 12.7-mm machine gun and the angles of fire in the lower hemisphere be increased. The Conclusion on the test results dealt with the oil cooling problem. It was noted that powerplant/oil system operation was satisfactory; the additional oil coolers kept the oil temperature within the stipulated limits at ambient temperature of +35°C (+95°F) near the ground. At ambient temperatures below 0°C (+32°F) there was a possibility of the oil coolers freezing and bursting in flight. The installation and removal of the oil coolers according to the season was a cumbersome procedure; in consequence, it was suggested that the installation of additional oil coolers be permitted as a temporary measure only.

The report was endorsed on 9th September 1942. A day earlier, order No.0174 of the Red Army Air Force was issued, stipulating that henceforth the PS-84 aircraft be designated Li-2 (Lisunov-2). It was followed on 17th September by Order No.72 to the same effect issued by GU GVF Chief Lt. Gen. Fyodor A. Astakhov and GU GVF Military Commissar, Brigade Commissar Antonov; it was titled 'On the renaming of the PS-84 aircraft'. At that time Boris P. Lisunov was chief engineer of Plant No.84.

The emergence of the new designation appears rather strange because a new procedure for allocating the designations of aircraft had been introduced in keeping with a GKO directive issued in December 1940 and the NKAP Order dated 9th December 1940. Instead of the role designator used hitherto (PS for *passa**zheer**skiy samo**lyot*** – airliner, I for *istre**bi**tel'* – fighter, DB for ***dahl'****niy bombardi**rov**shchik* – long-range bomber and so on), the aircraft's designation should include the first letters of the designer's last name, followed by an odd number for 'light' aircraft (such as fighters) or an even number for heavy aircraft such as transports and bombers. The designation for each specific aircraft type was introduced by an order issued by the People's Commissar of the Aircraft Industry.

In this case the first letters referred to a person who was not the aircraft's designer. Though Lisunov undeniably did an enormous job organising PS-84 production in Tashkent, it would have been far more logical to rename the aircraft Se-2 (in honour of chief designer A. A. Sen'kov) who created the military versions, or Mo-2 in honour of his successor I. P. Mosolov who introduced various design improvements, or even Sem-2 (to honour both). What's more, the order on the PS-84/Li-2 designation change appeared nearly *two years* after the new system had come into effect. Besides, the wording of Astakhov's order contained one rather unusual phrase: '*...pursuant to an Order of the VVS KA'* (Red Army Air Force). This could only be a reference to an order of the Air Force Commander-in-Chief. *Whose* order was it, then?

Thus, from the summer of 1942 onwards the PS-84 became a dual-purpose aircraft: after having been fitted with the bombing equipment, it retained the capabilities of a transport machine. Despite the fact that the aircraft was renamed, the new designation began to appear in Air Force documents only in the second half of 1943.

In September 1942 a number of alterations were introduced into the aircraft's design. The single hydraulic system was divided into two independent systems. The autopilot was actuated by the hydraulic pump installed on the starboard engine, while all other hydraulic equipment was served by the pump on the port engine. Sure enough, this reduced reliability by eliminating the element of redundancy; on the other hand, this made it possible to fill up the main system with a cheap mixture of alcohol and glycerine instead of the costly MVP grade oil.

An attempt was made to install wooden propellers. The VISh-21-D-22 propeller had blade shanks made of so-called 'delta-timber' (wood impregnated with phenol formaldehyde resin) and the rest of the blade was ordinary pinewood. However, tests conducted by a crew commanded by Maj. M. A. Nyukhtikov showed that top speed with the VISh-21-D-22 propellers was reduced by 12-25 km/h (7.4-17.5 mph), the vertical speed above 1,800 m (5,910 ft) also deteriorated, and the service ceiling was diminished by 500 m (1,640 ft). Eventually the idea of using wooden propellers was abandoned. Also in September 1942, improvements were made to the airframe's metallisation (the electric resistance between airframe units and subassemblies was reduced), which helped increase the range of radio communication.

From Batch 62 onwards all machines were equipped with de-icers. The wing leading edges were heated by hot exhaust gases passing through pipes along the whole span. Heating of the stabilisers was also tried on some aircraft. The stabiliser leading edge was coated with a conductive graphite compound through which electric current passed. Such experiments had been undertaken earlier; for example, two aircraft had been similarly equipped at the Vnukovo repair facility by 5th November 1942, and a dozen more machines by the end of the year for the purpose of holding service tests. However, eventually the electro-thermal de-icers were deemed inefficient and were deactivated on most of the PS-84s thus equipped.

The PS-84 aircraft manufactured earlier and retrofitted with armament but lacking the structural reinforcement measures were operated with limits imposed on the all-up weight and maximum speed.

Beginning with the Battle of Stalingrad, bomber-configured PS-84s were used successfully in all major operations of the Red Army, including the Berlin operation. The results of their actions were sufficiently impressive, especially when used against enemy communications. For example, during the Battle of Stalingrad, on the night of 26th August 1942, a group of PS-84 aircraft destroyed German pontoon bridges over the Don River near the hamlets Vertyachiy and Luchenskiy with direct hits of FAB-250 bombs, which helped ease the situation of Soviet troops defending the approaches to Stalingrad. In the Battle of Kursk the Li-2 bombers operated by ADD units dealt tangible blows first and foremost against railway junctions. In these cases the combat losses of transports-turned-bombers were relatively low. Getting ahead of our story, we may note that the overall losses of the PS-84 (Li-2) aircraft during the war were close to 600 machines, which was about 26% of the type's total wartime production.

In the opinion of the military, the Li-2's main drawback in the bomber role was the inconvenient workstation of the navigator, who had a very poor view from his seat. The ADD command turned to NKAP with a request for a modification of the aircraft: its nose section should be lengthened and glazed in order to accommodate the navigator/bomb-aimer with the necessary instruments, day and night bombsights and bomb release switches. There were plans for replacing the fixed nose machine gun with a ShKAS in a ball mount (of the same type as on the IL-4 bomber) with 500 rounds of ammunition. On 4th November 1942 the People's Commissariat sent a letter to Plant No.84, tasking it with developing such a version and constructing a mock-up of the forward fuselage, but there is no evidence as to whether this work was actually performed. Much later, in the post-war years, a similar design was used on a purely civil version – the Li-2PR fishery reconnaissance aircraft (see below).

In 1943 further improvements were introduced on the Li-2s intended for front-line operation. To improve the airframe's aerodynamics, the cargo door was made completely flush-fitting (earlier it had protruded slightly above the fuselage skin when closed), the gaps between the flaps and the wings, between the ailerons and the wings, and between the propeller spinners and blade shanks were made smaller; flush riveting was introduced on the leading-edge skin of the wing de-icer. From Batch 67 onwards electro-thermal de-icing was introduced on production aircraft, after all; from Batch 90 onwards the flightdeck featured ultra-violet lighting which considerably improved the crew's working conditions during night flights.

The use of the Li-2 in the night bomber role was seriously hampered by the absence of flame dampers/mufflers on the exhaust pipes because the exhaust flames gave the aircraft away to German fighter pilots and anti-aircraft artillery crews. After a series of tests involving several types of flame dampers the Air Force selected the most efficient model, the GAM-10 which had been developed by A. I. Tsepov at the Central Aero Engine Institute (TsIAM – *Tsen**trahl'**nyy insti**toot** aviatsionnovo mo**tor**ostro**yen**iya*). One machine fitted with flame dampers (c/n 1842606) was transferred to NII VVS for operational tests, and then for service tests in the 1st ADD division which were completed in July 1943. From Batch 93 (August 1943) onwards the GAM-10 flame dampers/mufflers were fitted to all Li-2s. From Batch 107 onwards, hoists for hooking up bombs were introduced (prior to that this work was done manually).

Li-2 Night Bomber with Internal Bomb Carriage

Yet, the Air Force had a practical interest in tackling the problem of accommodating a bomb load internally in the PS-84's fuselage. Using only internal bomb carriage could give an improvement of the bomber version's performance. A combination of internal and external bomb carriage would make it possible to increase the total warload.

Experimental work on internal bomb carriage was conducted as early as 1941, in the opening phase of the war (before the evacuation of the plant). Yet the first practical attempt to develop a night bomber version able to carry an internal bomb load of up to 1,500 kg (3,310 lb) was not made until the autumn of 1942. Such an aircraft (c/n 1845408) was built by 15th September and was passing manufacturer's tests in January 1943. It was flown by a single pilot; the right-hand seat was occupied by the navigator/bomb-aimer who used an NKPB-4 night bombsight. The machine was fitted with separate bomb suspension devices inside the fuselage.

The following internal bomb load variants were possible: 15 FAB-100 (or FAB-100M43) bombs or 15 TsAP-40 chemical spray tanks. The FAB-100 bombs were placed in three special cassettes: two of them were installed side by side in the forward fuselage immediately aft of the flightdeck, with a passage in between, and one in the rear part of the cargo cabin. Each cassette was to contain five bombs. The bombs were to be dropped through fuselage hatches which were closed by doors. A removable hand-driven winch was used for hoisting the bombs into position inside the fuselage. The external bomb racks for four FAB-250s or two FAB-500s remained unchanged. The maximum bomb load within the permissible all-up weight of 11,500 kg (25,360 lb) reached 2,500 kg (5,510 lb) at the expense of reducing the fuel load. The internal bomb stowage had practically no detrimental effect of the aircraft's aerodynamics and affected its performance but little.

The defensive armament comprised a UTK-1 dorsal turret with a 12.7-mm UBT machine gun which had successfully passed tests on a production PS-84 at the NIPAV test range in July 1942. As noted earlier, back in August 1942 the Commander of the Air Force pointed out the need to install the UTK-1 turret with the UBT machine gun instead of the then-current MV-3 turret with the ShKAS machine gun on all production PS-84s. However, the PS-84 (Li-2) began receiving these turrets with some delay because the IL-4 bombers enjoyed higher priority.

Serialled '5408' to reflect the c/n, the Li-2 night bomber with internal bomb stowage underwent state acceptance trials at NII VVS in February 1943 but didn't make the grade, primarily because of the too high force applied to the bomb release lever (up to 70 kg/154 lb). In addition, the proposed modification of the fuselage was regarded by the military as too complicated; they feared that the introduction of the new design would affect the rate of series production. In consequence, this version remained a one-off.

Li-2 Night Bomber with M-88 (M-82) Engines and Internal Bomb Carriage (Project)

As a development of the PS-84 night bomber version with internal bomb stowage, in the first half of 1943 chief designer of Plant 84 I. P. Mosolov prepared an advanced development project of a similar version powered by Tumanskiy M-88 or Shvetsov M-82 radials. The proposed versions also differed in defensive armament: the pintle-mounted ShKAS machine guns at the beam positions were to be replaced by 12.7-mm UBT machine guns. The project was not implemented.

Li-2VP Night Bomber with Internal Bomb Carriage

In September 1944 Plant No.84 undertook yet another attempt to improve the bomber version of the Li-2. This time the internal bomb carriage arrangement was considerably simplified. The unserialled aircraft (c/n 1846605) had the following main differences from the machine which had undergone tests in early 1943 (c/n 1845408):

- the bomb cassettes were installed directly in the cabin, and bomb release was effected through tunnels in the floor; three Der-21 cassettes also made it possible to accommodate up to fifteen FAB-100 or FAB-100M43 bombs in the fuselage. The external bomb racks were also retained;
- the nose-mounted machine gun was deleted (it was considered useless);
- the navigator/bomb-aimer had two bombsights at his disposal – the OPB-1R (*op**ticheskiy** pri**tsel** bombardi**rov**ochnyy*) for daytime use and the NKPB-7 for night-time use;
- the ESBR-3P main bomb release unit was replaced by the ESBR-6;
- a more modern AP-42 autopilot was installed.

The total bomb load was 2,500 kg (5,512 lb). The machine retained standard defensive armament – a UTK-1 dorsal turret and two ShKAS machine guns in rear fuselage side ports. The aircraft received the designation Li-2VP; contrary to popular belief, the VP suffix denoted ***vnoot**rennyaya pod**ves**ka* (internal [bomb] carriage), *not voyennoye* *prime**nen**iye* (military use).

In late December 1944 the aircraft was ferried to NII VVS where its state acceptance trials commenced. The aircraft was flown by a crew captained by Lt. Col. V. I. Zhdanov. The tests lasted, with intermissions, until 8th March 1945. The introduction of internal bomb carriage led to some improvement of the night bomber's performance, but not to the extent that would justify the trouble involved in changing the production process; for this reason the Li-2VP was not adopted for series manufacture. Nevertheless, some of the improvements tested and checked on the Li-2VP were gradually introduced on production machines. For example, Li-2s from Batch 147 onwards featured the AP-42 autopilot which was a copy of a US model. It was actu-

Above: The Li-2VP bomber prototype (c/n 1846605) during NII VVS trials in December 1944. Note the bomb-aimer's window in the baggage loading door on the port side of the nose.

ated electrically and had a quicker response in comparison with the previously used hydraulically-actuated autopilot. From Batch 156 onwards the nose-mounted ShKAS was deleted because it was used extremely rarely and became completely unnecessary at the end of the war.

The forward fuselage underside of the Li-2VP, showing the open internal bomb bay doors; FAB-100 bombs are visible. Note the external bomb racks with their release cables.

Li-2NB Night Bomber

From December 1943 (Batch 108) onwards the Tashkent Aircraft Plant No.84 began producing considerably modified transport/troop-carrier Li-2s which could be operated in the bomber role. The main alterations were as follows:

- the crew included two pilots instead of one;
- a navigator's station equipped with an instrument panel was arranged behind the captain's seat;
- a radio operator's station was placed behind the co-pilot's seat instead of the baggage compartment;
- one more window on each side was added to the flightdeck glazing near the new crew stations;
- two windows were added in the forward fuselage door; the lower one (the navigator's observation hatch) was horizontally split into two halves, the upper half opening outwards and the lower half inwards;
- a GEA-50 gas analyser was installed;
- an ESBR-3 electric bomb release unit was installed;
- a Bendix MN-26S direction finder was installed from Batch 117 onwards; the shape of the DF loop aerial fairing was changed;
- the RSB-*bis* radio was replaced by the RSR-1 model from Batch 117 onwards;
- the NKPB-4 night bombsight was replaced by the NKPB-7 model;
- an MSh-3 compressor was installed (from Batch 119 onwards); it was provided with a small engine of its own and produced compressed air even with the main engines inoperative, which eased the servicing of the aircraft at unequipped field airstrips.

In December 1944 the sixth machine of Batch 119 (c/n 18411906) was submitted for state acceptance trials; it already bore the official designation Li-2NB (*noch**noy** bombardi**rov**shchik* – night bomber). According to the assessment of test pilot M. A. Nyukhtikov and test navigator N. P. Tsvetkov, the aircraft's performance remained unchanged but the view from the navigator's station became much worse; there was no communication between the pilot and the navigator.

The trials of the Li-2NB showed once more the poor efficiency of the de-icing system, therefore a decision was taken to order BF Goodrich pneumatic de-icer boots (which had proved their worth on the DC-3/C-47) in the USA. Actually, the GKO had issued a directive authorising the purchase of 250 sets as early as 13th March 1944. Negotiations on this purchase lasted for a long time and resulted in the acquisition of only a small number of de-icers which were used as spares for the C-47s delivered to the Soviet Union under the Lend-Lease agreement.

Left: The two forward bomb cassettes of the Li-2VP, each holding five FAB-100s, with the passage to the flightdeck in between. Note that the apertures are closed by covers when not in use. Note also the hand-driven bomb hoist on the right and the step for the dorsal turret in the middle of the cabin.
Right: The rear bomb cassette of the Li-2VP, again with five FAB-100s. The propeller-like vanes on the detonators are fitted with safety pins.

Li-2 Transport / Troop-Carrier Aircraft with M-88B Engines

According to the Russian press, during the Great Patriotic War several examples of the Li-2 were fitted with 1,100-hp Tumanskiy M-88B radials as fitted to the IL-4. The aircraft were used in the transport role, but were armed with only one ShKAS or UBT machine gun in an enclosed dorsal turret. The machines were capable of transporting up to 25 troops with their sidearms. The speed reached 350 km/h (217 mph) at an altitude of 2,000 m (6,560 ft). (There are doubts as to the veracity of the claim; the engines may have been misidentified as M-88Bs by the shape of the cowlings and could be Shvetsov M-82s.)

Li-2 Glider Tug Version

During the war Li-2s were also used for towing Antonov A-7 and Gribovskiy G-11 assault gliders carrying supplies to partisan detachments far behind enemy lines. The fuselage tailcone was cropped and housed a device which permitted the towing of several gliders simultaneously – the so-called 'glider train'. Bombs weighing up to 100 kg could be suspended under the wing centre section.

Li-2 Special Mission VIP Aircraft

In late 1943, when Iosif V. Stalin was due to go to Teheran for a conference with Franklin D. Roosevelt and Winston Churchill, the question arose: what aircraft was to carry the Soviet leader to Teheran? Suddenly it became obvious that the 'great aviation power' had no suitable passenger aircraft; for decades all the numerous design bureaux and production plants had been preparing for the coming war and building only attack aircraft, fighters and bombers. Thus, there were only two alternatives: the VIP-configured Petlyakov Pe-8ON bomber in which Vyacheslav M. Molotov had flown to Great Britain in 1941, or the PS-84 (Li-2) or its US progenitor. Using a converted C-47 or a civilian DC-3 was extremely undesirable – after all, it was unbecoming for Stalin to go to a meeting with the leaders of the Allied powers in 'their' aircraft!

Stalin had some rather unpleasant recollections associated with the four-engined Pe-8 (TB-7). Several times he had had to pronounce his judgement on the destiny of this high-altitude strategic bomber, an aircraft that was unique for that period. At that time no nation in the world had strategic aviation, and the ATsN supercharger driven by a fifth engine in the Pe-8's fuselage and catering for the four cruise engines enabled the bomber to fly at altitudes unattainable for fighters and anti-aircraft artillery (as corroborated by Molotov's safe journey over the war-stricken Europe). Four times Stalin had signed directives ordering the Pe-8 into production, and four times he had abrogated them. As a result, by the time the war began there were very few strategic bombers in the USSR. The Li-2 was not the best option either, if only because it was built under American licence. Yet, it was this aircraft that the Air Force started preparing for the Supreme Commander-in-Chief's important mission.

Five Li-2s with pre-war type comfortable passenger cabins were specially manufactured in June 1943 to take the Soviet delegation to Teheran. They were assembled with particular thoroughness and were approved by a special commission. One more aircraft (three, according to some sources) was converted into a passenger version by the repair facility of the 1st Air Regiment of the NKVD security police in the town of Bykovo near Moscow. It had fewer seats than a standard

Above: An unserialled Li-2NB night bomber (c/n 18411906) during state acceptance trials at NII VVS in December 1944. Four FAB-250M43 are suspended under the wing centre section. Note the airflow control shutters fitted to the engine cowling fronts in winter to prevent excessive cooling.

Another aspect of Li-2NB c/n 18411906 at NII VVS.

Four views of the Li-2 2M-88B prototype during trials at NII VVS. The reshaped engine nacelles with the multi-petal cooling airflow control shutters are shown to advantage, as are the new propellers.

passenger aircraft and featured a luxurious interior. Yet, Stalin did not make use of any of these 'Teheran Specials', preferring a US-built C-47 with its greater speed and reliability.

Li-2 Transport and Troop-Carrier Aircraft with Extended Range

In 1943 ten production Li-2s were fitted with additional fuel tanks in the fuselage. These aircraft with an extended radius of action were intended for flights into the enemy's rear. They had no special designation.

Li-2 Fuel Carrier

In the same year of 1943 five production Li-2 aircraft were converted into 'fuel carriers' for use by the ADD; they were to transport fuel to front-line airfields.

Li-2 with Caterpillar Undercarriage Designed by S. A. Mostovoy

In 1942-43 an attempt was made to equip the Li-2 with a tracked (caterpillar) undercarriage designed by S.A. Mostovoy; this held the promise of considerably improving the aircraft's ability to taxi on soggy ground or slush. The undercarriage made use of the so-called 'Chechubalin caterpillars' (designed by N.A. Chechubalin) which had a width of 300 mm (11¹³⁄₁₆ in) and were composed of Textolite composite cylinders having a diameter of 50 mm (1³¹⁄₃₂ in). Earlier a similar device had been successfully tested on the Polikarpov U-2 and R-5 biplanes.

Fitted with a fixed caterpillar undercarriage, the aircraft (c/n 1841314) commenced manufacturer's tests in September 1942. Taxi runs, take-offs and landings were performed on a normal airfield, on a ploughed field (a potato field) and on a marsh covered with a water layer up to 70 cm (27 in) deep. In the concluding part of the test report it was noted that a caterpillar undercarriage could be utilised on all types of combat aircraft, enabling them to operate from a ploughed field, an airfield with a soggy surface and even marshland, all of which would be unsuitable for aircraft with a normal wheeled undercarriage.

The flight and field performance of the aircraft equipped with a caterpillar undercarriage, as well as its handling, were no worse than those of a standard aircraft with an extended wheel undercarriage. The designers of the undercarriage considered that minor modifications to the Li-2 would make it possible to retract the caterpillar undercarriage. The prototype installation weighed twice as much as the normal wheels and 1.25-1.3 times more than the skis used on the Li-2. The test commission noted that the experience accumulated in the process of developing and testing the caterpillar undercarriage for the Li-2 made it possible to start work on a similar undercarriage for combat aircraft immediately.

In April 1943 manufacturer's tests were conducted of another Li-2 (c/n 1846310) fitted with an improved version of the caterpillar undercarriage. Generally the report on the testing of this aircraft repeated the conclusions made after testing the first version of the caterpillars. It was stated that the undercarriage had passed manufacturer's tests successfully and the aircraft ought to be submitted to state acceptance tests.

No sooner said than done. Project test engineer Engineer-Captain Shoobralov and test pilot Major Khripkov were assigned to conduct the state acceptance tests of the Li-2 fitted with the caterpillar undercarriage. The aircraft's flight performance was determined with wheels only, as both sets of the caterpillar undercarriage had suffered damage in the course of testing. The trials showed that the caterpillars caused a marked reduction of ground manoeuvrability, the take-off and landing techniques became considerably more complicated, and the take-off run was increased. It was noted that the caterpillar design was not fully developed and its operation was unreliable. Even in its fixed version the weight of the caterpillar undercarriage was 290 kg (640 lb) heavier than the standard one.

It was stated in the Conclusions that the flights had confirmed the possibility of utilising a caterpillar undercarriage for single special flights, providing it was well manufactured, but the design was unsuitable as a standard undercarriage type for mass operation. The caterpillar undercarriage failed to pass state acceptance tests, and it was not recommended for series manufacture. Despite the fact that the trials report was a 'thumbs-down', it was nevertheless confirmed that N. A. Chechubalin's concept was feasible. The state acceptance trials protocol was endorsed on 2nd July 1943.

Li-2 Cannon-Armed Attack Aircraft

In early 1945 a Li-2 armed with two wing-mounted 45-mm (1.77 calibre) Nudel'man/Suranov NS-45 cannons was submitted for flight tests. The aircraft passed the tests successfully, but was not put into production because the war came to an end.

Li-2P Airliner

In the spring of 1945 it was obvious that the war had been won. Hence, in accordance with GKO directive No.8241 dated 22nd April 1945 and an NKAP order issued five days later, from 1st May 1945 onwards Plant No.84 was to manufacture only the ASh-62IR-powered Li-2P airliner (*passa**zheer**skiy* – passenger, used attributively) and the Li-2 transport without defensive armament (these designations were allocated in accordance with the GKO directive and NKAP order dated 8th March 1944). The Li-2P had only the starboard-side entry door. The passenger cabin featured 24 semi-cushioned seats (eight rows of three), the floor was covered with carpets. The common and individual ventilation, lighting, a heating system, heat- and soundproofing created the necessary comfort. A coat closet and a toilet were provided in the rear part of the cabin. Overhead bins for the passengers' personal belongings were installed along the whole length of the cabin.

A new c/n system was introduced in 1952. For instance, Li-2P CCCP-73976 is c/n 23440610 – that is, year of manufacture year of manufacture 1952, Plant No.84 (number of the non-existent Plant No.34 now became a code used for security reasons), Batch 406, 10th and final aircraft in the batch. The Li-2P remained in production until 1953.

Li-2T Transport/Cargo Aircraft

In accordance with the abovementioned GKO directive and NKAP order issued in April 1945,

One of the two PS-84s fitted experimentally with a caterpillar undercarriage for soft-field operations.

Above: A Li-2T with the post-1958 style registration CCCP-04215. Although it wears nothing more than Aeroflot titles, the 04xxx registration batch reveals this is a Polar Aviation aircraft.

Passengers disembark from Li-2P CCCP-84714 No.1 as a porter with a trolley stands by to take care of their baggage. This registration was later re-used for an Antonov An-2R agricultural aircraft.

on 1st May Plant No.84 started production of the ASh-62IR-powered Li-2T commercial freighter and military transport (T = *__trahns-__portnyy* – transport, used attributively). The Li-2T retained the cargo door but lacked armament. The prototype underwent state acceptance trials at NII VVS between 12th September and 13th October 1945 with V. Ya. Magon as project engineer.

The Li-2T was produced by Plant No.84 from late 1945 until 1953. In late 1946 the transport version also entered production at Plant No.126 at Komsomol'sk-on-Amur/Dzemgi airfield, where it was built until 1950. The machine could transport cargoes with a total weight of up to 3,000 kg (6,615 lb).

Li-2P Staff Transport (VIP) Version

Some ten aircraft were converted into a VIP/staff transport version designated Li-2 'Salon' (*samo**lyot**-'sa**lon**'* is the Russian term for VIP aircraft). The passenger cabin was equipped with comfortable seats in a club arrangement with tables in between. Separated from it by a partition was a small rest area provided with two sleeping berths, a coat closet and a toilet. The passenger cabin was finished with walnut and blue velvet. There were also other versions of the 'Salon' layout. In particular, one aircraft belonging to the 6th Special Mission Air Squadron of the Polish Air Force had its passenger cabin divided into two parts. One of them was provided with a sofa, a table and two comfortable seats; the other section had a table and a comfortable seat.

Li-2 Mailplane/Passenger Aircraft with ASh-82FN Engines

In 1942 I. P. Mosolov, who succeeded A. A. Sen'kov as chief designer of Plant No.84, started developing a military version of the PS-84 powered by Shvetsov M-82 14-cylinder radials; at the same time studies were made of an airliner version powered by these engines. In 1943 a prototype Li-2 with 1,950-hp ASh-82FN engines was built in a military version with a dorsal turret; it was readily identifiable by the new tapered engine cowlings (similar to those of the Lavochkin La-5FN fighter) and the large propeller spinners. In 1944, in accordance with an NKAP order, the aircraft was converted into a mailplane/airliner seating 21 passengers and intended for trunk lines.

In March-April 1945 the ASh-82FN-powered Li-2 underwent manufacturer's tests at the Flight Research Institute (LII – ***Lyot**no-is**sled**ovatel'skiy insti**toot***); a report on these tests was endorsed on 29th April. G. I. Popov was the engineer in charge, with S. F. Mashkovskiy as project test pilot; Aleksey N. Grinchik, an LII test pilot, also participated in the tests. The use of ASh-82FN engines led to a substantial increase in the maximum speed. The flight performance of the Li-2 powered by ASh-82FNs was noticeably superior to that of the Douglas C-47. The maximum speed reached 418 km/h (260 mph), the cruising speed was 360 km/h (224 mph) and the service ceiling was raised to 8,800 m (28,870 ft).

Li-2 Glider Tug (Post-War Versions)

During the first post-war years the Soviet Air Force attached much importance to the use of transport (assault) gliders as a means of enhancing the potential of the military airlift arm. Several types of heavy transport gliders were developed; of these, the Tsybin Ts-25 and the Yakovlev Yak-14 achieved series production and service. The Li-2 was among the aircraft that were used for towing these gliders. It was capable of towing the Ts-25 with an all-up weight of 4,200 kg (9,260 lb).

An interesting experiment was conducted, in which two Li-2 aircraft were to tow one Ts-25 glider. The purpose of the experiment was to simulate the proposed use of two Il-12 transports for the towing of one Il-32 heavy glider in the *Veyer* (Fan) project; the name referred to the fanlike spread of the towing lines. The Ts-25 was piloted by Ye. S. Oleynikov, and the Li-2s by A. D. Alekseyev and F. U. Kolesnichenko. The two tugs flying in echelon formation had to keep extremely close to each other because the slightest increase in the lateral spacing led to sharply increased pedal forces.

The Yak-14 transport glider with an all-up weight of 6,750 kg (14,880 lb) was appreciably heavier, and a single Li-2's power was clearly insufficient for towing it. A scheme was devised involving the use of two Li-2s to tow a single Yak-14. This was a forced measure brought about by the shortage of the more powerful IL-12D and IL-12T aircraft specifically equipped for towing.

In 1950 OKB-153 led by Oleg Antonov conducted the development of a pilotless glider intended for the transportation of weapons and hardware of the Airborne Troops. This glider was projected in several versions bearing the common designation 'B'; it was intended to be attached by a rigid towbar to an IL-12 or a Tu-2 bomber. The Li-2 was also considered as a possible tug aircraft in the project. After some experiments involving the use of an An-2 the development of pilotless gliders was abandoned

Li-2 as a Helicopter Tug

The Li-2 was considered in the unusual role of a helicopter tug. The towing of a helicopter,

Above, below and bottom: The prototype of the Li-2T post-war unarmed transport version (c/n 18421001) at NII VVS during state acceptance trials in the autumn of 1945. Note that the cooling air control shutters have been removed for the summer season.

with its rotor in autorotation mode, was supposed to increase the helicopter's range. No information is available if such experiments were actually conducted or what types of helicopters were involved (the obvious choice would be the Mi-1 helicopter). Naturally, the helicopter would have to fly at some elevation over the towing aircraft; should it descend below the tug, hard-to-tackle safety problems would arise.

P-82A, P-82B, P-82L, P-83, P-30B and P-30F Airliners (Projects)

In 1944 work was under way on several derivatives of the Li-2 airliner with a view to increasing the speed, range and payload, greatly enhancing passenger comfort and developing a project of a 'standard' airliner for the post-war period. The following project versions powered by Shvetsov ASh-82FN radials and Charomskiy ACh-30B liquid-cooled diesels were considered (the P- designation prefix denoted *passa**zheer**skiy* [*samo**lyot***]):

- the P-82A 30-seater with an all-up weight of 16,000 kg (35,280 lb);
- the P-82B extended-range version;
- the P-82L (*lyuks* = de luxe) 'special mission' VIP version for government flights;
- the P-83 powered by 1,900-hp ASh-83 radials (a version of the ASh-82);
- the P-30B airliner with 1,500-hp ACh-30B diesel engines and seating arrangements for 21 or 32 passengers;
- the P-30F airliner with 1,900-hp ACh-30BF engines (*for**see**rovannyy* – uprated).

None of these projects materialised.

T-82, T-30 and G-30F Transport and Cargo Aircraft (Projects)

Chief designer of Plant No.84 I. P. Mosolov also developed the following projected versions of the Li-2:

- the T-82 transport and troop-carrier version with ASh-82FN engines (T = ***trahns**port-nyy* [samolyot]);
- the T-30 transport and troop-carrier version with ACh-30B engines,;
- a pure cargo version with ACh-30BF engines, designated G-30F (G = *groozo**voy*** [*samo**lyot***]).

None of these projects was implemented, either.

T-82M Transport Aircraft

From 1946 onwards further development of projected Li-2 derivatives with ASh-82FN and ACh-30 engines was conducted by Aleksandr P. Golubkov, chief designer of OKB-30. He directed the work on re-engining the Li-2 with ASh-82FNs, a measure which made it possible to raise the all-up weight by nearly 50% and, if turbosuperchargers were fitted, to raise the service ceiling. The latter was of particular importance for operations in mountainous areas.

For example, in 1947 the project of the T-82 aircraft emerged. The aircraft had a maximum all-up weight of 15,600 kg (34,400 lb) and a maximum speed of 415 km/h (258 mph) at an altitude of 5,000 m (16,400 ft). It was

Above: Li-2T CCCP 03505 No.1 in basic Air Force olive green colours. This registration was also re- used for an An-2R

'Heave-ho! Heave-ho!' Ground personnel use a thick board for loading a 200-litre fuel drum into a Li-2. Note the twin Venturi tubes aft of the cargo door.

planned to operate this aircraft in six main versions optimised for:

- cargo carriage;
- transportation of paratroopers;
- transportation of wounded or sick personnel;
- transportation of paradroppable cargoes;
- glider towing;
- bombing.

Like the Li-2T, the T-82 featured an entry door on the starboard side of fuselage and a port side cargo door incorporating a smaller door. A novel feature was the special hatch in the cabin floor for airdropping cargoes. The aircraft was equipped with cargo handling devices which comprised a hoist and a carriage with a lifting platform; the carriage ran on tracks mounted on the floor and was moved by a winch.

According to information published in the Russian press, a T-82M prototype was completed at Plant No.84, but Golubkov himself suspended further work on the project.

Li-2 Transport Aircraft with Wright Cyclone G-102 Engines (Li-3)

Several Li-2s that remained in Yugoslavia after the end of the war were re-engined with Wright Cyclone G-102s (some sources say Pratt & Whitney Twin Wasps) and were unofficially dubbed Li-3. However, these aircraft were no longer used as military transports. One such aircraft, serialled 7011, survives in the Aeronautical Museum in Belgrade.

PS-84-T (Li-2MT) Mine Countermeasures Aircraft (Project)

In 1943 People's Commissar of the Navy Admiral N. G. Kuznetsov addressed the State Defence Committee with a request that a special aircraft be developed for clearing magnetic mines. He stated that the British had such aircraft but they had turned down a request to supply nine such aircraft to the Soviet Union. The idea was not new; a year earlier the Germans had developed a similar machine based on the Junkers Ju 52/3m transport. It was designated Ju 52/3m (MS), the suffix denoting *Minensuche* – or minesweeping.

The task of developing a Soviet mine countermeasures (MCM) aircraft was issued to A. P. Golubkov, chief designer of OKB-30 based at Plant No.89, who conducted the development of military versions of the PS-84 (Li-2) during the war. In the same year Golubkov submitted an advanced development project of the PS-84-T aircraft intended for clearing magnetic mines (T = ***trahl'****shchik* – minesweeper). On 23rd August the People's Commissariat of the Navy examined this project and submitted it to NKAP for approval. The project was approved by Deputy People's Commissar of the Aircraft Industry Aleksandr S. Yakovlev.

The main problem met while developing the MCM aircraft lay in creating an electromagnetic mine sweeping (degaussing) device that would detonate the German magnetic mines efficiently enough. The Electrotechnical Engineering Research Institute (NIEI – *Na****ooch****no-is****sled****ovatel'skiy* ***elek-****trotekh****nich****eskiy insti****toot***) headed by Academician A. G. Iosif'yan was involved in tackling this problem. The institute was to develop an electro-magnetic coil which would create a magnetic field strong enough to trigger the German mines, as well as a generator for supplying the coil with electricity and the appropriate equipment for controlling the magnetic mine clearing device. The task posed before Golubkov included selecting the type of aircraft engine to drive the generator, developing the control system and fuel supply system for this engine, and determining the best location and installation of this engine in the aircraft. It was necessary to accommodate the whole equipment of the mine clearing device and optimise its design features for operation on an aircraft; the system had to be convenient to operate, and the admissible weight stresses and CG position had to be kept in mind. The biggest problem was how to locate and attach the ring-shaped electro-magnetic coil with due regard to the aerodynamic requirements. TsAGI was involved in tackling the questions of aerodynamics.

In accordance with Golubkov's project, the mine clearing device consisted of a mine degaussing loop shaped as a huge ring with a coil inside; the ring was attached to the nosecone and the underside of the wings by bracing struts, while part of it was supported by a bracing wires attached to a wire-braced mast on top of the fuselage. A generator driven by a 220-hp MV-6 six-cylinder inverted inline engine (a licence-built version of the Renault Bengali 6) housed in the fuselage supplied the electric current in the coil. Flying 20 m (65 ft) above the water with a speed of 200 km/h (124 mph), the aircraft could sweep a lane 45 m (150 ft) wide, destroying mines at a depth of up to 30 m (98 ft).

In 1944 a different version of the MCM aircraft was proposed at Plant No.456; it featured the use of the more powerful Klimov M-105 Vee-12 engine as the generator drive.

Development of an 'aerial minesweeper' for the Navy required the co-operation of organisations subordinated to three authorities: NKAP, the People's Commissariat of the Navy and the People's Commissariat of the Electrical Engineering Industry. Bureaucrats are the same all over, and coordinating the efforts of the three ministries took a long time. Not before the war ended, on 8th June 1945, did Admiral Nikolay G. Kuznetsov issue an order stipulating that two Li-2 aircraft be converted into 'aerial minesweepers', with the first test flights to be undertaken in December.

Two examples of the MCM version were completed by the summer of 1946; in documents they were referred to as the Li-2MT (***minnyy trahl'shchik*** – minesweeper). In accordance with an order issued by Deputy People's Commissar of the Aircraft Industry Aleksandr S. Yakovlev, one of the prototypes was to pass flight tests at LII; P. Ye. Genayev was appointed captain of the test crew. It is not known whether the Li-2MT was actually tested. However, there is one more document which mentions the Li-2 in the mine countermeasures version. Pursuant to an MAP order called 'On the preparation of aircraft for participation in the [Tushino] Air Display on 18th August 1947' chief designer of OKB-30 A. P. Golubkov was tasked with preparing two

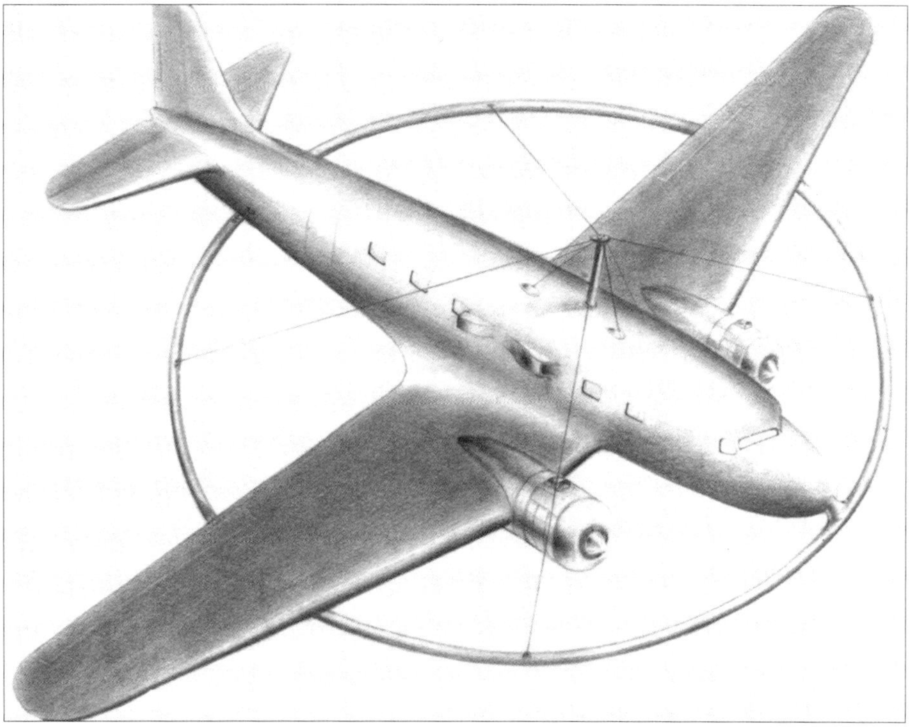

An artist's impression of the PS-84-T (Li-2MT) mine countermeasures aircraft with a mine degaussing loop attached to the wings and fuselage. Note the inlet and exhaust for the generator drive above the wing.

Li-2 aircraft in the aerial minesweeper version, but with the more powerful ASh-82R engines (the authors have no information about this version of the ASh-82 engine). (Note: In 1947 the one-time People's Commissariats had been reorganised as ministries; thus, NKAP became MAP – *Ministerstvo aviatsionnoy promyshlennosti*). It is also known that one more Li-2MT prototype powered by production ASh-82FN engines had been built by 1951. However, yet again there is no information as to whether it was flight-tested.

The last known mention of the Li-2MT in documents is dated 1949, when a project was developed envisaging the use of the new 225-hp Ivchenko M-14 (AI-14) nine-cylinder radial as the auxiliary engine. In August of the same year OKB-30 signed a contract with the Navy Command on the commencement of the ADP work; a contract on the development of the system's main component (the mine degaussing device) followed in December.

UchShLi-2 (UshLi-2, Li-2Ush) Navigator Trainer

During the war the Li-2 was easily adaptable for the training of navigators, bomb-aimers, or radio operators, because the machine could take on board a fairly large group of trainees and instructors. From 1942 onwards the Li-2 was used by the 1st Higher School of Navigators, which was then based in Central Asia. In 1945 one US-built C-47 was converted into a 'flying classroom' by the Military Air Academy named after Nikolay Ye. Zhukovskiy (VVA – *Voyenno-vozdooshnaya akademiya*), utilising a project developed by Lt. Col. A. S. Vartanyan and Major P. P. Tyurev. In early 1946 this machine passed tests at NII VVS. The military were pleased with the converted aircraft, and a decision was taken to build a similar version of the Li-2. In September 1946 the modified C-47 was transferred to A. P. Golubkov's OKB-30 for familiarisation.

In 1947, in response to an Air Force order, the designers of OKB-30 developed a navigator trainer version of the Li-2 which received the designation UChShLi-2 or UShLi-2 (both acronyms stand for *oochebno-shtoormanskiy* Li-2 – navigator trainer [version of the] Li-2). The first prototype (c/n 18424702) was converted from a production Li-2T. It was fitted with ten workstations for the future navigators who underwent training under the guidance of two instructors. The trainees' workstations were provided with the necessary navigation equipment which made it possible to teach various methods of navigation, bomb aiming and aerial photography.

Mounted under the wing centre section were bomb racks from the Po-2LNB night bomber, on which 12 concrete training bombs weighing 15 kg (33 lb) apiece could be suspended. A mechanical bomb release unit was provided. The OPB-1 bombsight was mounted in a blister located on the port side ahead of the cargo door. Apart from this blister, the UchShLi-2 differed externally from the standard Li-2T transport in having a profusion of various aerials (if only because inside there were three different types of radio compasses and a radio altimeter) and a large revolving

Above: An artist's impression of the UchShLi-2 navigator trainer showing the astrodome and the various dorsal aerials.

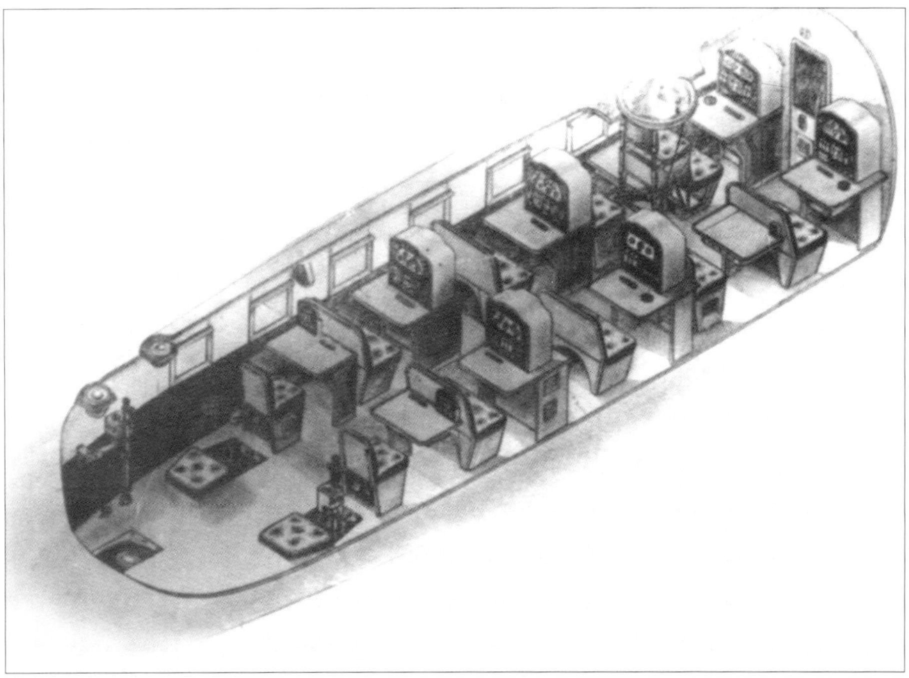

This drawing shows the layout of the UchShLi-2's cabin

astrodome in the cabin roof. The machine's weight was increased by 920 kg (2,030 lb) over the Li-2T; to keep the all-up weight within the normal limits, the fuel load was reduced.

On 26th April 1947 the UChShLi-2 prototype was submitted for state acceptance trials which proceeded at GK NII VVS (the State Red Banner Air Force Research Institute) in May-June. The increased all-up weight and the generally worse aerodynamics due to drag generated by the astrodome and aerials reduced the maximum speed to 308 km/h (191 mph), but that was considered to be quite acceptable. The State commission noted that the aircraft had passed the state acceptance tests and was recommended for the training of flight personnel in various kinds of aerial navigation.

On 29th September 1949 Commander of the Air Force K. A. Vershinin asked the Ministry of Aircraft Industry to convert in a similar way a further 40 Li-2s which were supplied by the military. The conversion was entrusted to Plant No.86 in Taganrog. The first machine of the batch (c/n 18426105) began its factory tests on 15th November 1948; the tests continued until 8th December. It was flown by a crew commanded by Lt. Col. S. G. Plygunov. The aircraft differed from the prototype mainly in having more efficient cabin ventilation, a Soviet RV-2 radio altimeter (instead of an American unit) and in having buried loop aerials of the RPKO-10 direction finders. A further aircraft (c/n 18427804) was tested on 21st-23rd March 1950, serving as the pattern aircraft for subsequent conversions.

The UChShLi-2 navigator trainers were widely used by the Soviet Air Force; a few were supplied to other countries, including China. Many navigators who flew on the Il'yushin IL-28 twin-jet tactical bombers took their initial training on these aircraft. Later versions (now referred to as the Li-2USh) were fitted with bomb racks from the Mikoyan/Gurevich MiG-15 fighter and electrical bomb release units for eight 50 kg (110 lb) bombs. The machines that were converted to UChShLi-2s came from late-series batches having a metal cabin floor; there were no longer any US (Lend-Lease)-supplied instruments in the equipment complement.

Li-2R Radar Operator Trainer

The Li-2R version, which was intended for training aircraft radar operators (hence the R), was built on a much smaller scale. OKB-30 led by A. P. Golubkov started work on this project in 1948. Initially the aircraft was to be equipped with the Rym-S radar (*rym* is a nautical term for 'lifting lug') whose antenna was to be accommodated in a new, more elongated nose, while the radar set and the operator workstations were located in the aircraft's passenger/cargo cabin.

In April 1949 the Li-2R prototype, which was being converted from a production Li-2T transport/cargo aircraft, was ready for installation of the radar, but the radar itself was still unavailable. GK NII VVS agreed to accept the aircraft in the incomplete configuration, and in July it passed state acceptance trials successfully.

In 1950 the Li-2R was modified to accept the Toriy-A (Thorium-A) aerial intercept radar intended for several Soviet all-weather fighters (such as the Mikoyan/Gurevich I-320). On 12th January 1951 the Ministry of Aircraft Industry terminated the programme on the grounds that there was no decision on putting the version into series production. However, in the same year Plant No.84 manufactured five such aircraft for the Air Force.

Li-2 Gunner/Radio Operator Trainer

There was one more trainer version of the Li-2. In 1954 three Li-2s were operated by the Balashov Military Air School for Long-Range Aviation Bomber Pilots (that's how it was called then; later the name was changed to the Balashov Military Pilot College). For some reason these aircraft were known at the school as 'flying laboratories' (a term usually

Above and below: The UchShLi-2 prototype (c/n 18424702) during trials. Note the ventrally mounted oil coolers characteristic of late-production examples.

applied to all sorts of testbeds or research/survey aircraft). These machines were converted from night bombers and were equipped as flying classrooms for the training of gunners/radio operators. Each aircraft had three workstations with RSB-3 radios; on these machines trainees recruited from conscription service personnel acquired the necessary skills. Only the dorsal turrets were left for teaching the gunnery techniques, the beam positions being eliminated. Initially the trainers were fitted with the UBT machine guns, but this weapon proved to be too potent for training purposes, shooting the towed sleeve-type targets to shreds too quickly; hence the UBTs were replaced by ShKAS

Three views of the navigator trainee workstations in the cabin of the UchShLi-2.

Above: The first 'production' UchShLi-2 trainer (c/n 18426105) at Taganrog during trials in December 1948.

Above: The additional ventral DF loop aerials and aerial masts on the same aircraft; these were characteristic of the UchShLi-2.

CCCP-31136, an Aeroflot Li-2F photo survey aircraft, is seen here immediately after touchdown; the port side observation blister is clearly visible.

machine guns. Lest some naughty trainees should be tempted to try their skills on the target-towing aircraft, the turret's rotation angle was limited to 180° in the rear hemisphere.

Aerial gunners/radio operators were also trained at the school for aircraft radio operators in the town of Kansk, Kranoyarsk Territory, where the training was conducted on suitably converted Li-2s (later supplanted by trainer versions of the An-24 and An-26).

Li-2Gr Cargo/Passenger Aircraft

Among the numerous versions of the Li-2 there was also a cargo/passenger version designated Li-2Gr (*groozo***voy**) which was designed to carry ten passengers and 1,200 kg (2,650 lb) of cargo.

Li-2F Photo Survey Aircraft

A small number of Li-2 aircraft were manufactured in the aerial photography version designated Li-2F (*fotos"***yom***ochnyy*). The passenger cabin accommodated a camera operator compartment equipped with AFA-TE-35 and AFA-33N-20 cameras (one of each type) and two AFA-TE-100 cameras (AFA = ***aerofot****oappa****raht*** – aerial camera). The cameras 'fired' through ports in the fuselage underside closed by sliding protective doors for take-off and landing.

Observation blisters were located on both sides of the fuselage, each of them accommodating an NKPB sight; for ease of work the port side blister was provided with an armrest. The rear baggage compartment was transformed into a darkroom suitably equipped for recharging film cassettes and processing the films.

Li-2FG Photogrammetry Aircraft

Another aerial photography version equipped for photogrammetry (that is, for determining the shape, size and location of different objects by measuring their images on aerial photos) was designated Li-2FG.

In addition to the USSR, such machines were used in Poland, where the technical department of LOT Polish Airlines developed the conversion in 1952. A Swiss-made Wilda RC-5 camera was mounted in the cabin, the camera port being closed by a belt-driven door when not in use. An exposure measurement blister was added on the port side, with a rather crude sighting blister in the starboard flightdeck window, and the rear baggage compartment was transformed into a darkroom. An oxygen system for the crew was provided to permit high-altitude flights.

Five machines thus converted saw service with a special photo survey squadron of the Polish Air Force, and a further three machines (including SP-LAB, c/n 18422703) were operated by LOT. Other examples were operated by the Czechoslovak Air Force.

Li-2SKh (?) Agricultural Aircraft

In 1948 the first experiments were made involving the use of the Li-2 for agricultural purposes. LOT Polish Airlines converted eight of its Li-2Ps, including SP-LAA (c/n 18422702), SP-LAD (c/n 18422705) and SP-LAM (c/n 18422610), into crop-dusters for fighting pests afflicting crops and forests. In Russian literature this version was referred to, rather misleadingly, as the Li-2SKh (***sel'skokhozi-aistvennyy*** – agricultural). However, this designation is obviously Russian; the Polish word for 'agricultural' is *rolniczy*, so the Polish designation would have been Li-2R.

The converted aircraft originally had a hand-driven crusher in the cabin for pulverising dry chemicals, the powder exiting via an orifice in the lower fuselage; the chemicals were loaded manually. Later the primitive crushers gave way to twin hoppers holding 1,500 kg (3,310 lb) of chemicals each; they were filled by mechanical loaders via a dorsal hatch. A mixer was fitted in the lower part of each hopper to prevent the chemicals from caking. A tunnel-shaped duster with a capacity of 20 kg (33 lb) of chemicals per second was fitted under the aircraft.

The operation of the aircraft in 1948-1955 demonstrated their high efficiency in combating vermin. However, the Li-2s required fairly long runways, and their operation was appreciably more costly than that of the An-2R biplane. For this reason they were not used on a wide scale and their operation was discontinued after agricultural work in Poland was delegated to the air clubs in 1955.

Above: Li-2F CCCP-71228 No.1 in an overall natural metal finish with no trim whatever. Note the double set of radio altimeter dipole aerials. The registration again passed to an An-2R biplane later.

Li-2 Polar Aviation Version

As early as 1946 General Papanin, Chief of the Main Administration of the Northern Sea Route, addressed N. A. Voznesensky (who headed the State Planning Agency at that time) with a request that a transport aircraft be developed specially for the needs of Polar explorers; he mentioned specifically Igor' V. Chetverikov's amphibians as possible types for adaptation. However, Minister of Aircraft Industry Mikhail V. Khrunichev suggested that the Li-2 transport aircraft re-engined with ASh-82FNs be used for this purpose, since it would have considerably greater payload, range and speed. This proposal was not implemented either; the Soviet Polar aviation had to make do with standard Li-2 (PS-84) or Li-2T aircraft with a fixed ski landing gear which were operated on a wide scale from snow-covered airfields.

Initially the skis were of wooden construction and incorporated an ash-tree or oak running surface, two spars, two side stiffeners, the forward and rear bosses, 12 frames and six stringers. The upper surface was skinned with 3-mm ($0\frac{7}{64}$ in) plywood to which a layer of fabric was glued. As the aircraft were fitted with skis the main wheels were removed together with their axles and braking flanges, the rear bracing struts were replaced with girder-type struts. The tailwheel was removed from the fork and a tail skid was mounted on its axle. Late-series Li-2s were fitted with all-metal skis. A retractable version of ski undercarriage was also under development.

In the winter the Li-2s were often operated on skis; since the skis were non-retractable, they created extra drag and increased fuel consumption. An alternative to the fixed skis was that provided by the jettisonable skis which were developed at NII GVF (the Civil Air Fleet Research Institute) during the war. The aircraft was rolled into special recesses in these skis (as if these were 'galoshes') by a tractor, using special ramps, or taxied onto the skis under its own power; the rear fuselage was jacked up for installing the tailskid. After the take-off the skis, which were not attached in any way to the wheeled undercarriage, simply fell off. The landing was performed on wheels as usual. The jettisonable skis were produced in a small production batch, but they did not gain widespread use.

Some examples of the 'polar' Li-2s were fitted with additional fuel tanks in the wings (see below). These aircraft were used on a wide scale for delivering teams of polar explorers to the SP series (***Sev**ernyy **Pol**yus* – North Pole) research stations, including stations deployed on drifting ice floes. The 'polar' Li-2s remained in operation for a long time; for example, in 1968 the Sever-14 (North-14) expedition had one such machine at its disposal. The Li-2 was able to perform prolonged flights in adverse weather, in rarefied air, in ambient temperatures down to –70°C (–94°F) and in the conditions of strong icing. This, and the ability to operate from ice runways of limited size, including strips chosen from the air, coupled with simplicity in servicing, ensured it a long career in Polar aviation alongside the IL-12 and IL-14.

Li-2V High-Altitude Transport/Airliner

The Li-2 was widely used by Polar explorers. Li-2s performed ice reconnaissance for the purpose of guiding ship convoys through ice fields, delivered research expeditions to their sites, including sites in the North Pole

Li-2F CCCP-54931 at a Soviet airport. Many Aeroflot Li-2s lacked the Soviet flag on the tail.

Top and above: The Polish and Czechoslovak Li-2FGs had a crude 'homebuilt' sighting blister and a makeshift sighting device on the starboard side of the nose.

area and in Antarctica; as a rule, ski undercarriage was used in such cases. During operations in Antarctica the standard Li-2s started suffering problems: it proved virtually impossible to take off from airstrips located at an altitude of 2,000-3,000 m (6,560-9,840 ft) above sea level. The somewhat reduced power output of the engines at these altitudes made the aircraft incapable of starting its movement at take-off, because under the very low temperatures the snow became coarse like sandpaper and the skis simply would not slide.

To tackle this problem, the Polar Aviation Administration asked the design bureau led by Oleg K. Antonov (then based in Novosibirsk and called OKB-153) to produce a batch of four Li-2s equipped with a 'high-altitude' version of he powerplant. There was one more reason for developing a high-altitude version of the Li-2. Aeroflot needed such an aircraft in connection with mastering the operation of the Stalinabad-Khorog air route passing over the Pamir mountain ridge.

In 1953 OKB-153, working under a contract with NII GVF, started work on equipping ASh-62 engines with TK-19 turbosuperchargers (***toor**bokom**press**or*) designed by A. B. Treskin. This supercharger located on the outboard side of the nacelle had a centrifugal compressor powered by a turbine driven by exhaust gases. The engines equipped with TK-19 superchargers drove V-516-P2F four-blade propellers designed by Zaslavskiy. The shape of the engine nacelles was altered, with prominent dorsal fairings for the intercoolers being added. The aircraft, which received the designation Li-2V (*vy**sot**nyy* – high-altitude), was provided with standardised oxygen equipment for the crew and passengers. The work proceeded under the guidance of A. P. Eskin and Yu. M. Kirzhner.

The prototype (c/n 18422804) passed manufacturer's tests and was delivered to the customer. The tests were conducted by V. Z. Krivoy, a NII GVF test pilot. The tests sowed that the stipulated service ceiling of 8,000 m (26,240 ft) was attained without difficulty. In 1955 a small number of Li-2s underwent appropriate modifications at a production plant in Kiev. The 'production' Li-2V differed a little from the first high-altitude machine; they had three-blade propellers and the superchargers were located on the outer faces of the nacelles.

Several Li-2Vs, including CCCP-H465 (that is, SSSR-N465 in Cyrillic characters), CCCP-H495 (c/n 18430708), CCCP-H496 (c/n 18430801), CCCP-H501 (c/n 18430705), CCCP-H502, CCCP-H552 and CCCP-H556, were used by the second and third Soviet Antarctic expeditions for flights on routes over mountainous areas and for weather reconnaissance flights. *Note:* Under the Soviet civil aircraft registration system used in 1932-1958 the CCCP- country prefix was followed by a letter designating the agency to which a particular aircraft was assigned, plus up to four digits. Thus, CCCP-Лxxxx (that is, SSSR-Lxxxx, for *lee**ney**nyy* [*samo**lyot***] – aircraft in airline service) denoted the Main Directorate of the Civil Air Fleet (GU GVF) which operated scheduled passenger/cargo services. Cf. CCCP-Hxxx (the Cyrillic N) for the Main Directorate of the Northern Sea Route (GU SMP – ***Glahv**noye oopravl**en**iye* ***Sev**ernovo mor**sko**vo pu**tee***) which included the Polar Aviation branch, CCCP-Cxxxx (the Cyrillic S) for the Osoaviakhim organisation running Soviet air clubs, CCCP-Axxxx for the agricultural division, CCCP-Khxxx (khoziaystvennyye *organizahtsii* – national economy organisations) for aircraft owned by industrial enterprises and so on. The rendering of the registrations as actually applied is used throughout.

CCCP-H495 gained fame when it was used by a Soviet crew in the search for a Belgian aircraft that had been lost in the Antarctic. As a result of the expedition, the Belgians were rescued. In the 1960s Aeroflot Li-2Vs

Ski-equipped Polar Aviation Li-2T CCCP-04221 comes in to land on a snow airstrip.

Above: The prototype of the Li-2V high-altitude version (c/n 18422804); the TK-19 supercharger can be seen on the outer side of the engine nacelle.

transported sheep and calves to high-mountain pastures in Uzbekistan. According to newspaper reports, the 'passengers' of the aircraft included 70 sheep or 14-17 calves, the payload reaching some 2,000 kg (4,410 lb).

Li-2D Transport/Passenger Aircraft

To increase the range, some Li-2s were provided with four additional fuel tanks in the outer wing panels. Each tank had a capacity of 350 litres (77 Imp gal), the overall fuel load being thus increased by some 1,200 kg (2,645 lb). This version referred to as the Li-2D (***dahl'****niy* – long-range) was used primarily on air routes of the High North and the Far East, as well as in the Polar aviation.

Li-2D Transport (second use of designation)

Confusingly, the Czechoslovak Air Force referred to some of its *Cabs* as Li-2Ds. In this case the D probably stood for *desantový* (for paradropping).

Li-2LP (Li-2PPL) Forest Patrol Aircraft

A special version of the Li-2, known as Li-2LP (Li-2PPL), was developed for forest fire patrol duties (LP = *les****noy****, pat****rool'****nyy*). This aircraft was fitted with observation blisters on both sides of the fuselage; dispensers with illumination and signal flares were mounted in the rear part of the fuselage. The cargo cabin was fitted out to a troop-carrier standard; it accommodated fire-fighters equipped with parachutes who were air-dropped near the site of a forest fire.

Li-2PR Fishery Reconnaissance Aircraft

Several Li-2s, including CCCP-63052, were converted into the Li-2PR fishery reconnaissance aircraft (PR = *promys****lov****yy raz****ved****chik* –

Above: Front view of the Li-2V prototype's port engine. The prototype was equipped with V-516-P2F four-bladed propellers fitted with An-2 style large spinners.

The intercooler fairing on the Li-2V prototype's port engine.

Above: A 'production' Polar Aviation Li-2V on wheels; note the reshaped engine nacelles resembling those of the Vickers Wellington.
Right: Close-up of the supercharger on the starboard engine of a ski-equipped Li-2V in Antarctica.

fishery reconnaissance aircraft). They were used for monitoring the ice situation and the congregations of sea mammals (seals, walruses and others), for discovering shoals of fish and directing fishing vessels towards them. For this purpose the standard 'solid' nose was replaced by an elongated, extensively glazed 'bomber nose' housing an observer; the passenger cabin was used to accommodate hydrologists' workstations and additional fuel tanks, and the rear baggage compartment was outfitted with devices for the air-dropping of cargoes. The Li-2PR was also fitted with some additional equipment items: an S-1 siren, an NI-50 attitude indicator (*navigatsi**on**nyy indi**kah**tor*), an AB-52 drift indicator, an SGU-15 loud-hailer system (*sig**nahl'**no-**grom**kogovo**rya**shchaya ooosta**nov**ka*), and some machines also had aerial photography equipment.

Li-2 ELINT and ECM Aircraft

In 1953 a number of Soviet Air Force Li-2s were equipped with two sets of active jammers and electronic intelligence stations. Mounted on the wing leading edges were two ram air turbines driving 5-kW generators. Large polystyrene fairings fitted under the wings accommodated the antennas of devices intended to detect enemy radars. In the 1950s these aircraft performed patrol flights along the borders with China and Iran.

These may well have been the first ELINT and ECM aircraft in the Soviet Air Force.

Li-2 TV Relay Aircraft

At least three Li-2s were used as TV relay aircraft; they were referred to as Li-2RT (*retrans**lya**tor televizi**on**nyy* – TV relay aircraft).

In the 1950s, TV broadcasting over long distances was a major problem because the ultra-short waves used by TV stations propagated only within the radius of direct vision and could not be received farther than 100 km (62 miles) from the TV aerial masts that were in existence at that time. A group of specialists of the Moscow TV laboratory of the Ministry of Electronics Industry (MRP – *Minis**ter**stvo **rah**dioelek**tron**noy pro**mysh**lennosti*) led by P. Kirillov conducted work on measuring the intensity of the signals emitted by the transmitters of the Moscow and Minsk TV centres at different altitudes and distances. It was established that these signals could be confidently received within a radius of 250-300 km (155-186 miles), providing that the receiver was placed at an altitude of 3,500-4,500 m (11,480-14,760 ft). This is how the idea of relaying TV transmissions with the help of specially equipped aircraft was born.

The laboratory's personnel developed transmitting and receiving TV equipment which was fitted to a Li-2 aircraft at a repair facility in Minsk (later known as the Civil Aviation aircraft repair Plant No.407). Tests showed that the equipment ensured a good relaying of signals at a distance of 150-200 km (93-124 miles). It was decided to organise the broadcasting of programmes released by the Moscow TV centre to Minsk with the help of the modified Li-2RT aircraft. In addition to aircraft, a ground-based station located in Smolensk was used for this purpose.

In 1957, on the opening day of the World Festival of Youth and Students in Moscow, two Li-2RTs began loitering in the designated areas. The special tracking equipment mounted on the aircraft maintained a constant direction of their antennas during turns. One aircraft received the signals of the Moscow TV centre and relayed them to Smolensk. Then the image was transmitted to the second aircraft, which relayed it to Minsk where the signal was received by the local TV

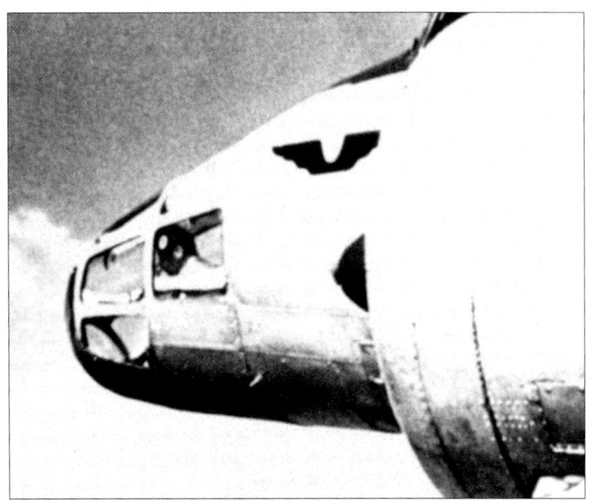

Two views of the distinctive glazed nose of the Li-2PR fishery reconnaissance aircraft.

centre. Thus, the inhabitants of Smolensk and Minsk saw the Festival's inauguration ceremony and then, in the course of two weeks, had a possibility to watch broadcasts from Moscow for six to eight hours daily (that was the endurance of the Li-2RT). The operation of the aircraft was ensured by a group of engineers, technicians and pilots which included leading engineer I. Litvak, engineers A. Pankratov, P. Gisig, I. Pokrovskiy, V. Khodak, technicians A. Lookin, A. Koorochkin et al. On the last day of the Festival the inhabitants of Kiev were also given the possibility to watch TV programmes from Moscow; a third Li-2RT aircraft was used for this purpose.

In the autumn of 1957, on the eve of the 40th anniversary of the October Revolution, an airborne relay line was established between Moscow and Gor'kiy (now renamed back to Nizhniy Novgorod). In 1958 the specialists of the Odessa Electrical Engineering Institute used one Li-2 for relaying TV programmes by way of experiment from Kiev to their own city. For this purpose a three-section rotating receiver antenna was mounted on the centre fuselage; it was supplemented by a fixed transmitter antenna designed by Rappoport and Khachatoorov which was mounted aft of the tail unit. Experiments were also made with the reception of TV programmes from Bucharest. Transmissions from Bucharest were received with good quality at an altitude of 4,000 m (13,120 ft).

Li-2 Meteo Weather Research Aircraft

The Li-2 Meteo weather research aircraft ('meteorological laboratory') was created at the Minsk Aircraft Repair Plant No.407 after the war. The aircraft was fitted with the necessary set of equipment; workstations for aerologists were outfitted in the cabin. The aircraft was intended for:

- exploration of the atmosphere and clouds within a wide range of altitudes, using the methods of contact and remote measurements;
- studying the characteristics of electric zones in the atmosphere that could be dangerous for air traffic;
- exploration of the laws of propagation of radio waves in different meteorological conditions;
- monitoring the operation of other aircraft;
- monitoring the environment with a view to detecting pollution zones.

One of the first Li-2s to be converted to a Li-2 Meteo weather research aircraft was CCCP-Л4890. Subsequently several other examples were modified for this role; these included CCCP-54909, CCCP-83962 No.1 and CCCP-84713 which differed in the equipment fit; for instance, CCCP-83962 had a nose-mounted sensor boom.

Li-2 Avionics Testbed for Developing the KS Cruise Missile

Development of the guidance system for the first Soviet anti-shipping cruise missile, the Mikoyan KS (*izdeliye* K), was conducted initially on two converted Li-2 aircraft. One of the modified Li-2s emulated the cruise missile, while the other posed as the carrier aircraft. This was followed by experiments with the specially equipped MiG-9L (*izdeliye* FK) and MiG-17K (*izdeliye* SDK) testbeds, and only thereafter by tests of the *izdeliye* K proper. (*Izdeliye* (product) such and such is a common term for coding Soviet/Russian military hardware items.)

Li-2 Avionics Testbed for Developing the K-10 Cruise Missile

Codenamed Looga-S in the USSR, the K-10 anti-shipping cruise missile system (whose development was initiated by a directive of the Soviet Council of Ministers dated 3rd February 1955) was destined to remain in the inventory of the Soviet Naval Aviation for more than 30 years. Design and development work on the system began in January 1958 and was conducted simultaneously on four aircraft, including a Li-2 converted into an avionics testbed. This aircraft featuring the seeker head of the K-10 missile on an elongated adapter attached to the fuselage nose (the result looked like a sharpened pencil) and fitted with some other additional devices flew test missions from the airfields of the Black Sea Fleet's Air Arm.

This machine was accidentally caught on camera and a glimpse of it could be seen in the Soviet feature film *Bar'yer neizvesnosti* (The Barrier of the Unknown), provoking curiosity on the part of many persons who wondered, what it could be. In some publications it was called Li-2LL IRE or Li-2IRE (LL means *letayushchaya laboratoriya*, literally 'flying laboratory' – the Russian term for testbeds or research/survey aircraft). The IRE acronym denoted *Institoot rahdioelektroniki* – the [Moscow] Elelectronics Institute to which the aircraft allegedly belonged, although no information was published to corroborate this claim.

Li-2 Avionics Testbed with Oval Radar

The OKB-30 led by A. P. Golubkov was tasked with preparing technical documentation for the installation of the *Oval* radar on a Li-2. One production Li-2 was converted to this configuration.

Li-2 Avionics Testbed with Proton-M Radar

Six production Li-2s were equipped with the Proton-M radar; this version was, likewise, developed by OKB-30.

Top and above: The Li-2RT television relay station was fitted with distinctive revolving aerials on top of the fuselage and aft of the tail unit.

Li-2 with 'Azimuth' SLAR

A single Li-2T coded '08 Red' (c/n 33444205) was fitted with the Azimuth side-looking aircraft radar (SLAR) which was accommodated in the aircraft's cargo cabin. The aircraft was also fitted with equipment for remote IR sensing of the Earth, which was located near a special hatch on port side of the rear fuselage. This equipment was developed in 1958 and flight-tested in 1959.

Li-2 in Experiments with Studying Information Characteristics of Targets

In late 1950s intensive work was conducted in the Soviet Union on various airborne missile strike systems. For the purpose of creating new airborne radar target designation and guidance systems intended to direct cruise missiles towards high-priority maritime surface targets, it was necessary to perform an analysis of the characteristics of radar signals reflected by targets. To this end, in 1960 the MoD's Central Research Institute No.30 (TsNII-30) together with NII-2 (Research Institute No.2), NII GKRE (Research Institute of the State Committee for Radioelectronics, responsible for the development of radar target designation and guidance systems) and Institute No.4 of the Soviet Navy (NII-4 VMF) organised and conducted test flights intended to examine the mentioned characteristics within the framework of the framework of the *Saksaool* (a kind of steppe grass) research and development programme.

Two types of target illumination radars and experimental equipment for recording the parameters of the reflected signals were installed in a modified IL-28 and a modified Li-2. The role of targets was played by cruisers, destroyers and minesweepers of the Black Sea Fleet which were moored on the roadstead of Feodosiya or moved along a predesignated route. The aircraft took a course which was at right angles to the movement of the ships. Recording of the characteristics took place in 38 flights at altitudes

Left: CCCP-54909, a Li-2 Meteo weather research aircraft with wing-mounted sensors.
Above: Close-up of the sensor on the starboard wing of a similar aircraft.

between 2,000 and 5,000 m (6,560-16,400 ft) and at flight speeds of 110-167 m/sec (360-548 ft/sec), the distance between the aircraft and the target ranging from 10 to 50 km (6-31 miles). 43 recordings of reflected signals from a cruiser, 64 signals from a destroyer and 40 signals from a minesweeper were used for the purposes of processing. The recorded signals were processed on a computer.

Li-2 Meteo CCCP-83962 No.1 features nose- and wing-mounted sensor probes. The registration later passed to the An-12BK prototype.

Other Li-2 Military Avionics Testbeds

The Li-2s were used as flying testbeds by various organisations dealing with the development of avionics for military purposes. For example, one of the aircraft (confusingly, bearing the Polar Aviation registration CCCP-04368) was used for developing the bomb-aiming radars which were planned for installation on the Tu-4 bomber; the radar was housed in a large teardrop radome under the wing trailing edge.

Another Li-2 served as a testbed for the Ton-2 (Tone-2) radar warning receiver developed for fighters.

There was also a Li-2 coded '08 Yellow' (c/n 23440603) which was referred to as the Li-2REO in some documents (REO stands for ***rah****dioelek****tron****noye obo****roo****dovaniye* – electronic equipment). Again, it featured a ventral radome (this time of hemispherical shape); it was used for the development of various types of radio equipment for military use.

Li-2 Radiation Reconnaissance Version

From the very beginning of the Soviet nuclear weapons programme a large number of different aircraft were involved in the nuclear tests; among other things, aircraft were used for the taking of samples of radioactive substances directly from the mushroom cloud appearing after the explosion. The 647th Special Support Composite Air Regiment (SAPSO – ***smesh****annyy* ***a****via****polk*** *spetsi-****ahl'****novo obespe****chen****iya*), which was based in the vicinity of the Air Force's 71st Test Range in Semipalatinsk, Kazakh SSR (assigned for nuclear tests), comprised aircraft and helicopters of different types: Po-2s, Yak-12s, Li-2s, IL-14s, Il-28, IL-28s, Yak-25s, An-8s, An-12s, An-24s and Mi-6s. These aircraft were to fulfil the following tasks:

- sampling of radioactive substances from the cloud of a nuclear explosion (Li-2, IL-14, IL-28, Yak-25);

• liaison and cargo transportation flights (Po-2, Yak-12, Li-2, IL-14);

• recording the various stages of nuclear tests by means of aerial photography and filming (Li-2, IL-14).

In addition to pilotless assets, Li-2 aircraft were also equipped for taking samples of radioactive substances from a nuclear mushroom cloud; they were fitted with air sampling pods developed by TsAGI. Inside the cylindrical pods there were metal nets with a filtering material. After the flight the nets were removed from the containers, and the material detached from the nets was sent for radiation chemistry analysis and for assessing the ratio of the use of fissionable materials. The aircraft was possibly designated Li-2RR (*radiatsionnyy razvedchik* – radiation reconnaissance aircraft). The crews of the modified Li-2s had virtually no protection against the harmful radiation during the flight through the cloud and the subsequent flight in the contaminated aircraft to the landing site, which cost them their health later.

On 18th October 1951, after the first Soviet above-ground nuclear explosion had been conducted, the specially-equipped Li-2s were used for taking air samples. Since the aircraft did not have sufficient altitude performance, it proved possible to take samples only from the 'stem' and the 'skirt' of the nuclear 'mushroom'. To enhance the safety of the taking of air samples from a nuclear cloud, the specialists of the OKB-240 design bureau headed by Sergey V. Il'yushin, in response to a technical requirement from the 71st Test Range, modified two IL-28 bombers which were fitted with compressed air bottles in bomb bays. This made it possible to pressurise the crew cockpits, thereby excluding the ingress of contaminated air. The OKB-30 design bureau, which equipped two Li-2 aircraft with sampling devices, did not take special measures to protect the crews against radiation. After the modification the Li-2s were tested in accordance with special programmes, after which approval was given to their use in the course of the forthcoming real nuclear tests.

On 12th August 1953, for the first time in the world, a thermonuclear device (a hydrogen bomb) was tested at the Semipalatinsk test range. Samples from the nuclear cloud in the 'stem' of the 'mushroom' at low altitudes were again taken by a pair of Li-2s captained by I. I. Kooz'min and V. Ya. Gorbatov. In September of the same year, for the purpose of additional research, a series of nuclear tests was conducted, involving the dropping of the RDS-5 nuclear bomb from a Tu-4 bomber. The bombs were dropped from an altitude of 9,000 m (29,530 ft), and the sampling of radioactive substances was conducted by the specially equipped IL-28s and Li-2s.

Li-2SIP Airborne Measurement Station

Development of the R-7, the first Soviet intercontinental ballistic missile, was completed in 1956. At the same time ground-based measurement posts (telemetry pick-up/relay stations) were established for the purpose of monitoring the behaviour of the missile at the active stage of its trajectory. In order to test the effectiveness of these systems before the missile was launched, it was decided to use airborne measurement posts (SIP – *samolyotnyy izmeritel'nyi poonkt*). The first of these was obtained by converting a Li-2 which was fitted with all the radio engineering equipment of the missile. During the tests the Li-2SIP piloted by N. Khlynin loitered in designated areas at an altitude of 3,000 m (9,840 ft), while ground-based radar and telemetry stations adjusted their equipment with the help of signals from this aircraft.

Soon a suitably modified IL-28 bomber joined the programme; it was used at higher altitudes. In this way it proved possible to simulate a considerable part of the active stretch of the missile's trajectory. Subsequently, when the launches of the first space vehicles began, a further four Li-2SIP aircraft were converted from standard machines; they featured a different set of equipment. The new Li-2SIPs were telemetry pick-up/relay aircraft intended for receiving information from satellites when those were flying over areas where there were no ground-based measurement posts.

Li-2 as a Compound Helicopter ('Kh' Project)

In 1951-52 a project was developed in the USSR which envisaged converting the Li-2 into a compound helicopter (*vintokryl*, in the Russian parlance of the day). The machine was to combine the helicopter's ability to take off and land vertically with the aeroplane's high speed. These design studies were made in the design bureau headed by Niklay I. Kamov. The in-house designation of the project was 'Kh' (Cyrillic 'X', which should not be confused with the Latin X).

The machine was to be fitted with a Kuznetsov TV-2 gas turbine engine above the fuselage in the area of the wing centre section; it was to drive co-axial three-bladed rotors via a special gearbox. The Li-2 retained its standard powerplant comprising two ASh-62IR engines which ensured forward propulsion in cruise flight. After a vertical take-off the machine was to perform a gradual transition to level flight in normal aeroplane mode; the TV-2 engine would be throttled back from its take-off rating of 4,650 ehp to 1,000 ehp to provide a measure of power drive to the rotors.

The *vintokryl* was to carry 25 troops or various items of military hardware (mortars, guns, motorcycles and so on). The estimated

This still from the movie *Bar'yer neizvesnosti* shows the Li-2REO testbed for the K-10 missile's guidance system.

performance of the aircraft was not going to be overly impressive: the speed would not exceed 320 km/h (199 mph), with a service ceiling of 6,500 m (21,320 ft) and a range of 450 km (280 miles). Actually, the 'Kh' machine would be roughly equivalent in performance to the standard Li-2 but would have the advantage of vertical take-off and landing capability. However, after the successful testing of the Mi-4 and Yak-24 helicopters in 1952 there was no point in continuing the work on this project and it was shelved, having progressed no further than wind tunnel tests.

Li-2 Bomber Trainer (Polish Modification)

In March 1947 three Polish Li-2NBs ('3 White', c/n 18416208; '4 White', c/n 18416110; and '12 White', c/n 18416204) were converted into bomber trainers. The trainer-specific equipment was located in such a way as to retain the possibility of transporting people and cargoes. Twelve Der-7 bomb racks were mounted under the wing centre section. There was only a mechanical bomb release unit. In 1953 this machine was modernised: instead of the Der-7, racks for drop tanks from the MiG-15 fighter were installed, coupled with an electric bomb release unit. A year later, the armament was reworked once more; this time it comprised eight racks for 50-kg (110-lb) bombs.

Li-2 Staff Transport Aircraft (Polish Modification)

Some Li-2Ts were modified into staff transport aircraft in Poland.

Li-2 Navaids Calibration Aircraft (Polish Modification)

In 1963 Li-2P SP-LKE (c/n 23442002) was converted into a navaids calibration aircraft for the Polish Civil Aviation Authority (ZRLiLK – *Zarząd Ruchu Lotniczego i Lotnisk Komunika-*

Above: In spite of the civil registration in the Polar Aviation series, Li-2 CCCP-04368 adorned with a ventral radome is not an ice reconnaissance aircraft but a military avionics testbed.

Li-2REO '08 Yellow' (c/n 23440603) seen near Leningrad in 1958. It subsequently became CCCP-13386.

cyjnych, Air Traffic Control & Commercial Airfields Administration). Outwardly it could be identified by the smart red/white livery and the additional blade aerials on top of the fuselage.

Li-2 Conversions Impersonating Aircraft of Other Types

On several occasions the Li-2 was used – after some radical 'surgery' – to represent aircraft of the Second World War period for filming purposes because 'the real McCoy' was unavailable. Of course such conversions were non-flyable.

One of these conversions was the transformation of the Li-2 into the IL-4T torpedo bomber, undertaken in the USSR in the process of shooting the feature film *Torpedonostsy* (The Torpedo Bombers) devoted to wartime Soviet Navy pilots in action against the Kriegsmarine. The original forward fuselage with its stepped flightdeck glazing was replaced by a new forward fuselage section to match the contour and the glazing of the Il-4T navigator's cockpit; an IL-4 style pilot's cockpit was added above the fuselage, as well as a dorsal turret aft of it. The fin-and-rudder assembly received new contours resembling those of the bomber.

In another Soviet film a suitably modified Li-2 performed the role of a Junkers Ju 52/3m transport; the transformation was achieved by adding a fake third engine to the aircraft's nose and altering the shape of the cowlings of the wing-mounted engines; the vertical tail contours were also altered.

No less interesting is the story of a Li-2 forming the basis for a resurrected Vickers Wellington B.1 bomber. This job was undertaken in Czechoslovakia in connection with the shooting of the film *Nebesti jezdci* (The Sky Raiders). Made in 1969, this film told the story of mixed British-Czech squadrons serving in the RAF Bomber Command in the early years of the war. In the film the Wellington is seen taxying across an airfield under its own power. The conversion, using a surplus Li-2 supplied by the Czech Air Force ('2209', c/n 23442209), was undertaken at the Aero Vodochody plant. A completely new, longer nose section was built on to the Li-2's fuselage, and a wooden structure with fabric covering was added around the remainder of the fuselage to obtain the correct contours. The nose section incorporated a working nose turret, a bomb-aimer's position and crew entry hatch for close-up shots. The Wellington's fuselage side windows were simulated in the new structure. The fin was made taller, a completely new rudder fitted, and a tail turret built into the rear fuselage. The wing structure of the Li-2 was not changed and, although the engine nacelle contours were altered to approximate those of the Wellington, the original engines and propellers were retained. The characteristic ground angle of the Wellington was obtained by shortening the main undercarriage legs and lengthening the tailwheel strut. The result looked very realistic, despite some inevitable compromises.

Unfortunately, different sources give different figures of the total production of the PS-84/Li-2 aircraft. The figure most often quoted is 4,863 machines. In Vladimir R. Kotel'nikov's publication *Li-2 transport aircraft* one can find a table listing the PS-84/Li-2 production figures as shown on this page.

In the same book the 'standard' total of 4,863 machines is quoted, but simply adding up the figures in the table gives you a different figure, namely 4,924 machines. Yet another magazine feature gives the figure of 5,207 aircraft. Several publications state that Plant No.126 in Komsomol'sk-on-Amur produced 353 Li-2Ts, but, according to the information published by the plant itself, 434 machines were built! One more publication claims that 'in the course of 15 years (between 1938 and 1953) 4,937 copies of the aircraft were built'. Thus, it appears very difficult to inform the reader about the real number of series-produced PS-84/Li-2 aircraft. However, it will not be a fallacy to consider, with a degree of approximation, that the total output of the type in the Soviet Union was of the order of 5,000 machines.

Plant	Year of manufacture															
	1938	1939	1940	1941	1942	1943	1944	1945	1946	1947	1948	1949	1950	1951	1952	1953
No.84	1	6	57	237	423	618	626	458	163	351	277	296	293	313	312	130
No.124	–	–	10	–	–	–	–	–	–	–	–	–	–	–	–	–
No.126	–	–	–	–	–	–	–	–	–	40	148	157	8	–	–	–

Chapter 3

The PS-84/Li-2 in Detail

Type: Twin-engined transport aircraft and airliner. The airframe is of all-metal construction. The main structural material used for the wings, fuselage and tail surfaces is D-16T duralumin. The airframe subassemblies feature wide use of parts produced by injection moulding (casting) from AL-7 and AL-9 aluminium alloys (*alyuminiy* ***li*****tey***nyy*), as well as by swaging (drop forging) from AK6 aluminium alloy (*alyu****mini****y* ***kov****ochnyy*). Some airframe units are made of 30KhGSA, S20 and S25 grade steel.

The military version of the PS-84 had a crew of six: a pilot, a navigator/bomb-aimer, a radio operator, a flight technician and two gunners. The Li-2P passenger version had five crew: captain, first officer, radio operator, flight engineer and flight attendant.

The permissible CG range is 14-26% of the mean aerodynamic chord (MAC). The CG position is 19.75% MAC for the unladen aircraft, 20.0% MAC with a full fuel load and 11 passengers, and 24.88% MAC with a maximum payload (21 passengers) and an 11,500-kg (25,350-lb) take-off weight. Landing gear retraction causes a 1% forward shift of the CG. The rearmost CG position occurs when a minimum quantity of fuel (500 litres/110 Imp gal) is in the forward pair of tanks, which equals a 45-minute reserve, and the oil quantity is 50 litres (11 Imp gal).

Fuselage: Semi-monocoque structure of beam-and-stringer construction and basically circular cross-section with a relatively thin skin reinforced with numerous light L-section stringers. There are 42 stringers in the centre section of the fuselage; they are partly disrupted by windows, the entry door and, on some versions, the cargo door. The fuselage structure comprises 48 (some technical manuals say 50) frames which are mostly of a light sheet-metal type; box-type main frames are used in highly stressed areas of the fuselage. The fuselage skin thickness is mostly 0.6 and 0.8 mm (0.023 and 0.031 in), increasing to 1.0, 1.2 and 1.6 mm (0.039, 0.047 and 0.06 in) in some highly stressed places. The stringers are of the bulb angle type; they pass through recesses in the frames and are affixed by a single rivet to deflected parts of each sheet-metal frame. This design reduces the fuselage's weight per cubic metre of its volume.

The *forward fuselage* houses the flightdeck with workstations for the pilots, and the radio operator; it also provides accommodation for the flight engineer and houses the forward baggage compartment holding up to 800 kg (1,760 lb) of baggage. The flightdeck is separated from the cabin by a bulkhead.

The forward fuselage of an Aeroflot Li-2P pictured in front of a brand-new terminal building at Moscow-Vnukovo. The sliding flightdeck window and the baggage loading door are visible.

Above: The forward and centre fuselage of a Soviet Air Force Li-2 transport in wartime armed configuration (note the open cargo door).

Above: The nose of an Aeroflot Li-2 with an upgraded avionics fit, including an SP-50 Materik instrument landing system whose U-shaped aerial is mounted on the flightdeck roof. Note the extra pitot heads.

The nose of an UchShLi-2 navigator trainer.

The nosecone ahead of the flightdeck windscreen is split horizontally, the upper half hinging upwards to provide access to equipment and control runs. The flightdeck glazing frame located between frames 3-7 comprises four stamped frames and the upper skin. The V-shaped windshield has four panes made of triplex glass 6.4 mm (0¼ in) thick; 6-mm (0$\frac{15}{64}$ in) Plexiglas is used for the two side windows, which are sliding direct vision windows. On military versions the seats of the pilot (to port) and the navigator (to starboard) are fitted with armoured backs. The window of the radio operator is located on starboard side between frames 7 and 9; located between frames 7 and 8 on the port side is the window of the flight engineer's station (on aircraft up to Batch 238 the radio operator's station was located to port). An escape hatch (or, on some aircraft, an astrodome) is provided in the flightdeck roof. A baggage loading door with a semi-circular top is located on the port side between frames 7-8, opening outward and forward.

The *centre fuselage* houses the cargo/troop cabin or, on the Li-2P, the passenger cabin. The cabin has seven rectangular windows with wooden frames on each side. Two windows on the port side and one window to starboard incorporate overwing emergency exits opening outwards and upwards on piano hinges. A large ventral cutout for the monobloc wing centre section is located between frames 13 and 25.

The Li-2P was manufactured in three versions: the basic version with 15 to 21 seats, a 15-seat version with improved comfort (for long-haul routes and for VIP transportation), and the so-called economic version with 24 seats (eight rows of three), the seat pitch being suitably reduced. The seats are cushioned and feature adjustable seat backs. Overhead bins for small luggage and headgear and individual reading lights are located under the ceiling along the cabin walls. The cabin is lined with heat- and soundproofing blankets and provided with ventilation and a heating system. Access to the cabin is provided by an entry door with a semi-circular top measuring 0.657 x 1.44 m (2 ft 1$\frac{55}{64}$ in x 4 ft 8$\frac{43}{64}$ in) located on the starboard side between frames 31 and 33; it opens inward and aft.

The Li-2T was manufactured in the same standardised configuration for both military and civil purposes. The cargo cabin was provided with 25 wooden tip-up seats. As an alternative, uprights could be installed for mounting stretchers intended to accommodate 18 patients. The Li-2T's cargo cabin lacks thermal insulation and internal lining. In addition to the abovementioned entry door, an upward/outward-opening rectangular cargo door with rounded corners (incorporating two windows) is located on the port side.

The *rear fuselage* carries the tail surfaces (the horizontal tail is inserted into lateral cutouts) and a detachable tailcone; it mounts the tailwheel, for which a cutout is provided between frames 43-46. On the passenger versions the rear fuselage also accommodates a toilet, a wardrobe and the rear baggage compartment holding up to 680 km (1,500 lb) of baggage. The rear baggage compartment is accessible both from within and from outside via a rectangular baggage loading door located to port between frames 37-40 and opening upwards/outwards on a piano hinge.

All changes were introduced on the civil and military versions virtually in parallel, with Plant No.126 in Komsomol'sk-on-Amur slightly lagging behind as compared to the Tashkent Plant No.84. When it came to the Tashkent-built Batch 250, the changes were introduced only on the Li-2T. Previously the main entry door (on the starboard side) had opened outward and forward through 180°; now it opened inward and aft (as had been the case on the pre-war PS-84-K prototypes) to enable paradropping. Two steel cables were mounted near the ceiling in the cargo cabin; they were used for attaching the paratroopers' parachute static lines.

Batch 262 saw yet another upgrade to the Li-2T: it was provided with an additional small door ('wicket-gate', in the Russian parlance) incorporated into the large port side cargo door; the small door also opened inward and aft. At the same time the aircraft was fitted with detachable seats for paratroopers – these were very simple benches made of wood and plywood, each bench intended for two persons. The commander's seat was located in the port side row, close to the door. When the aircraft carried cargoes, the benches were removed to save weight or simply tipped up against the walls.

On Batch 266 the cargo hold floor, previously made of plywood, was manufactured of corrugated metal so as to enhance its ability to sustain concentrated loads. The floor was covered with rubber runners. In Batch 277 the Li-2T was equipped with a device for towing assault gliders, which required the tailcone to be cropped, making the aircraft look still more like the Douglas C-47. The crew kept the glider under observation through a periscope mounted on the ceiling above the work stations of the radio operator and the flight engineer; this was a reworked OP2-LM bomb sight.

In October 1947 the airframes of the Li-2P and the Li-2T were brought to a common standard (except for the cargo door). The layout of the forward fuselage of the cargo version was altered to correspond to that of the passenger version. Thereby the volume of the cargo cabin was slightly reduced due to the introduction of three baggage holds.

Above: The Li-2NB night bomber's forward baggage door was modified to incorporate a three-piece window. Here it is seen in the closed position.

Above: The Li-2NB's bomb-aiming window in the open position, showing the NKPB-7 bombsight slid into position for aiming.

The open cargo door of a Li-2T. Note the emergency exit immediately forward of the door. The objects hanging from the door are window curtains.

Above, left and right: The centre fuselage. The wing/fuselage joint is covered by a large fairing.

Left: The open port entry/paradropping door of the PS-84-K; note the jumpmaster's seat beside the cargo door.
Right: The starboard (main) entry door. Instead of a boarding ladder this Li-2 is provided with detachable boarding steps of the kind used on some Mil' helicopters.

Wings: Cantilever low-wing monoplane. The three-spar wings utilise the NACA 2215 airfoil at the root and the NACA 2206 airfoil at the tip. The wings are built in three portions: a rectangular centre section spanning 7.214 m (23 ft 8 in) and two detachable outer wing panels of trapezoidal planform featuring rounded tips, an unswept trailing edge and a swept leading edge. Sweepback at quarter-chord 15°, dihedral 5° on the detachable outer portions, incidence 2°; root chord 4.318 m (14 ft 2 in), tip chord 1.305 m (4 ft 3⅜ in).

The *wing centre section* comprises the forward part (up to the third spar) and the trailing edge part; it carries the engine nacelles and is mated to the centre fuselage frames by means of eight fittings made of AK-1 aluminium alloy and lengthwise angle pieces. Each outer wing panel comprises the forward and trailing edge parts and a wingtip section. The trailing-edge portions of the outer wings and the wingtips are detachable. The wing leading edge houses the piping of the hot-air de-icing system and incorporates the landing lights. The starboard outer wing panel mounts the sensor of the PDK-45 potentiometric remote-indicating compass. The wings are fitted with hydraulically actuated Schrenck slotted flaps, two of which occupy the whole of the wing centre section trailing edge and the other two are located on the outer wing panels. The ailerons are aero-

Above: The cargo cabin of the PS-84-K, looking towards the tail; note the open doors, the folded troop seats along the cabin walls and the manually operated cargo loading hoist.

The passenger cabin of a Li-2P, looking towards the tail. The doors at the end lead to the toilet (left) and the rear baggage compartment.

Above: The lovingly restored cabin of what is now the last remaining airworthy Li-2 in the world – the Gold Timer Foundation's Li-2P HA-LIX. Note the 'quilted' heat- and soundproofing blankets on the walls and the decidedly non-authentic seats dating back only to the 1970s or even more recently.

A view of the same cabin, looking towards the nose; note the commemorative plaques on the front bulkhead. Here the meal trays in the seat backs sound an even more jarring note; to be sure, the seats are of Soviet origin but they come straight from a Tupolev Tu-134 or a Tu-154.

Above: A peek inside the flightdeck of Li-2P HA-LIX. The baggage compartment aft of it is occupied by modern storage lockers.

dynamically balanced and partially mass balanced. The starboard aileron has a trim tab.

The wing spars are of the H-beam type with a sheet-metal web and spar caps formed by a pair of shaped bulb angle sections. The wing centre section skin has an average thickness of 1.0 mm (0.039 in); on the upper wing surface it is reinforced by spanwise corrugations between the spars. On the underside the skin is made up of removable panels attached by bolts in order to provide access for the installation of fuel tanks. The skin of the outer wing panels has a thickness of 0.8 mm and 0.6 mm; it is reinforced by numerous bulb angle stringers. The wing outer panels are joined to the wing centre section with the help of flanges, using external angle fittings and 8-mm (0$^{5}/_{16}$ in) bolts made of 30KhGSA grade steel (94 bolts on the upper side and 132 bolts on the underside).

Tail Unit: Cantilever conventional tail surfaces of basically trapezoidal planform with rounded tips. The *vertical tail* consists of a detachable multi-spar one-piece fin with a duralumin skin 0.6 and 0.8 mm thick and a one-piece rudder with a metal framework and a skin of AM-100 linen fabric. The vertical tail utilise symmetrical airfoils (NACA 0009 at the root and NACA 0006 at the tip).

The structurally similar *horizontal tail* consists of stabilisers and one-piece elevators.

The tail unit of Li-2T '03 Yellow' (c/n 23441605) seen in the 1970s. Note how the rudder ribs show through the fabric skin.

Above: The port ASh-62IR engine and AV-7N-161 propeller of a Li-2T. Note the chin-mounted oil coolers introduced on batch 231. The small upper intake is for the carburettor.

The port main landing gear strut of Li-2P HA-LIX. This view shows the 'knee-action' struts, shock absorbers, brake flange and the V-shaped drag strut.

Again, symmetrical airfoils are used (NACA 0011 at the root and NACA 0006 at the tips). The stabilisers have zero dihedral and zero incidence and are joined along the aircraft's axis to form a monobloc assembly. The empennage is attached to the fuselage by bolts: the fin is attached by means of a reinforcing strap, the stabilisers make use of angle fittings on the rear fuselage sides.

The rudder and the elevators are aerodynamically balanced and partly mass-balanced provided with trim tabs.

Landing Gear: Tailwheel landing gear with a single wheel on each unit; all units are equipped with oleo-pneumatic shock absorbers. The wheel track is 5.639 m (18 ft 6 in) and the aircraft's ground angle is 11°30'.

The main units attached to the wing centre section retract forward and upward into the engine nacelles, the wheels remaining partially exposed when retracted; they have 1,200 x 450 mm (47.25 x 17.7 in) wheels fitted with low-pressure tyres and two-pad hydraulic brakes. Each main unit has dual 'knee-action' struts, whose lower halves incorporate shock absorbers with a stroke of 250 mm (9²⁷⁄₃₂ in), and a rear drag strut with a fork fitting around the wheel. The non-retractable castoring tailwheel measuring 600 x 250 mm (23.6 x 9.8 in) has a low-pressure tyre and is set in a fork. During take-off, landing and in flight it is locked neutral to align with the aircraft's longitudinal axis. Retractable skis can be fitted for winter operations.

Powerplant: Two Shvetsov ASh-62IR nine-cylinder single-row air-cooled radial engines rated at 1,000 hp (746 kW) at 2,200 rpm for take-off with a 5-minute limit; nominal (maximum continuous) power is 820 hp (611 kW) at 2,100 rpm at sea level or 840 hp (626 kW) at 1,500 m (4,920 ft), and cruise power is 410 hp (306 kW) at 1,670 rpm. Displacement 29,870 cm^3 (1,822 cu in), bore 155.5 mm, stroke 174.5 mm, compression ratio 6.4. Length overall 1,130 mm (3 ft 8½ in), maximum diameter 1,375 mm (4 ft 6⅛ in). Dry weight 560-579 kg (1,234-1,276 lb), depending on the series. The late-production ASh-62IR has a 6,000-hour service life.

The crankshaft turns anti-clockwise when seen from the front and has two torsional vibration dampers; power is transmitted via a planetary gearbox with a reduction ratio of 0.6875. The ASh-62IR has a single-speed mechanically driven centrifugal supercharger; manifold pressure is 1,050 mm Hg at take-off power and 900 mm Hg in cruise mode.

The engine uses aviation gasoline (Avgas) with an octane value not less than 91, such as Soviet B-91/115 grade Avgas. Specific fuel consumption 0.3 kg/hp·hr (0.66 lb/hp.hr) at take-off power and 0.26 kg/hp·hr

Above: The port nacelle of a Li-2T with the front cowling plate removed, exposing the ASh-62IR's reduction gear casing, valve actuation gear and propeller speed governor. The Soviet tyres make an interesting comparison with the ones on HA-LIX.

Above right: A Li-2 in winter configuration with the front cowling plate in place and the shutters closed. Note the ski restraining cables and the retaining stop on the main gear drag strut making sure the ski is correctly aligned after retraction.

Right: This Li-2 has a different type of skis and is a fairly early example with buried main oil coolers and an extra external oil cooler.

(0.57 lb/hp·hr) in cruise mode. Fuel is fed to the engine via an AK-61IR carburettor with automatic mixture controls.

Normally the ASh-62IR is started by an RIM-U-24IR electric inertia starter controlled from the flightdeck. The engine is also equipped with the following accessories: an R-9SM constant speed governor, a GSN-3000M generator, an AK-50M1 or AK-50P compressor, two BSM-9 magnetos,

A late version of the ski landing gear with retractable all-metal skis.

an MSh-8 oil pump, a TTsM-25 centrifugal oil purifier, an MFM-25 oil filter, a BNK-12B fuel pump and a fuel shut-off cock.

The engines are installed in nacelles on the wing leading edge and carried on truss-type bearers. Each bearer is composed of four Y-shaped struts made of welded steel tubes and a hefty stamped ring made of AK-6 aluminium alloy; the engine bearer is attached to the nacelle's firewall via four vibration dampers.

Each engine is enclosed by a broad-chord NACA cowling blended into the nacelle contour. The cowling comprises a circular forward plate featuring nine cooling apertures with shutters (this plate is removable and mostly used in cold climates), three detachable portions (port, starboard and upper) and adjustable cooling air outlet flaps. The carburettor intake fairing is located ventrally.

The ASh-62IR has a nine-section exhaust manifold made of EYa1T heat-resistant steel; on the Li-2 this is blended into a large exhaust pipe exiting the outboard side of the nacelle.

The engines drive three-blade variable-pitch metal propellers measuring 3.6 m (11 ft 9¾ in) in diameter. Three types of propellers were used:

- batches 1 through 284 had VISh-21 automatic non-feathering propellers; their hubs were enclosed by ogival spinners with Hucks starter dogs for starting the engines with the help of starter trucks.
- batches 285 through 328 had AV-7NYe-161 feathering propellers featuring a single-channel hydraulic system for automatic pitch control in flight and for feathering;
- from batch 330 onwards the Li-2 was fitted with AV-7N-161 propellers featuring a two-channel hydraulic system for automatic pitch control.

The engines and the gasoline valves of the fuel system are controlled mechanically from the flightdeck. For this purpose the following control levers are grouped on a special panel: carburettor air heating lever, throttles, propeller pitch levers, carburettor altitude-sensing corrector levers, oil cooler shutter levers; engine cowling shutter levers; shut-off valve levers.

Control System: Dual mechanical controls with cable linkages. The control cables from the control wheel, control column, rudder pedals and the trim tab handwheel run through a system of rollers and Textolite slides to the bellcranks of the ailerons, rudder and elevators, as well as to the trim tab control drums. To provide easy access to the control linkages, the floor of the flightdeck/cabin aisle is easily removable.

Roll control is provided by one-piece ailerons with a maximum deflection of 27° up and 18° down. The starboard aileron incorporates a trim tab with a deflection of ±12°. Directional control is provided by a rudder with a travel of ±30° which features a trim tab with a deflection of ±13°30'. Pitch control is provided by one-piece elevators with a maximum deflection of 30° up and 20° down; again, the elevator trim tabs have a maximum deflection of ±13°30'.

Early-production PS-84s were equipped with an AVP-12 hydraulic autopilot, succeeded by the AVP-12*bis* model on later aircraft. Later (from batch 330 onwards, manufactured in 1946) the aircraft were equipped with the AP-42 autopilot, succeeded by the AP-42A and, later still, by the AP-45 autopilot.

Fuel System: The fuel system comprises four tanks which are made of welded and riveted AMTs aluminium alloy sheet 0.8 mm thick, two-way, three-way and four-way distribution cocks, a filter, a hand-driven pump, a check valve, hand primer gun, two gasoline pumps, piping with accessories, an electric fuel gauge and two manometers.

The fuel tanks are installed in the wing centre section between the front and middle spars, and between the middle and rear spars; for CG reasons the fuel in the rear group of tanks is used up first. Each of the forward tanks holds 795 litres (174.9 Imp gal) or 600 kg (1,322 lb), each of the aft tanks holds 760 litres (167.2 Imp gal) or 560 kg (1,234 lb). Total fuel capacity is 3,110 litres (684.2 Imp gal) and the total fuel load 2,320 kg (5,114 lb). The fuel used is B-91/115 or B-92 grade Avgas or equivalent.

Oil System: The oil system of each engine comprises an oil tank holding 128 litres (28.16 Imp gal, some manuals state 145 litres/31.9 Imp gal), normally filled to a level not exceeding 90 litres (19.8 Imp gal), a Model 812A oil cooler, plug-type drain cocks of the oil tank and of the engine oil feed line, piping consisting of tubes made of AMrM aluminium alloy (with the exception of the pipe from the oil tank to the engine's oil pump which was made of 20A grade steel). The oil grades used are MK-22, MS-20 and MS-24 mineral oils suitable for all seasons. In the summer an additional uncowled oil cooler was mounted on the outside of the engine nacelle in a horizontal position.

Beginning with c/n 18423110, the location of the oil coolers was changed. The two big cylindrical oil coolers, which had previously stood almost vertically in the engine nacelle, were moved down to the carburettor air intake and suspended horizontally, being covered by a common chin fairing. The adjustable shutters had previously been placed at the entrance of the air stream; now they were placed at its exit. As a result of all this, a characteristic 'chin' appeared under the engine nacelle.

Electric System: The electric system uses a twin-wire layout (with live and neutral wires). The electric system caters for the normal functioning of the gauges controlling the powerplant and its accessories, the radio equipment, the lighting and signalling equipment used for night-time flying, the de-icers of the propellers and stabiliser, and the windshield wipers. The electric circuit is designed for 24V DC. On aircraft from Batch 300 onwards the electric circuit used a single-wire layout, the airframe structure acting as the neutral wire. The power supply was provided by GS-1000 aircraft generators (one on each engine) or by two 12-A-30 storage batteries. All power sources worked in parallel supplying electricity to a common onboard circuit.

The aircraft is fitted with FS-240 landing lights buried in the wing leading edges, AB-37 navigation lights at the wingtips (red to port and green to starboard), a KhS-37 white navigation light on the tailcone and a system of internal lighting.

Hydraulic System: The hydraulic system actuates the undercarriage, flaps and wheel brakes, and caters for the hydraulically actuated units of the autopilot and the compensation cylinders of the undercarriage which ensure a speedy retraction and smooth extension of the main undercarriage units. Hydraulic pressure is created by two engine-driven MSh-3A six-stage hydraulic pumps.

In the course of production the PS-84/Li-2 was equipped with hydraulic systems of two basically different designs. One of these featured undivided feed to all hydraulic equipment (Batches 1 through 47 and from Batch 200 onwards to the final batch), the other provided separate feed (batches 48 through 199). The basic difference between the two versions was that in the second version the pump of the starboard engine catered only for the autopilot units.

The hydraulic system uses MVP grade oil; total capacity is 23 litres (5.06 Imp gal). The working pressure is 56 kg/cm^2 (797 psi).

Heating System: The heating system maintains a temperature inside the aircraft within a range of +12-15°C (+53-59°F) at an ambient

Above: The captain's instrument panel and control wheel.

Above: The first officer's (co-pilot's) instrument panel and control wheel.

The centre portion of the instrument panel, the bank of throttles and the propeller and mixture controls.

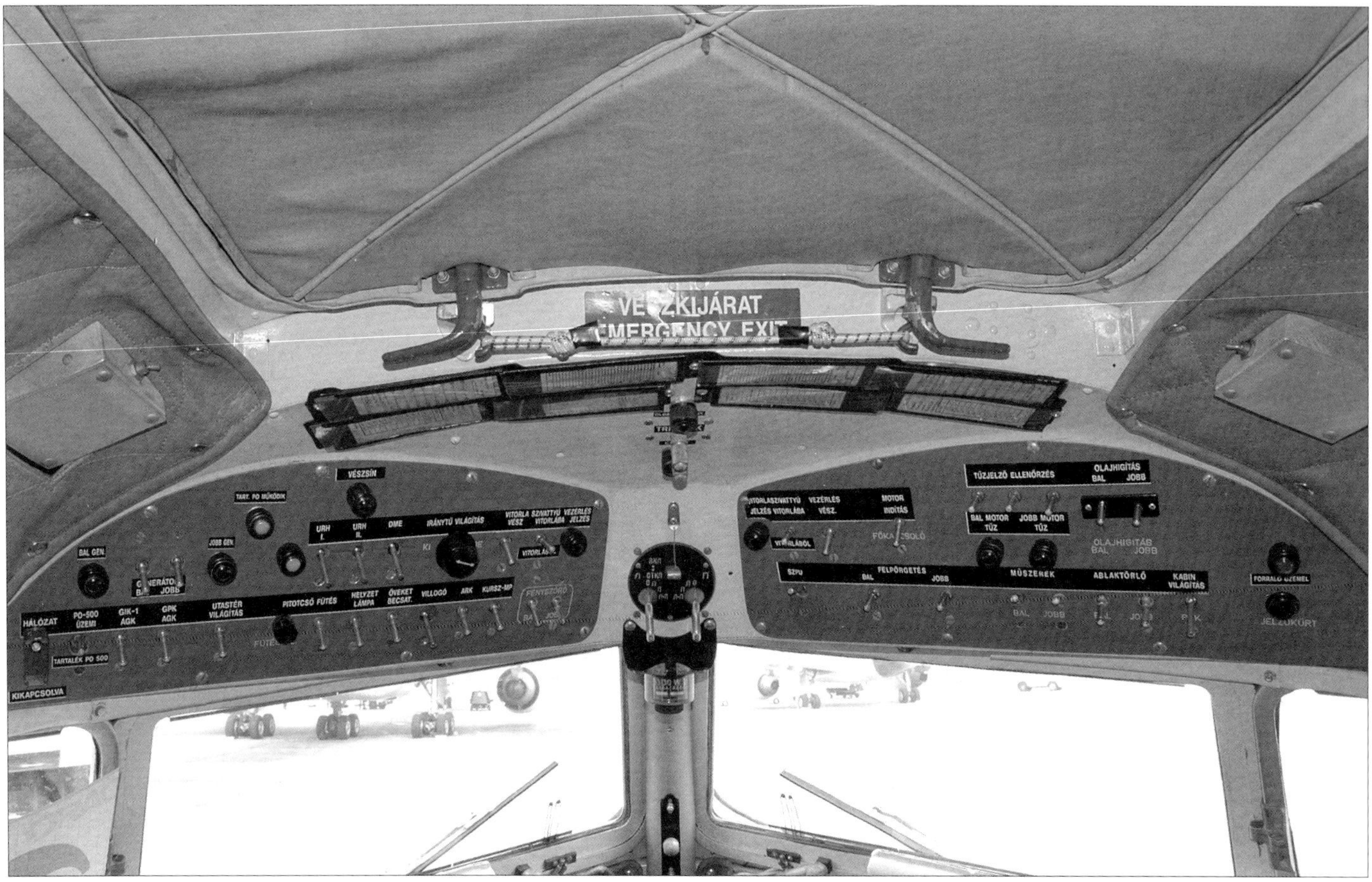

Above: The overhead circuit breaker panels, the bank of caution/warning lights and the flightdeck escape hatch on Li-2P HA-LIX. On this particular aircraft all flightdeck placards are in Hungarian.

The instrument panel of HA-LIX is pretty much the way it has always been – except for the addition of a modern communications radio in the middle. Compromises are inevitable if you want to fly an old-timer and still comply with current flight safety regulations.

temperature of –30°C (–22°F). The cabins of late-production Li-2s (beginning with Batch 280) were heated by a steam/air heating system. Its main units comprised a boiler fitted around the exhaust pipe of the starboard engine's exhaust manifold, a water tank placed in the forward baggage compartment, a radiator accommodated under the floor of this compartment, and piping. In the boiler the water was turned into steam which went to the radiator and heated the cold air coming from the outside; the heated air passed through a mixing chamber into air ducts mounted along the sides of the passenger cabin on its floor and escaped into the cabin through louvres. The mixing chamber was fed by cold air through a pipe; in case of need it was possible to regulate with the help of shutters the amount of hot and cold air supplied and thus to adjust the temperature in the cabin.

Ventilation System: Fresh air is fed through an aperture in the forward fuselage via piping into air ducts with individual ventilation nozzles which are located above the passengers' heads. The suction of air is effected through louvres located in the cabin roof. The influx of fresh air is regulated by a variable metering orifice placed in the forward fuselage air duct.

De-icing System: Hot air de-icing for the wing leading edges, electro-thermal de-icing for the horizontal tail and a fluid (alcohol) de-icing system for the windshield and propellers. To remove precipitation, the windshield is provided with AS-2 electric wipers.

Avionics and Equipment: The *radio equipment* serves for two-way telegraphic and voice communication of the crew with ground control centres or with airborne aircraft, for radio navigation of the aircraft with the help of signals transmitted by radio beacons or broadcasting stations, and for calculating a landing approach in poor visibility conditions. It comprises:

- an RSB-*bis* command link radio (telephonic transceiver) whose wire antenna ran from a mast above the flightdeck to the top of the fin; later it was replaced by an RSI-6 radio (from Batch 325 onwards);
- an RPK-2 direction finder (its loop aerial was housed in a teardrop fairing above the forward fuselage); later it was replaced with the RPKO-2B model (from Batch 257 onwards but not on all machines) which enabled the crew to use broadcasting stations as radio beacons;
- a marker beacon receiver (from Batch 300 onwards);
- an RV-2 radio altimeter (from Batch 300 onwards);
- an ARK-5 radio compass (from Batch 300 onwards);

Above: An MV-1 'ball turret' with a 7.62-mm ShKAS machine gun on a Li-2NB night bomber. Note the stabilising fins which make it easier to rotate the turret when tracking a target.

Above: One of the ShKU-1 beam positions, also with a ShKAS machine gun. The aperture is mostly closed by a plate to prevent draughts when the machine gun is not in use.

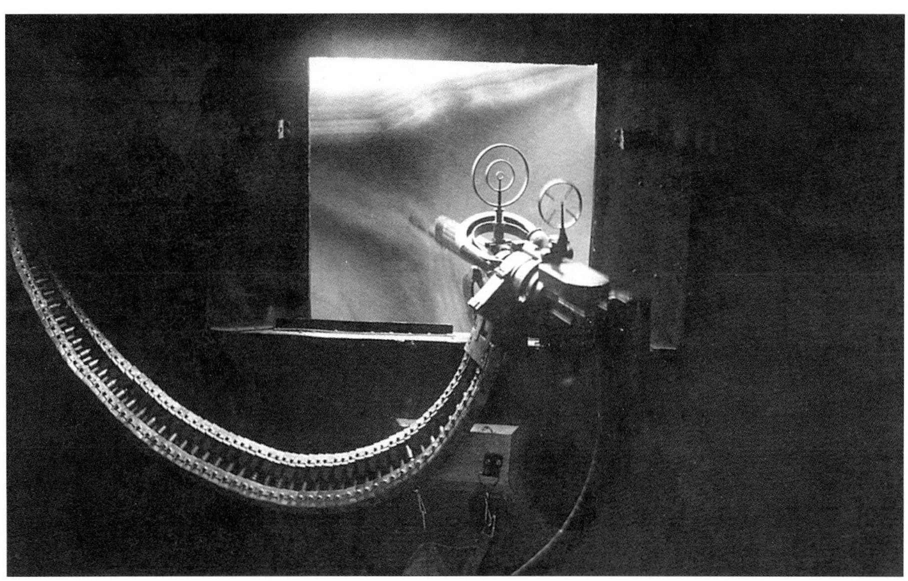

The ShKU-1 installation seen from the inside, ready to fire. Note the ammunition belt and the ring-and-bead sight.

Above: A forward-firing ShKAS with angled spent case chute in the nose of an early bomber-configured PS-84 (note the protective visor ahead of the flightdeck window enabling the bomb-aimer to stick his head out of the window). The 5T-275U fixed installation proved impractical and was soon deleted.

Here the upper half of the nosecone is opened for access to the 5T-275U machine gun installation. Note the ammunition belt and box, and also the early-style cowlings and VISh-21 propeller.

• a Noch-1 (Night-1), or *Kor**don*** (Border) instrument landing system; later replaced by the SP-50 *Mate**rik*** (Continent) ILS (from Batch 325 onwards;

• an SPU-3 intercom and other equipment.

The main units of the radio equipment are located in the radio operator's compartment (with the exception of the radio altimeter transceiver which is installed in the aft fuselage).

The *flight and navigation equipment* comprises:

• a KI-11 compass (supplemented by an A-4 compass up to Batch 229);

• two VD-12 altimeters;

• two US-350 airspeed indicators;

• a VR-10 vertical speed indicator;

• an AGP-2 artificial horizon;

• a UP-2 turn indicator;

• a PDK-45 remote-indicating compass (from Batch 300 onwards);

• a TVE-41 or TVE-45 outside air thermometer;

• an AChKhO clock.

In 1946 the 'antiquated' AVP-12*bis* hydraulic autopilot was replaced by the AP-42 electric autopilot (also a copy of a US prototype, but a more modern one, dating to the years of the war). On Batch 252 the autopilot was replaced by the improved AP-42A model.

Armament: The machine gun armament of the military PS-84 (Li-2) initially comprised four 7.62-mm (.30 calibre) Shpital'nyy/Komaritskiy ShKAS machine guns. The 5T-275U fixed nose installation had an ammunition complement of 450 rounds. It was worked by the pilot with the help of a button placed on the left control wheel via the M-10 electric trigger. The recharging was effected mechanically with the help of a handle and a Bowden cable. The KPT-5 sight was mounted externally on the nose skin to port. Spent cartridge cases were expelled through a chute downwards and rearwards, the links were collected in a compartment in the lower portion of the forward fuselage.

Above: The fuselage underside of a PS-84 bomber (c/n 1843603) fitted with four bomb racks. Note the bomb release control cables.

Above: The same aircraft with four FAB-100 bombs hooked up.

The same aircraft again, this time with RRAB-250 cluster bombs. As the bomb fell. rotating around its axis, the thin outer shell was torn apart by the centrifugal force, scattering the submunitions.

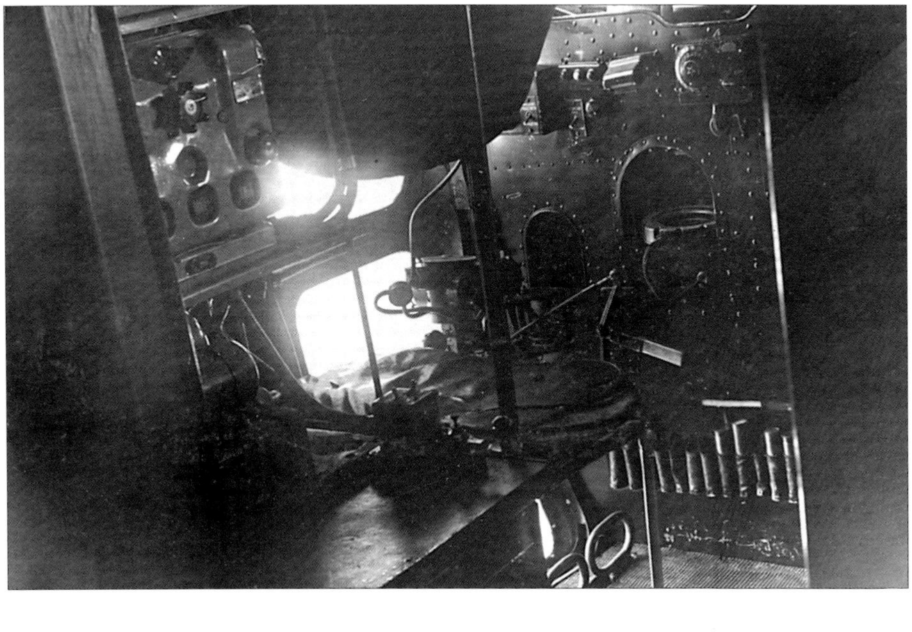

Mounted above the fuselage was a Mozharovskiy/Venevidov MV-3 shielded dorsal turret provided with three ammunition cases, each holding 500 rounds (some sources indicate an ammunition complement of 1,200 rounds). The dorsal installation was operated by a gunner who stood on an adjustable support. The gunner made use of the MPT-1 sight. Spent cartridge cases and links were collected into a common bag. Subsequently a UTK-1 dorsal turret with a 12.7-mm (.50 calibre) Berezin UBT machine gun was fitted. The turret was aerodynamically balanced and could be easily rotated manually in flight. Attached to the fuselage behind the turret was a tubular frame which restricted the movement of the machine gun and prevented its fire from hitting the vertical tail.

Two machine guns were mounted on ShKU-1 gun pivots which were placed in the rear fuselage between frames 36 and 39 in special ports on both sides that had served previously as baggage hatches. Each machine gun had an ammunition complement of 500 rounds. When not in use, the ports were covered by shields with a slit for the machine gun barrel. In combat position the shield slid inwards and upwards. The sights were of the KPT-5 type. The overall ammunition complement for the two machine guns was 1,000 rounds. Spent cartridge cases and links were collected into a bag. The machine guns mounted on gun pivots in the rear were operated by the radio operator and the flight engineer who moved to the tail of the aircraft when the danger of an aerial attack arose.

The bomb armament of the PS-84K comprised a removable transverse beam with Der-19 and Der-31 bomb racks. They could carry such loads as eight 100-kg bombs, PDMM paradroppable cargo sacks and PDBB paradroppable gasoline delivery tanks. The external stores were released by means of an ESBR-3 electric release mechanism and an ASBR mechanical emergency release device. The Li-2NB night bomber could carry four 250-kg (551-lb) bombs or two 500-kg (1,102-lb) bombs. The NKPB-3 collimator bomb sight was mounted near the starboard side window of the flightdeck and was protected by a deflectable shield. The ESBR-3P electric main bomb release unit and the back-up mechanical bomb release unit were placed to starboard of the navigator's station.

Top left: The bomb-aiming window of a Li-2NB night bomber closed for cruise flight.

Centre left: The same window opened for business, with the NKPB-7 bombsight moved into position.

Left: Overall view of the navigator/bomb-aimer's station on the Li-2NB. The workstation was extremely cramped.

Chapter 4

Comparison and Assessment

It would be of interest for the readers to learn a comparative assessment of the transport aircraft that were produced in different countries during the war, especially of those that were, in fact, reproductions of the famous DC-3.

The Li-2, in the configuration manufactured during the war by the Aircraft Plant No.84, was a dual-purpose aircraft – it was used both as a transport/troopship and as a long-range night bomber; in contrast, the C-47 was a pure transport/troopship (though it was also used for towing assault gliders). Therefore, in the Soviet Air Force the Li-2 was supplied primarily to long-range bomber regiments, while the C-47s obtained under the Lend-Lease agreement were issued to transport air regiments, although several C-47s were usually supplied to regiments operating the Li-2.

The C-47 was reliable and fuel-efficient. For example, in the first six months of 1945 the number of flight incidents per one machine of this type was 2.5 times lower as compared to the Li-2. Moreover, the US aircraft was superior in many characteristics to the PS-84 (Li-2). The powerful R-1830 Twin Wasp two-row radials ensured a higher speed – up to 360-370 km/h (223-230 mph) at an altitude of 2,300 m (7,540 ft) – and a higher service ceiling; the cargo-carrying capacity was also higher. The engines were mounted in a very rational way and were easy to service. It took 62 man-hours to replace one Soviet ASh-62IR engine, while the replacement of the US engine, together with the engine mount, took only 10 man-hours! On the Li-2 the VISh-21 propellers had a service life of only 50 hours before the first overhaul. In contrast, the US Hamilton Standard Hydromatic propellers, featuring a more complicated design and provided with the very important automatic feathering device, had a company-guaranteed service life of 750 hours. In practice, the imported propeller had a service life approximately five times longer than the Soviet one! In case of need two bag-type tanks holding 375 litres (82.5 Imp gal) each could be installed in the cargo cabin, increasing the range to 3,400 km (2,111 miles). Expert technicians could fit non-standard extra tanks of even greater capacity.

The C-47 was characterised by its higher manufacturing standards and superior quality in the manufacture of the airframe. The American aircraft was more reliable, its smoother surface finish created less drag. In comparison with the Soviet aircraft, it had a much more efficient fuel system and hydraulics (Soviet-produced valves leaked, thus placing an extra burden on the ground personnel). The clamshell cargo doors of the C-47 were considerably wider than the one-piece upward-opening cargo door of the Li-2 which was introduced on production aircraft as late as 1945.

The American instruments and radio equipment proved to be much more advanced than those of the Li-2. Not only did the C-47 have a considerably more comprehensive complement of instruments, but they were also more precise and reliable and had a longer service life. The Li-2's radio operators

A Pratt & Whitney-powered Douglas DC-3 (not a C-47 – there is no cargo door) in Soviet Air Force colours; the '085' on the tail is in all probability the last three digits of the USAAC serial. Note the pneumatic de-icer boots on the wings and tail and the distinctive shape of the engine nacelles.

Wearing a somewhat unusual three-digit registration for a GU GVF aircraft, Oklahoma City-built Douglas C-47B-10-DK CCCP-Л976 (c/n 26332) still carries its original USAAC serial 43-49071 on the tail.

could only envy their colleagues flying the US-built machines: these lucky guys had at their disposal three different radios, a radio altimeter, an instrument landing system (ILS), an automatic direction finder; the Soviet licence-built transport aircraft from the early batches had a much more primitive set of equipment. In addition, the radios of US manufacture were five to six times more powerful than the Soviet ones and ensured greater stability of operation while having lower weight and smaller dimensions. On the C-47 the radio operator's station was located outside the propeller rotation plane and accommodated in a special soundproof compartment. The only cause of vexation was the fact that the C-47s intended for export were fitted with an incomplete set of equipment: the USAAC machines featured many additional equipment items, as evidenced by empty support brackets and unnecessary inscription plates on the export aircraft.

The American designers had given much thought to easing the aircraft's operation at low ambient temperatures. They provided all the devices that were in existence at that time – de-icers on the wings and tail surfaces, fluid de-icing for the propeller blades and flight-deck glazing, heaters for the flightdeck and the cargo/passenger cabin. The BF Goodrich pneumatic de-icer boots were more effective than the thermal de-icers of Soviet design. The hydraulically-actuated glazing wipers

Another C-47 in Aeroflot service after the war. Like most aircraft in GU GVF (mainline) service, it has a four-digit registration, CCCP-Л1015. The very bold Aeroflot titles are noteworthy.

were also considered to be superior to the electrically-operated wipers on the Li-2.

The crews also liked the heaters installed on the C-47s. The Li-2 was equipped with a steam/air heating system using a boiler. The flight engineer operating the system got the scathing nickname of 'stoker'. It took a lot of trouble to get the 'stove' to function reliably, otherwise the heater produced a cloud of steam filling the flightdeck. The Soviet-built aircraft had to be warmed up for 40-45 minutes before a winter take-off, while the US-built machines were provided with a system for diluting the oil with gasoline (not only in the engines but in the propeller hubs as well), which eased cold-weather operations a lot. The fluid in the C-47's hydraulic system was frost-resistant. During frosty weather the only place on the C-47 that had to be encased for warmth was the breather tubes between the engine and the oil tank.

After the cessation of military hardware deliveries from the USA to the Soviet Union, difficulties arose with obtaining spare parts for the US-supplied transport aircraft. When they underwent repairs, some elements of the electric equipment and some instruments often had to be replaced by Soviet-produced counterparts. In the USSR the R-1830 engines underwent two or three overhauls, but they could not last indefinitely. Therefore, on the basis of a project developed by N. T. Mashovets and Zinoviy M. Lipskiy, the Civil Air Fleet's aircraft repair facility No.400 at Moscow-Vnukovo airport started to re-engine the US-supplied C-47s with ASh-62IR radials driving Soviet propellers. The machines thus converted received a new designation, TS-62 (***trahns**portnyy samo**lyot** [s **dvig**atelyami ASh-] shest'de**syat** dva* – 'transport aircraft with ASh-62 engines). The engines were provided with front shutters for winter operation after the fashion adopted on the Li-2, but the shutters were operated hydraulically, not by cables as on the baseline aircraft.

The 'hybrid' TS-62s were inferior in performance to the C-47s, but they were superior to the Li-2s thanks to the better aerodynamics. It was noted, however, that repainting these aircraft in the USSR always led to a reduction of the maximum speed (the paints used in the USA produced a smoother coat). These machines were operated by various directorates of the Civil Air Fleet (Aeroflot). The TS-62s were available in cargo and passenger versions (in the latter case the fuselage underwent a suitable modification).

The Tajik Directorate of the GVF operated similarly modified TS-82 aircraft – that is, C-47s re-engined with Shvetsov ASh-82FN two-row radials. As compared to the ASh-62IR this engine had not only greater power output but better altitude performance as well. The TS-82 could fairly easily outrun

Above: C-47B-35-DK '26 White' (44-76998, c/n 33330) was probably in use as a staff transport; note the red fin cap.

Above: Still wearing high-visibiity delivery insignia with the red star on a white circle, a C-47 is loaded with crates from a GAZ-AA (licence-built Ford Model AA) 1.5-ton lorry. The wide cargo door is clearly visible.

Red Army officers walk past a Soviet Air Force C-47.

Above: A Red Army reconnaissance/sabotage group armed with Mosin rifles and carriage-mounted Maxim machine guns waits to board a PS-84 which will insert them behind enemy lines.

Above: The personnel of a Long-Range Aviation (ADD) unit equipped with bomber-configured PS-84s stands to attention, preparing to pronounce the Guards oath as the unit receives Guards status.

Another scene at a frontline airfield with PS-84 '049 White'. War ain't all about shooting. When the guns fall silent, the muses take over.

necessary cargoes to the Soviet troops, thus enabling them to break out of the encirclement. In the Smolensk area the German command, having concentrated several tank formations, tried hard to penetrate the Soviet defences and reach the suburbs of Moscow. The Soviet troops were supported by the Air Force of the Western front and by the long-range bomber units. All the materiel that was necessary for the defence was delivered by transport aircraft of the MAGON which made 50 to 60 sorties to the battlefield area every day. Not infrequently the airmen had to perform several flights within every 24 hours, spending 14 to 16 hours in the air; on one occasion a crew captained by D. V. Kuznetsov logged nearly 20 hours!

During the Battle of Moscow frontline troops received assistance from three special aviation groups of the Civil Air Fleet: the Western group, the Moscow group and a special air communications group. During the very first days of the defensive operation near Moscow, in early October, a potent armour group of the Wehrmacht broke through the defences of the Western front, reached the town of Oryol and tried to launch an offensive against Moscow from the south. In this situation 30 PS-84 crews from the MAGON, acting under orders from the Supreme Command, effected a quick airlift of troops and materiel of the 5th Airborne Corps to the airfields of Oryol and Mtsensk. 30 of the group's aircraft took part in this operation; their crews flew 216 sorties in the course of three days, airlifting 5,440 troops and 12 tonnes (26,460 lb) of cargo.

When the 900-day siege of Leningrad began in September 1941, the PS-84 crews were tasked with delivering the necessary cargoes to the beleaguered city and evacuating children, women and specialists of various trades from Leningrad. Again, thirty MAGON aircraft were assigned for this task, supplemented by aircraft furnished by the Special Northern Civil Aviation Group (OSAG – *Osobaya severnaya aviatsionnaya grooppa*). The missions were flown from the airfields in Tikhvin, Kushever and Khvoynaya situated closest to the 'Northern Capital' (as St. Petersburg and, in Soviet times, Leningrad was – and still is – often called, as a reminder of the times when St. Petersburg was indeed the capital of Russia). Both groups performed their flights in the period between 10th October and 21st December, and when road haulage was organised on the ice of the frozen Lake Ladoga (known as 'The Road of Life'), the MAGON aircraft were reoriented to other operational areas. During that period the airmen airlifted 6,000 tonnes (13,230 lb) of food, medical supplies, ammunition and weapons and evacuated 53,000 persons to the 'mainland' (that is, the safety of the rear territories).

Probably, neither before nor after that operation had the Soviet PS-84 transport aircraft been used in such numbers and with such intensity for front-line flying in daytime. To reduce the danger of being attacked by German fighters, the airmen had to fly their machines as close to the ground as possible (at tree-top level, or 'shaving' flight, in the Russian parlance of the day), descending literally to a few metres above the tree tops or the waves of Lake Ladoga. During the first months of the war GVF pilots had to master the new method of flying virtually without training, directly during combat missions. The point was that, despite their great experience, the pilots had not had a chance to become 'old hands' at this kind of flying because, in Aeroflot, mainline pilots were strictly prohibited from flying close to the ground (nor was there any need to). No less difficult were formation flights, which had not been practised in the GVF either but became vitally important at the front. The defensive armament of the militarised PS-84 did not give a solitary aircraft many chances for survival in an encounter with a Messerschmitt Bf 109; yet, when flying in close formation, the PS-84s usually managed to hold their own against the enemy fighters that reigned supreme in the air.

For example, in September 1941 A. Pantelli, a MAGON pilot, was flying his PS-84 with a load of food supplies from Moscow to Leningrad – nothing out of the ordinary. All of a sudden, his machine was jumped by four Bf 109s. Imagine the surprise of the German pilots, who were accustomed to meeting no resistance from transport machines, when during the very first attack they came under machine gun fire. One Bf 109 dived into the waters of the lake; another disappeared behind the forest, trailing smoke. On 13th October 1941 the 3rd MAGON Squadron guided by Deputy Squadron Commander, Lieutenant (Senior Grade) A. Semenkov, used their dorsal machine guns effectively, quickly warding off a pair of Messerschmitts. Four days later, in another air battle, German Bf 109 fighters managed to break through the cover provided by the escorting Soviet fighters and knock out an engine on the rearmost PS-84 in a group (piloted by S. Frolovskiy). In this situation the leader of the PS-84 group ordered all the crews to reduce speed and thus prevent the damaged machine from lagging behind. When the Luftwaffe pilots tried to finish off the crippled transport, they were met again by a hail of defensive fire from the entire group; for one of the German fighters this attack became the last one.

The maintenance and service personnel of the air transport groups, too, displayed utmost dedication in their work. Not infrequently the aircraft came back from their missions literally riddled with bullets and shell fragments but, as a rule, the maintenance personnel quickly put them back into service. On many occasions technicians or mechanics doubled as gunners on the transport machines, replacing the crew members who had been put out of action. Sometimes they also took part in defending the front-line airstrips from enemy troops forcing their way towards them.

The maintenance and service personnel did a huge amount of work modifying the aircraft for front-line needs. Not only in regular repair facilities, but also under field conditions the aircraft were fitted with machine guns and bomb racks, and the crew seats were provided with armoured backs.

The flight engineers also had to shoulder a big workload. When their aircraft landed on field airstrips and at combat aviation bases, the flight engineers conducted the servicing and repair jobs on aircraft, engines and equipment which, before the war, had been performed by technical ground services in airports. When the situation required it, flight engineers displayed heroism and courage. Here is just one of the numerous examples. On 27th July 1941 a PS-84 from the MAGON evacuating gravely wounded personnel from the front-line was attacked by enemy fighters. The captain was seriously wounded; the machine turned uncontrollable. In this extremely dangerous and seemingly hopeless situation flight engineer I. S. Boolkin did not lose his nerve; he quickly seated himself

Top and above: The intensive operations took their toll on the aircraft, which quickly became weathered and worn, as exemplified by PS-84 '4054 White' (probably ex-CCCP-Л4054). Oddly, this aircraft wearing late-style white-outlined insignia appears to have no beam machine gun positions.

Above: Having delivered a load of crated supplies, a PS-84 with VISh-21 propellers is started up by means of a suitably modified ZiS-6 lorry. The temporary coat of chalk-based paint is well and truly weathered.

Li-2s often flew risky supply missions for the partisans behind enemy lines. Here the crew of a Li-2 armed with three ShKAS machine guns unloads supplies at an *ad hoc* airstrip while one of the airmen keeps a watchful eye for any Germans who might drop in.

in the pilot's seat and took the controls. Despite being wounded as well and having no prior experience in piloting an aircraft, Boolkin managed to choose a flat stretch of surface and land the heavily-loaded machine. He carried his captain out of the burning aircraft and helped the wounded 'passengers' to leave the machine. For his courage, valour and presence of mind I. S. Boolkin was awarded the Order of the Red Banner.

During the first days of the war a major tank battle took place in the vicinity of Lootsk and L'vov in western Ukraine. There the Soviet troops, supported by aviation, inflicted heavy losses on the enemy, holding back the Germans' advancement for as much as a week. The ground troops received substantial assistance from the pilots of the Kiev AGON. In the course of several days they delivered more than 33 tonnes (72,750 lb) of spare parts for tanks, 70 tonnes (154,320 lb) of ammunition, medicines, fuel and other cargoes.

In late January 1942 the regiments of the 1st Guards Cavalry Corps and several infantry divisions of the Western Front drove a wedge deep into the territory occupied by the enemy, reached his main communications and started active combat actions. Communication with these troops, delivery of food supplies and ammunition and evacuation of gravely wounded personnel was effected by the crews from MAGON GVF. The flights were performed in adverse weather, mainly at night.

By the spring of 1942 the military situation of the Soviet Union had become stable. In May 1942 the Chief Administration of the Civil Air Fleet (GU GVF) was subordinated to the command of the Red Army's Air Force. At that time the GVF's nine front-line air groups had some 870 aircraft on strength; a considerable number of these were PS-84s (Li-2s).

On 30th June 1942 thirteen Li-2 aircraft took off from an airfield near Sevastopol' in the Ukraine. They were carrying wounded personnel, valuable documents and military materiel. A machine captained by M. S. Skryl'nikov was the last to take off. Its passengers included Vice-Admiral F. S. Oktyabr'skiy, Commander of the Sevastopol Defence Region and the Black Sea Fleet; Division Commissar N. M. Kulakov, member of the Military Council; Major-General I. Ye. Petrov, Commander of the Seaside Army; chairman of the city defence committee B. A. Borisov and other prominent leaders. They left Sevastopol' at the order of the supreme Command, when no more could be done to defend the city.

When flying their missions, civilian airmen displayed courage, resourcefulness and mutual support. For example, a PS-84 captained by the same M. S. Skryl'nikov became mired in a bog just as it was about to take off from a small airstrip with wounded personnel on board; the aircraft had to be torched to stop it from falling into enemy hands. Three aircraft were sent to the rescue. Pilot V. P. Bibikov made a landing and evacuated the crew and passengers of Skryl'nikov's aircraft, while the crews of the aircraft piloted by A. I. Sukorkin and P. I. Kolesnikov used their machine guns to provide cover against enemy attacks for their comrades.

On 5th March 1942 the State Defence Committee of the USSR issued a directive establishing the Long-Range Aviation (ADD – *Aviahtsiya* ***dahl'****nevo* ***dey****stviya*); Major-General Aleksandr Ye. Golovanov was appointed its Commander. The ADD comprised long-range bomber and heavy bomber regiments which were no longer organisationally part of the Red Army Air Force, reporting directly to the Supreme Command. At that point an acute shortage of bombers arose due to considerable losses of aircraft at the front and to the drop in aircraft manufacture caused by evacuation of the aircraft factories; this prompted the use of the PS-84 (Li-2) in a role for which it had not been originally destined. These machines could carry up to four 250-kg (551-lb) bombs externally.

In April 1942 the first formation equipped with modified PS-84 (Li-2) aircraft was set up and included into the ADD. It was the 1st Air Transport Division commanded by Colonel V. Ye. Nesterov (the former MAGON). The division comprised the 101st and 102nd Air Transport Regiments (commanded respectively by Valentina S. Grizodoobova, an aviatrice renowned for her pre-war distance record flights, and B. P. Osipchuk). Each regiment included two squadrons consisting of five flights each, with three PS-84s (Li-2s) per flight. In all, a regiment had 30 PS-84s (Li-2s) and one Polikarpov Po-2 liaison aircraft on strength. In addition, it was envisaged that the regiments should have a reserve comprising 15 crews. These served as a basis for the 103rd Air Transport Regiment (commanded by Colonel Bozhko) which was formed in the division in the summer of 1943; it operated 30 PS-84s (Li-2s). A year later all three regiments were transformed into three-squadron units (in conformity with the three-squadron com-

Above: A Soviet Air Force officer wearing three medals gives the take-off signal to the crew of a Li-2NB adorned with the Guards badge. Several long-range bomber regiments flying the Li-2 had Guards status.

A PS-84 in two-tone camouflage takes off on a mission; the landing gear is just beginning to retract.

Above: Camouflage colours are applied in the field to a natural metal PS-84 – an early-production machine, judging by the main gear drag struts. Once again the aircraft appears to be armed only with a single ShKAS in an MV-3 dorsal turret, no beam machine guns being visible.

This Li-2NB made a crash landing after the port main gear unit failed to extend, suffering damage to the port propeller. Here, the aircraft has been trestled and repairs are already in progress.

position of the ADD regiments) with the same total number of aircraft. In all, the standard inventory of the division comprised up to 90 PS-84s (Li-2s) aircraft. Thus, from the first days and to the end of the war, MAGON and then the 1st GVF Air Transport Division of the ADD was one of the most potent and combat-ready military airlift units of the Supreme Command.

Originally the division operated only PS-84s in standard transport configuration at its disposal, hence the appellation. Very soon, however, the regiments began retrofitting their Li-2s with bomb racks *in situ*, and later Li-2s were delivered with the bomb armament already in place. Therefore the inappropriate 'transport' appellation was soon dropped. As Li-2 production grew, the bomber-configured aircraft were delivered to other ADD units, first and foremost the ones which still flew the hopelessly outdated Tupolev TB-3 bombers; new bomber units were also established.

The division's regiments equipped with the modified PS-84s (Li-2s) flew bombing sorties. For example, during the Battle of Stalingrad, on the night of 26th August 1942, the crews of the 1st Air Transport Division of the ADD destroyed German bridges over the Don River with direct hits of FAB-250 bombs. Inevitably, the use of this aircraft in the unusual role of a bomber created certain difficulties for the crew. The navigator, who acted as the bomb aimer and dropped the bombs, took up the station of the co-pilot which was utterly unsuitable for the navigator's work. The navigator was provided with a collimator sight mounted on the starboard side of the fuselage. This sight was extremely inconvenient to use: if the aircraft had a drift to starboard, no special problems arose and the aiming was more or less precise, but in the case of a drift to port the navigator could not see the target through the collimator. Naturally, bombing accuracy was inferior to that of a purpose-built bomber. Since the established airframe design of a transport aircraft did not allow making apertures of considerable size for bomb bay doors, the Li-2 had no bomb bay of the would expect to find on a bomber – only a small container for light bomblets. 100-kg (220-lb) FAB-100 and 250-kg (551-lb) FAB-250 bombs were carried on external racks, thus creating extra drag which reduced the Li-2's speed and increased the fuel consumption. However, the crews operating the PS-84 (Li-2) had an important advantage over the pilots of other Soviet bomber types – they flew their missions in a comfortable heated flightdeck; there was a galley and a toilet on board, and in case of need one could walk around and stretch one's legs.

True, the 'transports' were slower; on the other hand, they offered a sufficiently high level of crew comfort and, moreover, were provided with an autopilot.

After the catastrophic defeat on the banks the Volga River (the Stalingrad operation), followed by the winter offensive of the Red Army in late 1942/early 1943, the troops of Nazi Germany started suffering serious defeats on other crucially important sections of the Soviet-German front as well. The powerful blows dealt by the Soviet troops had a shattering effect on the German army. Still hoping to save the situation, the German High Command called a total mobilisation and sent new divisions from Western Europe to the East. They pinned their hopes on the summer offensive in the course of which Germany planned to regain the strategic initiative. The German command came to the conclusion that the most convenient section of the front for dealing this blow would be the salient formed by the front line in the Kursk area; it came to be known as the Kursk Bulge. In the vicinity of the towns of Oryol and Belgorod the Wehrmacht built up potent strike groupings comprising more than 50 divisions, including 16 armour and motorised infantry divisions.

Thanks to the efforts of the Soviet intelligence service the Soviet High Command became aware of the enemy's intentions in time. The Supreme Command evolved a plan of the forthcoming strategic operation designed to exhaust the enemy in defensive battles, and then to launch a counteroffensive and defeat him. The Soviet troops built up strong defence lines distributed in depth.

The Li-2 units of the ADD's 1st Air Transport Division were allotted the task of airlifting troops and materiel on the Kursk Bulge. Despite strong enemy opposition, each crew performed five to seven missions a day. The airmen of this division made 1,280 sorties; they transported to the front more than 2,000 tonnes (4,409,170 lb) of cargoes, 13,600 troops from reserve units and hospitals located near the front line, evacuated more than 12,000 casualties and relocated four hospitals.

On 5th July 1943 the German troops launched an offensive, with offensive thrusts converging on Kursk from the directions of Oryol and Belgorod. Thus began the Battle of Kursk, one of the greatest battles of the Second World War. The Soviet troops met with staunch resistance the onslaught of the enemy's armour units, artillery and aviation; they motto of the day was 'No retreat, no surrender!' The operations on the Central Front were catered for by the 62nd Guards Air Regiment of the GVF, and those on the Voronezh Front by the 8th Independent Air Regiment of the GVF. The needs of both of these fronts were served by the units of the 1st Air Transport Division of the ADD equipped with Li-2s and C-47s. Later, when the Soviet troops launched a counteroffensive, the 13th and 14th Independent Air Regiments of the GVF also took part in the Kursk Battle, as part of the Bryansk front and the South-Western front. Missions were flown day and night by the crews from elements of the 3rd Independent Communications Air Division of the GVF; they ensured operational communications between the Red Army General Headquarters and the headquarters of the Fronts and Armies fighting on the Kursk Bulge. The aircraft of this formation delivered to the front-line area not only mail, liaison officers and communications equipment, but also medicines, preserved blood, and current newspapers published in Moscow.

The crew of a PS-84 transport poses beside their aircraft, an early machine featuring the useless forward-firing ShKAS. In spite of the season the aircraft still wears summer camouflage.

The Military Council of the Central Front gave due credit to the actions of the crews belonging to the GVF regiments that formed a part of the ADD's 1st Air Transport Division. 75 airmen were awarded high government decorations for the excellent fulfilment of the High Command's tasks.

Considerable partisan forces were located in forests in the Bryansk area. The 6th Independent Air Regiment of the GVF was responsible for maintaining communication with them. The partisans prepared a landing site for the Li-2s and established radio contact with the Air Regiment's headquarters. To take their bearings during flights, the crews made use of direction finders and the directional radio beacons of the Air Army. The war effort of the personnel of the 6th Independent Air Regiment received a high appraisal. On 3rd February 1943 it became the first of the GVF front-line units to be accorded the Guards title – it was transformed into the 62nd Guards Air Regiment of the GVF. On 5th July 1943 A. P. Gorshkov, Chief of Staff of the partisans operating in the Bryansk area, wrote to GU GVF Chief, General F. A. Astakhov: *'We express to you and to the airmen of the 62nd Guards Regiment our exceptional gratitude for their heroic, selfless work in rendering assistance to the partisan detachments in the forests of Bryansk. Our glorious airmen came to our aid when we were in desperate straits. For those who had not been witness to this, it is hard to imagine the heroism and courage of such first-class pilots as Boris Lakhtin, Nikolay Repin, Aleksey Volkov, Nikolay Sel'demirov and others. Landing sites are unavailable, there is no communication. Yet these heroes set off for a free flight, they fly above the forest, establish voice communication with us and drop ammunition supplies for us.'*

When the partisans had a hard time beating off the attacks of the Germans' punitive units, or when they prepared major operations, the flights in support of the partisans became particularly intensive. In August 1943, in the course of a mere ten days the Li-2 aircraft delivered to the Belorussian partisans more than 100 tonnes (220,460 lb) of ammunition and explosives for a major operation then in progress which came to be known as the Rail Track War. The mining of railway tracks conducted simultaneously on a large scale paralysed German railway transportation for a long time.

Understandably, the German command did everything in its power to prevent the partisans from getting supplies by air. On the night of 23rd June 1943 a Li-2 captained by S. T. Basov was flying a mission to deliver

Above: The ground personnel made an immense contribution to the success of the Li-2's operations. Here, work is in progress on the starboard M-62IR of a Li-2. Note that the standing mechanic carries a TT pistol.

Li-2NBs also flew transport missions from time to time, as this photo testifies.

ammunition to partisans. As it approached the landing site, the aircraft was attacked by German fighters. A shell fragment badly injured Basov's right hand, flight engineer F. S. Teslyuchenko was also badly injured. Bleeding profusely and suffering severe pain, the brave pilot continued to control his burning aircraft with only his left hand on the control wheel. The flames were licking close to the explosives, but the crew managed to paradrop the whole load to the partisans in time, whereupon Basov succeeded in landing his aircraft on a small strip. Both heroes were decorated with orders for their courage.

In July 1943 a partisan formation commanded by A. N. Saboorov was compelled to move to the west under the onslaught of superior German forces. When they had run out of ammunition and food supplies, the partisans prepared an airstrip and radioed a request for an aircraft, while defending the site from enemy attacks. A Li-2 piloted by F. G. Radoogin was sent to bring aid to partisans. At night, deep inside enemy-held territory, the pilot discovered the landing site prepared by the partisans and delivered the necessary cargo. In all, Radoogin flew 247 sorties during the war; of these, 102 were missions into the enemy's rear. He delivered to partisans 120 tonnes (264,550 lb) of ammunition, weapons and medicines, and evacuated 385 heavily wounded persons. The pilot was awarded the Hero of the Soviet Union title and many Soviet orders and medals.

The increasing scale of PS-84 (Li-2) production, coupled with the training of airmen and technical personnel, made it possible to equip several more air regiments, in addition to the 1st GVF Air Transport Division of the ADD. In November 1942 the Long-Range Aviation alone had on strength 74 PS-84s (Li-2s); in July 1943 this number rose to 200, then to 266 at the end of 1943, and then to 412 as per 1st July 1944. From September 1942 onwards all PS-84 (Li-2) regiments of the ADD were transformed into three-squadron regiments, each squadron having 30 aircraft. This standard was retained until the end of the war. In connection with the establishment of eight Air Corps within the Long-Range Aviation, in the period between May 1943 and March 1944 divisions comprised two regiments, but in the spring of 1944 the third regiments were set up in all divisions. It was natural that precisely the formations and units of the Long-Range Aviation equipped with the PS-84 (Li-2) aircraft were usually called upon to fulfil airlift and airborne assault missions.

In addition to the Long-Range Aviation, the Li-2 aircraft were on the strength of the 2nd Special Mission Air Division (ADON – *aviatsi**on**naya di**vee**ziya o**sob**ovo nazna**chen**iya*) which was formed in the autumn of 1942. Until the end of the war it always comprised three transport air regiments with a total number of 100-105 Li-2s on strength. In March 1945 two air regiments (the 1st and 229th Airlift Regiments) were also re-equipped, receiving Li-2s (60 aircraft) instead of the Polikarpov R-5s, Po-2s and Yakovlev Yak-6 light bombers/transports they had operated. (Incidentally, the Yak-6 shared the general arrangement of the DC-3 and, by analogy, bore the affectionate nickname *Doogla**syo**nok* – Baby Douglas'.) Thus, by the end of the war the 2nd and the 4th ADON had a total of 160-165 Li-2s.

These aircraft were also delivered to the aviation of the Airborne Troops. In late 1942 it had only four PS-84s (Li-2s); not before late in 1943 did it receive enough of these aircraft to form a fully-equipped air regiment (30 machines). A year later, the Airborne Troops already had 43 Li-2s at their disposal.

From mid-1942 onwards and until the end of the war a small number of Li-2s (50 to 65 machines) were operated by front-line GVF units. In mid-1942 they began to receive US-built Douglas C-47A/Bs delivered under the Lend-Lease agreement. By 1945 the front-line GVF units operated 126 machines of this type, this number increasing to 486 by the end of the year; by the end of 1945 a total of 707 C-47s had been ferried from the USA.

Flying personnel for the Li-2 and C-47 were trained mostly in the flight centres and training detachments of the territorial GVF directorates. At the beginning of the war the State Defence Committee posed the GVF the task of training 300 crews. In July-December 1941 alone the GVF trained 377 pilots, 187 flight engineers and 177 radio operators. The total number of pilots alone who were trained or converted to transport aircraft in the GVF during the war amounted to 2,900. Crew commanders were also trained directly in the air units by upgrading the co-pilots.

Albeit the Li-2 was regarded as a military transport aircraft, it had limited capabilities as a troopship. The aircraft had a door 0.7 m (27½ in) wide which permitted the paratroopers with their personal firearms to be dropped only in a single line. Paradroppable bags weighing up to 80 kg (176 lb) were dragged to the door and pushed outside manually, which entailed a great dispersal of the bags. The loading of artillery pieces and self-propelled transport vehicles, to say nothing of their paradropping, was out of the question until the cargo door was introduced later in the war. Nevertheless, it would be wrong to underestimate the role of the PS-84 (Li-2) aircraft in paradropping operations.

For example, in January 1942, as a result of the offensive undertaken by the Western Front and the Kalinin Front, a situation arose in the western direction of the Soviet-German front which allowed the Soviet troops to surround and destroy part of the forces of *Heeresgruppe Mitte* (Central Group of Armies). In accordance with the concept evolved by the Supreme Command it was planned by means of outflanking thrusts of the troops of the right flank of the Western front in the Yookhnov – Vyaz'ma direction, with a simultaneous offensive of some forces against Sychovka and Gzhatsk in co-operation with the armies of the left flank of the Kalinin front, to surround, break up and destroy a German grouping in the Rzhev-Vyaz'ma-Yookhnov-Gzhatsk area. For this purpose the Supreme Command decided to paradrop a large airborne forces unit (the 4th Airborne Corps) in the area of Ozerechnya, south-west of Vyaz'ma. The decision to launch the airborne assault operation was taken on 15th January 1942. It was the Airborne Troops command that conducted preparations of the Corps for paradropping and the subsequent combat, but the overall guidance of the paradropping operation was the responsibility of the Commander of the Red Army Air Force.

The plan of the airborne assault operation developed jointly by the Air Force and Airborne Troops command on 16th January provided for the formation of an aviation group comprising 352 aircraft. These included: 65 transport aircraft (40 PS-84s from the MAGON and 25 TB-3 bombers in the transport role from the Air Force); 102 fighters for providing cover at the take-off area and for escorting the transports to the drop zone (DZ); plus 185 bombers and attack aircraft (45 Il'yushin DB-3 long-range bombers, 20 Il'yushin IL-2 attack aircraft, 20 Petlyakov Pe-2 dive-bombers and 40 obsolete R-5 attack and liaison aircraft). Air Maj. Gen. L. A. Gorbatsevich was appointed commander of the aviation group.

PS-84 '4117 White' was one of the Aeroflot aircraft pressed into military service, having flown earlier as СССР-Л4117. Thus, the reinforced main gear drag struts must be a late addition.

To perform the paradropping of an entire corps comprising three brigades in winter configuration (without tanks and transport vehicles) in the course of one mission, no fewer than 580 to 600 PS-84s (Li-2s) and TB-3s were required. The aircraft complement assigned for the paradropping would have to undertake at least 10 sorties, and this number would have to be increased to 12-15 with due regard to combat losses and malfunctions. That could be effected in the course of four or five nights under the most favourable circumstances.

Being fully aware of that, the command of the aviation group and of the Airborne Troops was looking for airfields that would be situated as close as possible to the paradropping area. In consequence, the take-off area was chosen in the vicinity of Kaluga, at a distance of some 30 to 40 km (19 to 29 miles) from the front line. The Kaluga airfield hub comprised three airfields: Grabtsevo (now the city's airport), Zhashkovo and Rzhavets. Being guided to a larger extent by the stipulations of the order issued by Army General Gheorgiy K. Zhookov, Commander of the Western Front, and not by the real possibilities and conditions of the operation's conduct, headquarters of the aviation group and of the Airborne Troops evolved a completely unrealistic plan for paradropping the 4th Airborne Troops Corps.

In accordance with this plan, the transport aircraft group was to comprise 30 TB-3s, 42 PS-84s with crews trained for night flying, and 15 PS-84s with crews rated for daylight operations only. It was planned to begin the paradropping of the lead detachment (a battalion from the 8th Airborne Brigade) at 14.30 Moscow time on 27th January. Thirty-six PS-84s were assigned for this task. The plans envisaged also a daytime paradropping of sabotage groups from five PS-84s. The remaining troops of the Corps were to be paradropped during the following two nights. It was assumed that during the first night the PS-84s and the TB-3s would fly six and five missions respectively.

The plan showed total disregard for possible combat losses and malfunctions that could disable the aircraft. Nor did anyone take into account the limits imposed on the crews by combat stress. A flight was to last not more than 2.5 hours. During that time the crew had to reach the DZ some 180 km (111 miles) away, make at least two passes for paradropping, return to base, refuel and inspect the aircraft, take on a fresh load of paratroopers and take off anew. The crew would have no more than 20 minutes for the preparation for a second flight. Needless to say, crews lacking sufficient experience of night-time paradropping operations could not sustain such a tempo. The conduct of the operation was further complicated by the almost complete absence of anti-aircraft defences in the take-off area and by poor organisation of the paradrop.

The fighter element of Kaluga's anti-aircraft defence, which was included in the aviation group, did not receive any specific instructions on providing cover for the transport aircraft and the airborne troops and was not subordinated to the commander of the aviation group. A fighter air group commanded by General Ye. M. Nikolayenko, tasked with providing cover to General P. A. Belov's mobile group, concentrated its efforts on the fulfilment of its main task and rendered support to the paradropping

Above: An armed Li-2 resting between missions.

A bomber-configured Li-2 coded '14 White' creates a local sandstorm as it taxies on a dirt airstrip. Oddly, the dorsal turret appears to be covered with a canvas cover.

operation with limited forces, despite being formally a part of the air group set up for supporting the paradropping operation. No steps were taken to organise the protection of the assault forces by anti-aircraft artillery, either.

As a result, the enemy's aerial reconnaissance pinpointed the transfer of Soviet troops already from the moment the 4th Airborne Troops Corps started crossing the Oka River. Nor did the Germans remain ignorant of the concentration of transport aircraft on airfields not far from the front line. During the very first night of the paradropping operation, the night of 28th January, the Luftwaffe raided Grabtsevo airfield. The navigation support of the operation was poorly organised, too. Contrary to the requirements of the Field Manual of the Red Army's Airborne Troops, no aerial photo reconnaissance of the DZ had been conducted. The landing sites were marked in a most primitive way. Before the first paratrooper detachment took off on its mission, the commander, presumably with the consent of the aviation group command, received instructions to the effect that he should mark the DZ for the assault troops 'by torching several sheds in the nearest village' (!). This method of marking the DZ proved to be very unreliable due to the large number of fires in the enemy's rear.

Paradropping of the Corps began in the afternoon of 27th January. The advanced detachment was delivered to the landing site by two group sorties on 29 TB-3s and 17 PS-84s from Zhashkovo airfield. Due to poor aircrew training the main part of the battalion was paradropped some 15-18 km (9.3-11.1 miles) to the south of the designated area. As a result of the big dispersal, the paratroopers and their materiel proved to be scattered over an area with a radius of some 25 km (15.5 miles) around the village of Tabory (instead of Ozerechnya). In these circumstances the advanced detachment proved unable to prepare the DZ intended to receive all the remaining units of the brigade. The detachment took all night to assemble, and by the morning the number of troopers who had reached the rendezvous was 476 out of the 648 that had been paradropped.

In the afternoon of 29th January the detachment approached the village of Ozerechnaya, wiped out the German garrison there and prepared the site for the arriving assault troops. However, the detachment was unable to establish communication with the Corps' headquarters because the radio operator had made a landing far from the commander and, having no secret codes, could not establish radio contact. Thus, the Airborne Troops Command had no information about the advanced detachment; yet it decided to continue the landing operation. During the night of 28th January the PS-84s made 62 individual sorties from Rzhavets and Zhashkovo airfields, inserting some 1,100 troopers. Some crews performed the paradropping near the village of Tabory because the advanced detachment had organised and marked a landing site there. Most of the crews, however, performed the drop in the designated area near Ozerechnya on an unmarked landing site.

On the very first night of the operation the transport aircraft group suffered heavy losses as a result of the enemy raid on Grabtsevo airfield. Eight TB-3s and a fuel dump were sent up in flames, 12 more aircraft were damaged by bomb splinters. For this reason during the first night no paradropping was undertaken from Grabtsevo. The PS-84 losses during the night amounted to five aircraft. On the morning of 28th January the transport aircraft relocated to airfields deeper in the rear because of the danger of a new air raid, and the airfields closer to the front line were used for intermediate landings.

On 29th January the aviation group had only 12 airworthy aircraft remaining – ten PS-84s and two TB-3s. Most of the PS-84s were damaged by anti-aircraft fire and needed repairs. This was due to the fact that GVF crews lacked experience and tactical training: they crossed the front line within reach of the anti-aircraft machine gun fire at altitudes of 110-150 m (360-490 ft), at the same altitudes at which they flew in daytime over their own territory in order to use terrain features for avoiding detection by enemy fighters.

The landing operation lasted five nights and was terminated on the night of 1st February when the tactical situation changed. By that time the personnel and materiel that had been paradropped included 2,081 troops, 120 general-purpose machine guns, 72 antitank rifles and twenty 82-mm (3.22-in) mortars, all coming from the 8th Airborne Brigade. Only 76 troops from the 214th Airborne Brigade had been paradropped.

However, there are also examples of good preparation and efficient execution of tactical assault operations involving the use of PS-84s (Li-2s). Such an example is provided by the operation in which the 1st and 2nd battalions of the 201st Airborne Brigade, with a total strength of 1,600 men, were landed in the enemy's rear (with the aircraft landing on airstrips) south-east of Vyaz'ma on 18th-22nd January 1942. The landing troops were tasked with rendering assistance to the 1st Guards Cavalry Corps in breaking through the enemy's defences from the rear. The aircraft assigned for participation in the landing operation included 21 PS-84s and three Tupolev G-2s (a civilian unarmed version of the TB-3 bomber) from the MAGON with crews that had been well trained for night actions. The operation started from Moscow's Vnukovo airfield, well protected by the assets of Moscow's anti-aircraft defence, which helped avoid losses on the airfield.

A good choice of the starting area and the landing area, coupled with good interaction with the local partisans in selecting and marking the landing sites, and good aircrew training made it possible to perform a paradrop successfully in two passes and deliver the initial group with a radio to the DZ codenamed *Zhelan'ye* (Desire). During the following three nights, with equal success, the main body of the landing troops was delivered by aircraft which landed on airstrips and disembarked the troops on the ground. At the end of January these troops, in pursuance of their task, joined the Cavalry Corps and continued their combat operations as a part of the Corps.

All troop-landing operations at the Soviet-German front, both those far behind the front line and tactical operations closer to the front line, were effected by paradropping (or disembarkation after landing) at night by groups of PS-84s (Li-2s) and TB-3s which followed one after another with a time interval of five to ten minutes; this entailed a considerable increase of the time required for the landing of troops. That was particularly noticeable in situations when the number of transport aircraft was insufficient and it was necessary to fly several sorties. In the example cited above four nights were required to effect a landing of 2,300 troops with light firearms.

On many occasions insufficient teamwork of the PS-84 (Li-2) aircrews and the lack of the necessary training of paratroopers, the absence or malfunction of radio beacons brought to naught all the efforts of the military. A vivid example of this is provided by the unsuccessful attempt to land assault troops on the Bookry bridgehead in September 1943. The operation involved the 53rd and 62nd Air Divisions of the ADD, as well as GVF transport regiments. Having encountered a strong opposition from the Germans, dispersed groups of the assault force failed to bring the operation to a successful conclusion; they retreated into woods in the Kanev area and joined the local partisans.

By the summer of 1943 the Soviet Air Force order of battle included three Air Corps which were almost entirely equipped with the Li-2s, both in the transport and the bomber versions; the 7th Air Corps of the ADD was one of them. By the end of the war there were 19 regiments equipped with these versatile aircraft.

In 1943 the 7th Guards Long-Range Air Regiment equipped with Li-2s was committed to preparations for a troop landing operation at Bookry; the operation's goal was to capture bridge-heads on the right bank of the Dnepr River for the purpose of ensuring the crossing

Above and below: This factory-fresh Yakovlev Yak-3 fighter coded '80 White' ran off the runway during a pre-delivery test flight at Saratov-Yoozhnyy, the factory airfield of Plant No.292, and collided with a parked Li-2.

of the river by Soviet troops. In addition to the Li-2 crews, a considerable number of GVF crews flying Douglas C-47s were involved in the operation, in which nearly 10,000 troops were to be landed. However, a number of tragic circumstances conspired to doom the operation. There was dense fog at the landing site; some of the civilian aircraft used in the landing operation were not adapted for paradropping, in some cases the GVF crews lacked experience of such operations. The operation turned into a dismal failure, with the loss of hundreds of paratroopers. Many of them, after leaving the aircraft, landed in the thick of the German positions, or fell into the Dnepr, or landed on the left bank of the river which had been liberated from the Germans. Flying in adverse weather, the airmen of the 7th Guards Long-Range Air Regiment did their best to fulfil their mission. On the night of 25th September 1943 a crew in which V. Prokof'yev acted as navigator took off and headed for the DZ. It took the crew a long time to find the designated site in the fog; finally, the aircraft happened to pass above the Fastov railway station near Kiev, where it was fired upon by German anti-aircraft artillery. Reluctant to subject the paratroopers to a risk, the crew refrained from performing the drop, turned east and, being unable to take their bearings because of the fog, flew eastward as long as the fuel reserves allowed. The aircraft landed at Starobel'sk (Lugansk Region).

On the night of 25th September a crew commanded by A. Vasil'yev (with L. Ageyev as navigator) took off with the intention to paradrop an auxiliary group in the Kanev area. Again, dense fog prevented the crew from observing the light signals marking the DZ which were to be deployed in the vicinity of Pereyaslavl'-Khmel'nitskiy. After a long flight, with great difficulty the crew noticed in the fog the piers of the destroyed Kanev bridge over the Dnepr. Using these as a landmark to take their bearings, they reached the designated area and effected the drop.

The 7th GvAP DD (*Gvar**deys**kiy **avia**polk **dahl'**nevo **deys**tviya* – Guards Long-Range Air Regiment) equipped with Li-2s, which in 1944 was incorporated into the 4th Guards Air Corps, took part in all major operations of the Long-Range Aviation. On 27th January 1944, as a reward for the bomb strikes against the enemy's defences in the Leningrad area, the regiment was given the honorary appellation *Gatchinskiy* ('Gatchina regiment'; Gatchina is a town near Leningrad to whose liberation the unit contributed). On 16th and 26th February 1944 the regiment took part in the bombardment of Helsinki. In the period from the spring to the autumn of the same year the 7th GvAP DD airlifted supplies for Czechoslovak partisans during the Slovak National Uprising. The flights were performed to Tri Duby ('Three Oaks'; pronounced *tree **doo**by*) airfield which was surrounded by mountains 1,500-2,000 m (4,920-6,560 ft) high and was often obscured by low clouds. Landings on this airfield became easier when a crew commanded by Lt. Col. Yezerskiy delivered a radio beacon to the airfield. The beacon enabled crews to perform precise landings in the 'cauldron' formed by mountains with the clouds as low as 300 m (1,000 ft) above the airstrip. In the course of the operation seven Li-2s were shot down and another seven were lost in accidents (including one on the return trip).

This picture (apparently taken during the winter of 1945-46) shows three Li-2s (including '408 Red') of the 334th Bomber Regiment which received the honorary appellation *Berlinskiy* in June 1945 for its part in the taking of Berlin. The aircraft bear the legend *Berlinskiy*; note also the red stars on the propeller spinners.

The combat achievements of the regiment include a troop-landing operation in the Carpathian Mountains. On 28th September 1944 German units approached the town of Zvolen which was under the control of Czechoslovak partisans. The town and Tri Duby airfield were in danger of being recaptured by the Germans. The scanty detachments of Slovak partisans defending them could not withstand the onslaught of the well-armed German troops and were retreating. At that time Li-2s from the 4th Guards air Corps started arriving at Tri Duby, airlifting a Czechoslovak assault brigade across the front line. The airfield's personnel worked like clockwork; the turnarounds took no more than 20 minutes. Almost out of nowhere a considerable military force suddenly appeared on this small strip of land and soon joined the fray; unexpectedly encountering serious opposition, the Germans had to retreat to a distance of 30 km (19 miles) from the town.

The 7th *Gatchinskiy* GvAP DD saw the end of the war as a purely transport unit. In the summer of 1945 it was transferred to the East of the USSR and in August, together with other Li-2-equipped regiments of the 4th Guards Air Corps, was committed to action in the war against Japan.

In the winter of 1943-44, for the first time in the course of the war, the Long-Range Aviation of the Red Army Supreme Command was transferred to the north-west of the USSR, which seriously alarmed Finland's military leadership. The Finns obtained credible information on the movements of the ADD units. On 12th December 1943 a transport-configured Li-2 carrying an advanced group of the 102nd Air Regiment of the 1st air Division of the ADD's 7th Air Corps was on its way to Levashovo airfield north of Leningrad. In the fog above Lake Ladoga the crew lost their bearings and started an approach for landing in the area of the Finnish airbase of Suulajärvi. Having discovered his mistake, the pilot tried to escape but the aircraft was shot down by Lieutenant Urfo Sarjamo from the Finnish Air Force's 24th Fighter Squadron (HLeLv 24) flying a Brewster Buffalo serialled BW-386. The crew was captured; during December-January the crew of the Li-2 was interrogated at least ten times. In the course of interrogation on 17th December Captain A. Korobov, the 102nd Air Regiment's executive officer, who had been heavily injured during the crash landing, gave the Finns very interesting information about the Soviet Long-Range Aviation, its organisation and control, whereupon he soon died of his injuries. According to Korobov, the main task of the Long-Range Aviation in the north was to destroy the German heavy artillery at the southern boundary of the Leningrad siege ring, which was a necessary precondition for starting an operation to break the siege.

In actual fact, in 1943-44 the ADD underwent considerable changes. Its inventory of combat machines consisted primarily of

Above: This unarmed Li-2 coded '31 Blue' was photographed in 1946. Note that the tactical code is carried on the rudder, as was normal practice in the final years of the war; in 1941 it was usually painted on the fuselage, a practice which was re-adopted after the war.

Ilyushin IL-4 bombers but also included many Li-2s. By early 1944 the ADD units equipped with the Li-2s included the 5th Air Corps, one Air Division of the 6th Air Corps and two Air Divisions of the 7th Air Corps – that is, ten units in all (see table on page 86).

The percentage of Li-2s among the long-range aircraft remained substantial even after 6th December 1944, when the ADD was reorganised into the 18th Air Army which was taken out of the direct control of the Supreme Command and re-incorporated into the Air Force. All the Li-2 units of the ADD listed above took part in the bombing raids against Helsinki mentioned earlier.

The raids against Helsinki were conducted with ten-day intervals on the nights of 7th, 17th and 27th February 1944. According to Finnish information, in the course of these three raids the Long-Range Aviation's IL-4 and Li-2 bombers flew 773, 497 and 850 sorties respectively. The first raid was conducted in two waves; the 216 aircraft taking part in the attack dropped 2,100 bombs, of which 331 (some 16%) fell on the city. In the two waves that formed the second raid, 416 aircraft dropped 4,200 bombs; the city's territory was

These unarmed Li-2T transports took part in the final phase of the Second World War when Soviet troops were deployed to the Far East to engage Japanese forces in Manchuria in the summer of 1945. Note the unusual style of the tactical code superimposed on a dark blue circle.

hit by 130 bombs (4% of the total number). The third raid was effected in three waves; the 900 participating aircraft dropped 9,000 bombs, of which 338 (only 3.6%) fell within the city bounds. The bombers approached Helsinki in the following array: the main attacking group of each Corps took up its place behind a weather reconnaissance aircraft, a pathfinder aircraft and aircraft tasked with lighting the targets with flare bombs and suppressing the anti-aircraft artillery. Rearmost in the array were aircraft tasked with post-strike reconnaissance. The main group was built up of individual aircraft which followed one another with 12- to 15-second intervals at an altitude ranging from 2,000 to 7,000 m (6,560-22,970 ft). The Li-2s based at the Karelian Isthmus flew up to three sorties each night.

The next massed attack of the Long-Range Aviation was directed against the southern coast of the Gulf of Finland: on the night of 10th March 1944 nearly 300 aircraft made a bombing raid against Tallinn. Since the German occupation troops had failed to organise sufficiently strong anti-aircraft defence in this area, the raid proved very effective: more than 53% of the buildings of the Estonian capital were destroyed and nearly 1,300 persons were killed.

Inevitably, the ADD units flying the Li-2 suffered losses, too. On the same night of 10th March 1944, after the raid on Tallinn, the LeR 4 bomber regiment of the Finnish Air Force, making use of information obtained by radio intelligence means, prepared an unpleasant surprise for the Soviet Long-Range Aviation. While the Soviet aircraft were on their way back from Tallinn to their bases on the Karelian Isthmus, 21 Finnish bombers, including some captured DB-3 and IL-4 bombers, gathered in a formation above the Gulf of Finland and made their way in the same direction. When landing lights were turned on alongside the runways at the Soviet airbases of Levashovo, Kasimovo, Gorskaya and Yukki, the Finns dropped their bomb load. The bombardment was accompanied by Finnish artillery strikes. During the attack against Gorskaya airfield on 9th-10th March one Li-2 from the 110th Air Regiment was damaged and two Li-2s from the 23rd Guards Air Regiment were destroyed.

Because of damage to the runways Levashovo AB was temporarily closed down, and the returning 4th GvAP DD Li-2s were directed to Kamenka and Pargolovo. Three Li-2s of the same regiment were damaged at Kasimovo, where damage was also inflicted on the airmen's hostel and a runway; two airmen were killed and one seriously wounded. An artillery raid against Kasimovo resulted in damage to two Li-2s; the pilots' mess of the 9th GvAP DD received a direct hit which killed five persons. An artillery attack against Levashovo AB resulted in six Li-2s being put out of action.

Above: Evacuees walk from a Li-2 that has flown them to safety.

By the end of the war the Li-2's production run had reached 2,362 machines. Many of these were sent to the front. The Air Divisions operating the Li-2 at the end of the war are listed in the table on page 88.

All these units and formations were part of the 18th Air Army. In addition, the following GVF air units were equipped with the Li-2: the 6th Independent Air Regiment (later renamed 69th Independent Air Regiment), the 19th Independent Air Regiment, the 10th Guards Transport Air Division (comprising the 1st, 2nd and 3rd Air Regiments).

Immediately before the end of the war a Li-2 piloted by a 19th Independent Air Regiment crew (captained by A. I. Semenkov) transported representatives of the Soviet Government to Berlin. The same aircraft brought back to Moscow the Act on the Unconditional Surrender of Nazi Germany. Finally, one more interesting fact from the war period: it was a Li-2 that brought the Banner of Victory from the vanquished Berlin to Moscow on 20th June 1945.

After the termination of hostilities in Europe two (some sources say three) divisions of the 18th Air Army were transferred to the Far East to take part in the war against Japan. These units included the 21st Guards

This Li-2NB looks definitely the worse for wear and is probably depicted after being withdrawn from use.

Air Division and the 54th Air Division which were incorporated into 12th Air Army of the Trans-Baikal Front, on the Manchurian theatre of operations. The 9th Air Army of the 1st Far Eastern Front was also committed to action in that area. In June the 281st Airlift Regiment, which was part of this Air Army, received six new Li-2s from the Tashkent aircraft plant. Before the beginning of combat the 21st Guards Air Division and the 54th Air Division performed preparatory work; between 8th and 20th July they airlifted cargoes that were necessary for the troops to regions difficult to access. The Soviet Union had concentrated a large number of 'true' bombers for engaging the Japanese Kwantung Army in Manchuria, and there was no need to use Li-2s for strikes against enemy targets. On the other hand, there was more than enough work for them in their primary role.

The war against Japan began on 9th August 1945 when the Hingan-Mukden operation of the Trans-Baikal Front started. In the course of this offensive operation, as early as 11th August the tank and mechanised infantry corps of the 6th Tank Army rushed ahead, leaving their supply bases some 400-450 km (249-280 miles) behind. The Army- and Front-subordinated vehicle convoys did not manage to ensure timely delivery of fuel. As a result, two-thirds of the tanks, all self-propelled guns and most of the transport vehicles were left without fuel, which placed the army in a most difficult situation. To ensure urgent deliveries of fuel, the 21st and 54th Airlift Divisions flying Li-2s and C-47s were committed to action. Every day 90 to 100 aircraft flew their missions. The task was made more complicated by the fact that the numerous flat stretches of land in Manchuria, which seemed quite suitable for landing from the air, often turned out to be covered with small sharp stones capable of damaging the tyres of a heavy aircraft. Therefore the crews were provided with maps showing the state of land surface in the combat zone. On 11th August alone they delivered 170 tonnes (374,780 lb) of fuel – two-thirds of the amount required for the needs of the 6th Guards Tank Army, and by 21st August they had carried 1,765 tonnes (3,891,090 lb) of fuel, 87 tonnes (197,800 lb) of ammunition and 42 tonnes (92,610 lb) of other cargoes. At the same time ammunition and fuel were delivered to front-line airfields used by bomber units. In all, in the course of the operation Red Army armour units received 2,042.3 tonnes (4,502,270 lb) of various cargoes, including 109 tonnes (240,345 lb) of fuel; 855 casualties were evacuated.

In order to speed up the disarmament and capture of the Kwantung Army, as well as to prevent possible destruction of industrial enterprises and other important objectives and removal of military hardware and valuable materials by the Japanese, on 18th-19th August the Soviet Command conducted 19 troop landing operations in which airborne assault parties numbering from 35 to 250 troops were landed. They were delivered to airfields of major cities of Manchuria, Liaotung Peninsula, North Korea, the south of Sakhalin Island and the Kurile Islands. On 15th August the air regiments of the 21st Guards Air Division and the 54th Air Division, as well as the 281st Airlift Regiment (operating nine TB-3s and six Li-2s) started the landing of troops on the airfields of Harbin, Girin, Yangtze, Kanko, Wangtsing and Heijio located in the rear of the Japanese army. In all, 1,347 troops with full kit were landed. The assault troops prevented Japanese aircraft from taking to the air and succeeded in preserving the airfield infrastructure intact until the arrival of the Soviet troops. On 18th August a Soviet plenipotentiary representative was sent to the Japanese headquarters in Harbin, he was accompanied by a landing party numbering 120 troops. In the presence of Soviet representatives the Japanese Commander-in-Chief Yamada signed the Act of Capitulation, and Chief of Staff General H. Hata was taken on board an aircraft to the command post of the 1st Far Eastern Front to receive instructions from the Soviet Command.

On 19th August more landing parties numbering from 150 to 225 troops were delivered by air to the cities of Liaoyuan, Changchung, Mukden, Girin and once more to Harbin. The following day yet another troop landing operation was conducted in Harbin. On 22nd August landing parties were delivered by air to Port Arthur (200 troops) and Talien (formerly Dal'niy, 250 troops), and on 23rd August to Yangtze (238 troops). On 24th August assault parties were delivered to North Korean cities – 166 troops to Heijio (Pyongyang) and 134 to Kanko (Hanmyn) – and to the settlements of Taiohara, Otirai, Sakaehama and Otomari in the south of Sakhalin Island (35 troops to each of them). The 10th Air Army rendered assistance to the troops which liberated Sakhalin and the Kurile Islands. The peculiarities of the Far Eastern theatre of operations made it imperative that the main attention should be concentrated on the preparation of maritime and airborne assault operations. From 12th August onwards the 344th Airlift Regiment equipped with Li-2s ensured the airlifting of cargoes for the troops on the offensive. As for the delivery of the landing troops, it was performed by GVF units flying C-47s. The landing of Soviet troops on Iturup Island (one of the four South Kurile Islands which are now a bone of contention between Russia and Japan) took place on 27th August. It should be noted that the demoralised Japanese troops offered practically no resistance; hence the main task of the landing troops was to ensure the acceptance of capitulation and to monitor the observance of its conditions.

Paradropping or disembarkation of landing parties was effected in daytime by aircraft flying in formations or singly, with or without fighter escort. The depth of delivery of landing troops was 150 to 600 km (93-373 miles). Landing operations were effected by Li-2 crews from the 21st Guards Air Division and 54th Airlift Division of the 12th Air Army. As a rule, this was done by disembarkation directly on the enemy airfields. Control of the disembarkation of landing troops was the responsibility of the Air Armies' commanders. The operations were preceded by careful aerial reconnaissance. To assess the conditions for the landing of an assault party on a given airfield, a fighter aircraft piloted by the commander of the escort fighter group would land there first; the pilot would then radio his assessment of the field. The pilot conducting the final reconnaissance on the ground doubled as an advanced and starting party and maintained contact with the help of his fighter's radio.

In all, during the whole period of the war against Japan in the Far East the Soviet transport aviation flew 5,473 sorties on the Li-2 and C-47 aircraft, transporting 2,777 tonnes (6,122.130 lb) of fuel, 2,045 tonnes (4,508,380 lb) of other cargoes and 16,497 persons.

By the end of the Second World War the 18th Air Army comprised 18 Air Regiments equipped with Li-2s. In early 1945 the 9th

Li-2 units in the ADD (Long-Range Aviation)

Corps	Division	Regiment
5th Air Corps	53rd Air Division	1st Guards Air Regiment
		325th Air Regiment
	54th Air Division	7th Air Regiment
		23rd Guards Air Regiment
6th Air Corps	9th Guards Air Division	4th Guards Air Regiment
		11th Guards Air Regiment
7th Air Corps	1st Air Division	101st Air Regiment
		102nd Air Regiment
	12th Guards Air Division	12th Guards Air Regiment
		110th Air Regiment

Guards Air Corps was formed within the Airborne Troops (or the Independent Guards Airborne Army, as it was called then). In this connection by April 1945 the number of Li-2s in the Airborne Troops had reached 80 machines. It was then that the Air Corps was incorporated into 18th Air Army. In all, during the Great Patriotic War the Long-Range Aviation received 1,214 Li-2s from the aircraft factories.

After the victory over Japan and the ending of the Second World War, in 1946, steps were taken towards the establishment of the Soviet Long-Range Aviation (now known as the DA – ***Dahl'****nyaya avi****ah****tsiya*, which basically means the same) on the basis of the 18th Air Army. The Li-2s were by no means suitable for the long-range bomber role, so they were gradually transferred to the military airlift units that were set up at that time. For example, one squadron was taken out of each regiment of the 54th Air Division based in the Khabarovsk Territory; these squadrons were united in the newly-formed 331st Independent Transport Air Regiment (OTrAP – *ot****del'****nyy* ***trahns****portnyy aviatsi****on****nyy polk*). In parallel, similar units were formed on the basis of tactical (front-line) aviation. For example, the regiments of the 6th Guards Attack Air Division stationed in the Kiev Military District were transformed into transport and assault air regiments. This made it possible to form the Military Transport Aviation (VTA – *Voyenno-****trahns****portnaya avi****ah****tsiya*) on their basis as a separate arm of the Soviet Air Force in April 1955, with Nikolay S. Skripko as its first Commander.

Air units equipped with the Li-2 were henceforth primarily intended for catering for the needs of the Airborne Troops (VDV – *Voz****doosh****no-de****sahnt****nyye voy****ska***). Hence, taking into account the experience gained in the Great Patriotic War, much attention in the course of combat training was accorded to raising the standards of formation flying, including flights at night and in adverse weather. An important element of this training was the assembly of the aircraft group in the area of the point of departure. At that time there was no shortage of fuel, and pilots quickly began to acquire the necessary flying skills, while the commanders learned the art of controlling large groups of transport aircraft. It took less than one hour to assemble a Li-2 regiment in the air.

It was the 353rd Air Regiment of the 6th Air Division that had achieved the best results in combat training. What else could explain the fact that this unit, located far from the capital, invariably took part in the Aviation Day displays at Moscow-Tushino during the first post-war decade? For the regiment these 'show performances' proved to be good training sessions which served to enhance their ability to fly missions in close formations. To undertake preparations for the Tushino air display, in May the regiment would redeploy to a base near Klin a short way north of Moscow (now Klin-5 AB) where it was supplemented by a fourth squadron sent from Tula. This was followed by intensive training in the course of three months. It was necessary to pass over Tushino in a line of squadrons, dropping paratroopers who would land in the centre of the airfield. For this purpose the lateral and longitudinal separation between the aircraft was to be around 20 m (65 ft), and lateral distance between groups of nine aircraft was 300 m (980 ft). Paradropping was performed at an altitude of 500 m (1,640 ft) and a speed of 250 km/h (155 mph).

The training began on the ground: the Li-2s were arranged in the order which they would have to keep in the air, and pilots marked on the flightdeck glazing the limits within which they were to keep the neighbouring aircraft in flight. In the final stage of the preparations 'dress rehearsals' were held over Tushino five or six times. During one of such rehearsals one of the squadrons was a bit late in starting the paradropping; as a result, the paratroopers, instead of a spectacular landing on the grass of the Tushino

Top and above: Maintenance in progress on the starboard engine of a Li-2. The partially removed cowling reveals the ventral oil cooler and parts of the engine bearer.

Paratroopers jump through the port and starboard doors of two Li-2s during an exercise. Note the circular plug closing the aperture in the roof of the nearest aircraft where the dorsal turret used to be.

airfield, came to hang preposterously on the lanterns and railings of the Riga Bridge which spanned the Moskva River, while some of them were even obliged to take a swim. This 'unpremeditated capture of the bridge' became the only incident in the history of the Tushino attractions of the 363th Air Regiment. The Tushino air displays themselves were always conducted in style and imbued the public and Iosif Stalin, who invariably attended these events, with pride for the country's Air Fleet.

Gradually the industry started supplying the armed forces with a steadily growing number of new aircraft. The transport air regiments began taking delivery first of the IL-12T and IL-12D, then of the IL-14T (augmented by Tupolev Tu-4 bombers converted to Tu-4D transports), and then of the more advanced Antonov An-8 twin-turboprop transport designed along entirely new lines. As early as 1949 the units of the 6th Air Division began converting to the Il'yushin machines. But there were also whole divisions which operated the Li-2 right up to the early 1960s, after which they converted straight to the even more capable four-turboprop An-12. This was the case, for example, with the Air Division stationed in Chernovtsy. After the delivery of the new aircraft the high-time Li-2s were struck off charge. Others, which were in better condition, were transferred to auxiliary air units catering for the needs of military district headquarters, army groups, air armies and armies of the land forces. A small number of the Li-2s thus made redundant was taken over by GVF and industrial enterprises.

The Soviet versions of the DC-3 also entered the inventory of military flying schools. For example, in 1948 the 408th Training Air Regiment equipped with Li-2s was formed in the Balashov Military Pilot College (VVAUL – ***Vys**sheye **voyen**noye aviat**sion**noye **oochil**ischche **lyot**chikov*).

The Soviet Air Force divisions and regiments operating the Li-2 at the end of the war

1st Guards Long-Range Air Division	31st GvAP DD, 32nd GvAP DD, 334th AP DD
12th Long-Range Air Division	12th GvAP DD, 33rd GvAP DD, 338th AP DD
21st Guards Long-Range Air Division	49th GvAP DD, 50th GvAP DD, 51st AP DD
22nd Guards Long-Range Air Division	11th GvAP DD, 220th GvAP DD, 339th AP DD
53rd Long-Range Air Division	1st GvAP DD, 239th GvAP DD, 336th AP DD
54th Long-Range Air Division	7th GvAP DD, 29th GvAP DD, 340th AP DD

It makes sense to dwell in some detail on the role the Li-2 has played in the training of Soviet Air Force pilots. In the early 1950s, Long-Range Aviation pilots continued to take their training on obsolete IL-4 bombers. As compared to these, the Li-2 had indisputable advantages in the training role. It had simpler handling and lower operating costs; it had a flightdeck with side-by-side seating for the trainee and the instructor (in contrast, the IL-4 had a fighter-type cockpit, making it impossible for the instructor to check the trainee's actions visually). In Balashov the Li-2s remained in service for more than a decade (the last graduation of trainees on these aircraft took place in 1960). Until 1955 they were used to train pilots for the DA, in subsequent years for the VTA. It should be noted that the aircraft delivered to the Balashov VVAUL were, without exception, well-worn machines (some of them had served throughout the war), and it required an almost heroic effort on the part of the trainees and technicians to keep them airworthy. Yet, even after all the vicissitudes of their flying career the Soviet *Cabs* remained reliable machines. True, there were three crashes involving the Li-2s in Balashov, but they were caused by the telltale human error.

The Li-2's participation in the training of airmen for the DA was not confined to its use in flying schools. In the 1950s the DA's first-line units started converting to the Tu-4 bomber. These aircraft were still scarce, they were flown primarily by experienced pilots, while the pilots that had just graduated from flying schools had few opportunities to fly these machines, and sometimes no chances at all. The Air Force Command realised in time that, should it wait until the industry supplied the necessary number of the Tu-4s, the new generation of pilots would run the risk of losing their skills.

An interesting method was devised to resolve this situation. Some 200 lieutenants who had just been promoted to this rank after graduation were included in a special group of officers-pilots of the DA which was sponsored personally by Air Force Deputy Commander-in-Chief S. I. Rudenko. They took appropriate training on the Li-2, received a 4th Class commercial pilot's licence and were posted to Aeroflot's civil aviation directorates. Subsequently the group received new 'manpower' several times. The work in Aeroflot gave the young pilots an opportunity to acquire considerable flying experience. They logged up to 500 flight hours per year – nearly ten times more than what pilots of the same age did in the Air Force. Three years later the pilots of the first enrolment in the group returned to the Air Force. They transitioned very easily to bombers, and soon many of them became Tu-4 captains; a few years later they were among the first to progress to the Tu-16, Tu-95 and Myasishchev M-4 bombers.

The post-war service of the Li-2 was concerned not only with everyday peaceful occupations. Several Li-2s were transferred to North Korea. In late 1947 North Korean military transport Li-2s and C-47s began performing scheduled flights from Pyongyang to the Soviet Far East (Vladivostok, Khabarovsk) and to China (Harbin). The flights were performed by mixed Soviet-Korean crews. The main purpose of these flights was the maintenance of regular communication between the 'Provisional Committee', then the government of North Korea, and the 'fraternal parties' (that is, the Communist Parties of other Soviet Bloc nations), delivery of diplomatic mail and various specialists. When the Korean War broke out, the aircraft of the 51st Guards Airlift Regiment, at that time stationed mainly at Komsomol'sk-on-Amur, were used for airlifting personnel and equipment of Soviet air units to the war zone.

In October 1956 the Chernovtsy-based division airlifted to Hungary a formation of Airborne Troops of the Carpathian Military District which, along with other Warsaw Pact forces, took part in the suppression of the anti-Communist uprising.

In the late 1950s a Li-2 regiment based in Fergana, Uzbekistan, supplemented by one squadron from Zaporozhye, the Ukraine (36 machines in all), was transferred to Vietnam, relocating to an airfield at Haiphong and joining the Soviet Air Force group in that country. The group's task was to perform transportation, including flights in support of the partisans of South Vietnam and North Laos, as well as to train local airmen.

The difficulties posed by the work in Indo-China are vividly described in the following account by M. M. Gamaris, who was the commander of that group in 1960-61. Here is just one episode from the events of those years: *'My predecessor in Vietnam was Colonel Somov. The destinations to which he had to send Soviet crews included Sam Neo airfield in Laos* (spelled Xam Nua in other accounts – *authors' note*) *which was noted for its extremely complicated conditions for take-off and landing. It was located at an altitude of some 2,500 m* [8,200 ft] *above sea level and was surrounded by mountains on three sides. Its dirt airstrip, slightly more than 900 m* [2,950 ft] *long and 32 m* [105 ft] *wide, was limited on both ends by the abrupt banks of a swamp and a small river. There was no communication with the airfield. To make matters worse, the ambient temperature there was +35-40°C* [+95-104°F]. *To make a safe landing at Sam Neo, it was necessary to touch down literally at the very edge of the swamp and be sure that the speed of the aircraft was down to an absolute minimum – around 130 km/h* [80 mph], *otherwise, given the rarefied mountain air, the runway length would be insufficient for the landing run.*

During the colonial period the French had lost 25 machines while attempting landings at Sam Neo, including several C-47s. Nor did our group steer clear of mishaps. Shortly before my arrival a Li-2 piloted by Captain Doobovtsev had made a crash landing. His machine touched down a mere 50 m [164 ft] *farther than required, but the wheel brakes proved to be in less-than-perfect condition; so, at the end of the landing run, with the speed reduced to a minimum, Doobovtsev had to ground-loop the aircraft to the right to avoid*

Li-2T '05 Red' (c/n 23441201) in Soviet Air Force service in the 1960s. Note the exposed dipole aerials of the RV-2 radio altimeter.

A poor but interesting shot of North Vietnamese Air Force Li-2s in action during the Pathet Lao insurgency in the 1960s.

crashing into the river bank. The Li-2 ran into a ditch near the 'cemetery' of French aircraft.

Despite the fact that nobody was hurt in the incident and the aircraft could be repaired (which no one dreamed of doing there), Doobovtsev could easily face court martial. As for Somov, he decided to play safe and banned further flights to Sam Neo – a decision which was met with acute incomprehension on the part of the Vietnamese and Soviet governments. The pilots found themselves in a no-win situation; if you fly, you can crash your machine and be prosecuted, if you don't fly, you may be accused of cowardice.

This had a most detrimental effect on the pilots' morale and physical condition, some of them even lost their sleep. Therefore, as soon as I took over from Somov, I immediately had a candid talk with the pilots. It came to light that it was Major Andropov who had the greatest experience of flights to Sam Neo (he had landed there eight times). I decided to make a flight to that place together with him, and then take the final decision as to the possibility of flying to that airfield. The reality surpassed all verbal accounts: the only possible approach to the runway was shielded by one more mountain, so that the finals had to be executed without visual contact with the airfield which became visible only after the fourth (last) turn. Andropov skilfully landed our Li-2, and soon the Laotians who had come running got busy turning our aircraft in the opposite direction (for take-off – *authors' note*) *– we would not be able to do that on our own because of the small width of the runway. Undoubtedly, further flights to Sam Neo would entail an unwarranted risk. But then it came to our knowledge that 400 wounded persons had been concentrated at the airfield; they had to be evacuated urgently, otherwise they would soon die. Therefore, upon our return to Haiphong, a decision was taken to evacuate the wounded and then terminate the flights to Sam Neo. When our pilots saw that the problem was going to be solved, they felt their spirits rise and tackled the task without any incidents. They picked up 40 persons; true, the wounded were emaciated and weighed little. They were placed in the cabin in a herringbone pattern, with their heads to the centreline, directly on the floor covered with tarpaulins.'*

The number of air regiments and Li-2 aircraft in the Soviet military transport aviation between 1940 and 1964

Years	*Li-2 (PS-84) and C-47*
1940	80
1943	355
1945	1046
1946	200 (10 regiments)
1949	230 (10 regiments)
1955	292 (16 regiments)
1956	576 (13 regiments)
1958	384 (9 regiments)
1959	288 (7 regiments)
1960	234 (4 regiments)
1962	142 (4 regiments)
1964	Withdrawn from service in 1963

An account published in the West adds some details, partly differing with those stated above. First, it mentions the dropping of supplies to units building the so-called Ho Chi Minh Trail through Laos and Cambodia; the task was tackled by the 919th Air Transport Regiment of the North Vietnamese Air Force in 1959-1960 by dropping supplies without parachutes – the so-called *Tha Vo* ('free fall' in Vietnamese) technique, using IL-14s, Li-2s and An-2s. Speaking about the North Vietnamese aid to Pathet Lao insurgency in Laos, this source states that 'in October of 1960 the first 44 Soviet aircraft arrived in North Vietnam. These comprised 20 Li-2s and 14 IL-14 transports and ten Mil' Mi-4 helicopters. An aerial supply bridge was established, starting in the Soviet Union, passing through North Vietnam, and ending in Laos. The Air Force Office created three units on the regimental level to perform the airlift. Two units were located at Cat Bi using the helicopters and the Li-2s with the help of Russian advisers. The third unit was assigned to Chu (later Kep) airfield and operated Li-2s with the assistance of Chinese advisers. The 919th ATR delivered weapons, food, and other military supplies to Laos and brought back wounded troops. Within the 919th ATR, 120 troops were divided among six squadrons and assigned to packing and air drop duties. New equipment was sent to the Vietnamese airfields at Gia Lam (near Hanoi), Cat Bi, Vinh, Na San and Dien Bien, while the airfield at Kep was urgently expanded. These airfields became the focal point for supplies sent from the USSR and China. On 11th December 1960 a new route was opened to Xam Nua airfield in Laos. Within a week Li-2s with mixed North Vietnamese and Russian aircrews had performed 184 flights into Xam Nua. In the meantime, the IL-14s and An-2s dropped supplies in the Laotian regions of Ban Hong, Muang Vanviang, Muang Phoun, and Sala Phou Khun.

With the help of the North Vietnamese and Soviet Air Forces, the Pathet Lao troops and their North Vietnamese allies attacked the Laotian districts of Xam Nua, Phong Sali, Xiang Khoang, and the strategically important plains of Chanh Dong Chum (Plain of Jars). The latter was 'liberated' on 1st January 1961. Following this victory, Li-2 and An-2 transports landed on the airfield at Chanh Dong Chum, delivering weapons to the troops and food supplies to the civilian population.

When US troops came to Vietnam the personnel of the Soviet Air Force group had already left the country. The Li-2s remained there and took part in the conflict that lasted nearly 12 years, performing the traditional tasks of transport aircraft.

The Li-2 aircraft remained in the inventory of the Soviet military transport aviation until 1964, whereupon some of them were transferred to the DOSAAF paramilitary sports organisation (*Dobro**vol'**noye **ob**schchestvo so**dey**stviya **ar**mii, avia**ht**sii i **flo**tu* – the Voluntary Society for the Support of the Army, Aviation (read: Air Force) and Navy). Others were taken over by the Ministry of Civil Aviation or were struck off charge.

The Li-2 also saw service with the Air Forces of other countries in the Soviet Bloc – Hungary, Poland, Romania, Czechoslovakia, People's Republic of China, North Korea and Vietnam. Almost everywhere they served for more than one decade, just as was the case in the Soviet Air Force where a few die-hard Li-2s were still flying in the early 1970s.

Chapter 6

In Civilian Service

In 1940 Aeroflot put the PS-84 airliner into service. The first PS-84s were concentrated in the Moscow Transport Directorate of the GVF. Operations were mastered on the routes between Moscow and Berlin, somewhat later between Tashkent and Kabul, and between Ulan-Ude and Ulan-Bator. On international air services the PS-84s were supplemented by US-built DC-3s. Also in 1940, Aeroflot introduced the PS-84 on three domestic routes: Moscow-Novosibirsk, Ashkhabad-Moscow and Moscow-Tbilisi. The type was operated primarily in a 21-seat configuration.

The pilots' comments were highly laudatory. While not being ideal in terms of piloting, the aircraft was sufficiently easy to fly, with agreeable handling. The PS-84 could fly with one engine inoperative, the passenger cabin was provided with ventilation and heating, as well as with individual lighting and overhead bins for small luggage, the flightdeck windshield was fitted with de-icing devices. The aircraft's equipment enabled it to perform night flights.

The Civil Air Fleet Research Institute conducted a large amount of work on the use of the PS-84 for operations under adverse weather conditions and in night-time. In 1940 a NII GVF Flight Training Centre was established at Zakharkovo airfield near Moscow; N. P. Shebanov was appointed its chief. The Centre was staffed with the best-trained pilots, navigator-instructors and technical specialists acting as teachers. The centre conducted the training of aircrews for the PS-84s. It was also used as a facility for retraining and upgrading the qualification of the flying and technical personnel in the Aeroflot management. The crews undergoing conversion training at the Centre performed their training flights on the Moscow-Leningrad, Moscow-Novosibirsk and Moscow-Tbilisi routes.

The first 100 PS-84s were allotted registrations within the CCCP-Л3400 to CCCP-Л3499 range; the next big batch of aircraft was registered within the CCCP-Л3900 to CCCP-Л3973 range. (It should be noted, however, that under the Soviet civil aircraft registration system used from 1932 to 1958 the registration batches were not necessarily allocated in sequence.) Several machines were delivered to the Chief Administration of the Northern Sea Route; they carried the logos and registrations of its air transport subdivision, Aviaarktika. Examples operated in the pre-war years included CCCP H-311 and CCCP-H455 (the registration may have been painted on as CCCP H-455).

Additionally, the PS-84 was actively operated by various subdivisions of the People's Commissariat of Aircraft Industry (NKAP). Known NKAP examples used before the war included CCCP-И682 (that is, SSSR-I682), И690 (*sic* – no prefix) and CCCP-И897.

By the summer of 1941 the aggregate length of the Soviet Union's air route network had reached a figure in excess of 146,000 km (90,680 miles), which was in no small measure due to the introduction of the new passenger aircraft on the routes. Moscow became connected by regular air communications with all the constituent republics, territories, regions and major industrial centres of Siberia, the High North, the Far East and Central Asia. The new aircraft were put into operation on the country's most important trunk air routes. As of 1 December 1940, the Civil Air Fleet had 26 PS-84s and seven DC-3s on strength. By June 1941 Aeroflot had 72 PS-84s at its disposal.

In the first six months of 1941 the total amount of traffic on Aeroflot's major air routes amounted to 17.8 million tonne-kilometres – almost 50% more than in the first six months

CCCP-Л3463 (that is, SSSR-L3463), an early Aeroflot PS-84 in the pre-war minimalistic livery – or rather no livery at all. Up to the end of the 1950s Soviet airliners flying domestic services usually did not carry the Soviet flag on the tail.

Above: Three Aeroflot PS-84s, including СССР-Л3415, await their next missions with canvas covers on the engines. Aeroflot Li-2s lacked propeller spinners.

of 1940. Traffic figures for the first half of 1941 included the transportation of 127,000 passengers, 3,000 tonnes (6,613,760 lb) of mail and 24,900 tonnes (54,894,180 lb) of various cargoes. The service introduction of the PS-84 was accompanied by a considerable improvement in the regularity of flights and an increase of the load factor.

With the outbreak of the Great Patriotic War the flights of the PS-84s on Aeroflot's routes were suspended and the aircraft were requisitioned by the military, serving with Civil Air Fleet units within the Air Force (thus, for instance, СССР-Л4171 received a camouflage finish and red star insignia but retained its civil registration less country prefix, becoming 'Л4171 White'). However, as early as 1944, when Soviet territory had been cleared of the Nazi invaders, the airline began to reinstate services, using PS-84s along with other types. After the end of the war a certain number of 'demobilised' machines, supplemented by new-build aircraft, formed a significant influx into the Aeroflot inventory. Virtually for a decade the Li-2 became the main airliner of the Soviet civil aviation.

The year of 1945 saw the resumption of regular air communications between Moscow and Kiev, Khar'kov, Donetsk, Odessa, L'vov and Dnepropetrovsk, and also between Khar'kov and Kuibyshev (now renamed back to Samara), Stalingrad (now Volgograd), Donetsk and Dnepropetrovsk. In late 1945 a 1,200-km (745-mile) air route connected Moscow with Kishinyov. The Li-2s resumed their operations in civil air communications in the Ukraine and Belorussia. Scheduled Li-2 services were started from Riga to Moscow, Leningrad and Minsk. In 1946 the Civil Air Fleet completed its changeover from wartime to peacetime operations. The final stage of this changeover was marked by the disbanding of all the wartime militarised enterprises, regiments and divisions of the Civil Air Fleet pursuant to the order issued by the Soviet Minister of Defence on 18th September 1946. The flight and ground crews, as well as the aircraft on strength, including numerous Li-2s (PS-84s), were transferred to the territorial directorates of the GVF, which allowed nine new transport flight detachments and 17 'special mission' (in this case, this means agricultural) flight detachments to be established within a short period.

By early 1947 there were 15 territorial directorates in the GVF structure. Each constituent republic had either a directorate or an independent flight detachment, while the Russian Federal Soviet Socialist Republic (the largest republic of the USSR) had several such directorates. Virtually all GVF directorates operated the Li-2. Two aviation groups were formed at Moscow-Vnukovo, which had recently become a civil airport. One of these, an independent aviation group commanded by V. M. Chernyakov, had 75 aircraft on strength and served domestic air routes; the other one, commanded by A. I. Semyonov, comprised 45 aircraft and was to fly international services. To cater for the needs of the Soviet military administration in the eastern part of Germany (the future German Democratic Republic) and of the Allied control commissions, an independent transport flight detachment was set up at Berlin-Tempelhof, supplemented by commandant's offices for receiving and dispatching Aeroflot aircraft in Sofia, Bucharest, Budapest and Helsinki.

Having completely restored the pre-war service network, Aeroflot went on establishing and mastering new routes, such as Minsk – Khar'kov, Minsk – Rostov-on-Don, Kishinyov – Kiev, Kishinyov – Odessa, which were flown by Li-2s. Flights were undertaken from Leningrad to Tallinn, Riga, Vilnius and Minsk and from Minsk to Kaliningrad. By the end of 1946 the total length of air routes of all-union significance increased by over 14,000 km (8,695 miles) as compared to 1945, reaching 32,300 km (20,060 miles); the total length of local routes increased in the same period by 16,400 km (10,190 miles) and amounted to more than 90,000 km (55,900 miles). The total length of Aeroflot's air routes as of 1st January 1947 was 172,400 km (107,100 miles).

The Soviet *Cabs* played an invaluable part in extending help to the inhabitants of the Turkmen SSR which was hit by a disastrous earthquake in 1948. On 5th October a seismological station registered subterranean tremors. Scientists pinpointed the earthquake's epicentre as being located in northern Iran, near the Kopet-Dag Ridge, 80 km (50 miles) from Ashkhabad, the capital of Turkmenia; they assessed the earthquake as having a force of 10 on the Richter scale in the

An airport scene of the late 1940s. Passengers disembark from a recently-demobbed PS-84 И-682 (that is, I-682, ex СССР-И682); PS-84 СССР-Л4293 in the background is unusual in having a lightning bolt cheatline.

epicentre and 8-9 in Ashkhabad. Numerous Li-2s took off from Moscow and other cities of the country and headed for Ashkhabad, bringing rescue workers and supplies. The first of the three aircraft that had been sent from Moscow was piloted by Pavel Taran, a bomber pilot who had earned the Hero of the Soviet Union title during the war. As they landed, the crews saw the airport apron packed with dozens of Li-2s that had arrived from the nearest cities on quake relief flights.

In February 1950 Li-2s from Aeroflot's Azerbaijan, North Caucasian and Moscow territorial directorates arrived in Astrakhan' for the purpose of transporting fodder to the places where large herds of sheep were caught by sudden snow storms in the midst of the steppes. The airmen did a wonderful job, helping to save a large stock of sheep of extremely valuable breeds. In February 1951 huge sheep herds were similarly afflicted on pastures in southern Kazakhstan. After a three-day snowfall the snow lay 35-45 cm (14-18 in) thick, and a sudden frost right after a thaw turned the snow surface into a crust of ice. The lack of fodder could lead to a massive loss of livestock. In the course of a month crews of Li-2 aircraft, sometimes flying under extremely harsh weather conditions, searched for the sheep herds lost in the boundless steppes and dropped hay and other fodder for them. As a result, hundreds of thousands of sheep were saved from death.

The more modern IL-12, followed by the IL-14, gradually supplanted the long-serving Li-2 on Aeroflot's services. By the mid-1950s the Li-2 could no longer meet the requirements of Aeroflot. For starters, it was replaced by newer types on international routes; in 1957 Aeroflot started to transfer the Li-2s en masse to local routes, and then to auxiliary subdivisions of Aeroflot and to the DOSAAF paramilitary sports organisation. After the introduction of the current five-digit civil aircraft registration system in 1958, under which the first two digits were a sort of code for the type aiding identification during radio exchanges with air traffic control, the civil Li-2s were reregistered in the CCCP-65***, -73*** and -84*** batches. (The CCCP-65*** series later passed to the Tu-134 jetliner.)

Scheduled operations of the Li-2 on Aeroflot routes continued until 1962. During the last years of operation on Aeroflot's local services the Li-2s were often flown by crews reduced from five to two persons. On the other hand, the type served on for many more years with various enterprises in the frameworks of the Ministry of Aircraft Industry (MAP), the Ministry of General Machinery (MOM – *Mini**ster**stvo **ob**schchevo ma**shin**ostroyeniya*) responsible for the Soviet space and missile programmes, the Ministry of Shipbuilding (MSP – *Mini**ster**stvo soodostro-*

Above: Bombs no more? This demilitarised Li-2NB (note the aiming window in the baggage loading door) appears to be saying 'humph' at the idea of farewell to arms as it undergoes an engine change.

Above: Crates of fruit are loaded aboard a Li-2T registered CCCP-Л42-something-or-other in ex-Air Force olive drab finish. Many 'war surplus' Li-2s joined Aeroflot's fleet in the late 1940s/1950s.

'Meet Pegasus, the flying horse!' Aeroflot Li-2Ts, exemplified by CCCP-Л4479, sometimes had to carry unusual cargoes, including livestock.

Above: Unfortunately unidentifiable, this silver-overall PS-84 equipped with streamlined non-retractable wooden skis almost certainly belongs to the Polar Aviation Directorate (Aviaarktika, as it was known before the war). Note the perfectly triangular drag braces (without wheel forks) that go with the skis.

Hiding behind an Aviaarktika Tupolev G-2 (which is being refuelled by means of a hand-driven pump), this PS-84 is a very early example with an outward-opening entry door. Only the Polar CCCP-H prefix is visible.

itel'noy promyshlennosti) and the Ministry of Electronic Industry (MRP – *Ministerstvo rahdioelektronnoy promyshlennosti*). The Li-2s operated by industry enterprises were registered in many more batches, including CCCP-06***, -08***, -133**, -215**, -26*** (later passed to An-26 transports), -272**, -291**, -46*** (later passed to An-24 airliners), -48***, -586**, -595**, -644**, -667**, -693**, -78***, -79***, -939** and -981**.

MAP aircraft were used by the aircraft factories in Arsen'yev (No.116), Gor'kiy (No.21), Irkutsk (No.39), Komsomol'sk-on-Amur (No.126), Kazan' (No.22 and No.387), Khar'kov (No.135), Kiev (No.473), Kuibyshev (No.18), Kumertau, Novosibirsk (No.153), Orenburg, Rostov-on-Don (No.168), Saratov (No.292), Tashkent (No.84), Taganrog (No.86), Tbilisi (No.31), Ulan-Ude (No.99) and Voronezh (No.64), the engine factories in Perm', Rybinsk and Ufa, as well as the Moscow-based Transport Aviation Production Association and the Flight Research Institute (LII) in Zhukovskiy. MOM enterprises operating the Li-2 included the plants in Kuibyshev (formerly MAP aircraft factory No.1) and Chelyabinsk, as well as the 'Strela' (Arrow) Production Association in Orenburg (the former MAP aircraft factory No.166). MRP divisions included NPO Vzlyot (the 'Take-off' Research & Production Association) and LNPO Leninets (the 'Leninist' Leningrad Research & Production Association).

Cabs on Polar Caps

During the post-war years the Li-2 was operated on a fairly wide scale in the Arctic and in Antarctica. Interestingly, crews from the

Soviet Air Force's military transport arm were among the first Li-2 crews to take part in the development of the high-latitude areas of the Arctic. It was the military who had accumulated the greatest experience of transporting cargoes in particularly difficult conditions during the war years. The Li-2 crews headed by Captain I. F. Popov, Lieutenant (Senior Grade) Faleyev and Lieutenant (Senior Grade) Belov were among the first to master flights in the High North. In December 1949 Major I. G. Sevost'yanov was awarded the coveted Hero of the Soviet Union title for his contribution to the development of the North and for reaching the North Pole; a further 31 persons were awarded orders and medals.

Among the participants in the high-latitude expedition of 1954 there were 31 Li-2s which delivered research equipment and life support cargoes for the SP-4 (***Severnyy Polyus*** – North Pole) Arctic expedition based on a drifting ice floe. The group of airmen flying the Li-2s was formed from the crews of the 281st TAD (Transport Air Division) and 556th TAP (Transport Air Regiment) based at Vypolzovo AB in what was then the Kalinin Region (now Tver' Region). A flight from Moscow to Cape Schmidt over a distance of 7,500 km (4,660 miles) with 12 to 15 refuelling stops took 15 days. The air group, which also comprised several aircraft of other types, as well as assault gliders, transported 22 tonnes (of cargoes and 60 passengers. One of the towed gliders delivered to the SP-4 a bulldozer whose weight exceeded by 700 kg (1,540 lb) the normal cargo-carrying capacity of the glider. After having delivered the Polar research team to the ice floe, the air group catered for their work in the course of March and April.

Not only military Li-2s, but also civil aircraft of this type delivered cargoes, food supplies and medicines to Arctic expeditions; those supporting the Soviet Antarctic expeditions were strictly civilian. Originally they retained the old-style registrations in the CCCP-H*** series; after 1958 the remaining Li-2s were reregistered in the CCCP-04*** batch allocated to Polar Aviation aircraft.

Not infrequently, both military and civilian crews had to conduct search-and-rescue operations. For example, on 11th December 1958 a telegram came to the Soviet Ice Station Mirnyy in Antarctica, sounding an alarm: an aircraft operated by the Belgian Antarctic expedition (an Auster lightplane) had set off in the direction of Crystal Mountains and failed to return to base. Nothing was known about the fate of the pilot and three explorers. The Soviet polar explorers were asked to give a helping hand.

The crew of a Soviet Li-2V (CCCP-H495, c/n 18430708) captained by Viktor M. Perov, Commander of the 3rd Soviet Antarctic

Above: Seen starting its engines, Li-2 CCCP H311 (that is, SSSR N-311) wears a smart white/orange livery with Aviaarktika titles. CCCP-H171 in the background is one of the three Tupolev ANT-6 Aviaarktika transports.

Above: One more view of the same aircraft; here, propeller spinners have been fitted. The eye-catching livery is designed for high definition against ice and snow in the event of a forced landing. Note how the registration it is applied (CCCP H-311 rather than CCCP-H311).

Open-air maintenance on PS-84 CCCP H-311 at Matochkin Shar airfield in February 1941. Note the highly polished propeller blades.

Above: View from the first officer's seat of PS-84 CCCP H-311 as the aircraft passes over one of the islands in the Arctic Ocean. The engine cooling shutters are open. The wings have orange tops.

Above left: The chief of the Polar research team (left) and the aircraft captain pose before PS-84 CCCP H-311, which is engine running with the shutters closed.

Left: One of the crewmembers has been lucky enough to trap a snowy owl and is examining his quarry in admiration.

Below: In contrast, Li-2 CCCP-H534 retains the standard olive drab finish with pale blue undersides. It has retractable all-metal skis; unusually, the front cowling plates have been removed.

Expedition's air detachment, sent a message to Moscow, to the management of the Chief Administration of the Northern Sea Route, informing them of their decision to set off on a search and rescue mission. The reply came immediately: 'Take all the necessary measures to save the Belgians'. Yet, to make matters worse, the weather was heavy; a snowstorm was raging, with the wind speed reaching 40 m/sec (80 kts) at times and almost zero visibility. On 12th December the crew took off with the intention of searching for the lost aircraft. They headed towards the Australian Ice Station Mawson. There the Li-2 made an intermediate stop after covering a distance of 1,320 km (820 miles). Continuing the flight was impossible because the weather had become absolutely devilish. The Australians accorded a warm welcome to the Soviet crew, helped to tie the aircraft down (this was a must to stop it from being wrecked by the high winds) and to refuel it.

On the morning of 13th December, having received a satisfactory weather forecast for the route, the crew took off. A strong fair wind imparted greater speed to the aircraft. A decision was taken to make an intermediate landing at the mothballed Japanese Ice Station Showa in order to leave a small supply of Avgas there – it could be needed on the return route, when the Li-2 might be confronted by a stiff headwind. Without delay the Li-2 continued the flight and soon arrived in the area where the Belgian Ice Station 'King Baudouin' was located. Another 1,660 km (1,030 miles) had been covered. The station itself could not be seen, it was all covered by snow. The landing was performed with smoke-pots providing orientation marks. The Belgians rejoiced at the arrival of the Soviet aircraft.

While the Soviet flight engineers got busy preparing the aircraft for the flight, a plan for further actions was being evolved. The Soviet crew was joined by the chief of the Belgian station and a physician on board the aircraft, whereupon the Li-2 took off again and headed deep inside the continent on its search. Having covered a stretch of 150 km (93 miles), the aircraft ran into an obstacle in the shape of heavy cumulus clouds which hid the mountains. Further flight was dangerous and, moreover, useless; the crew had to return to

Top right: A Polar Aviation Li-2 is reassembled on the Antarctic ice after being offloaded from a ship; Li-2V CCCP-H501 (c/n 18430705) stands in the background.

Centre right and right: Li-2T CCCP-H470 is offloaded from the supply ship M/S *Ob'* near Ice Station Mirnyy, Antarctica, in 1956. The aircraft is hooked up to a special T-bar for lifting by means of the ship's crane; the engines are under wraps to protect them from the ocean spray during the voyage to Antarctica.

Above: Li-2V CCCP-H552 is lowered onto the Antarctic ice from M/S *Ob'* before re-assembly; the bulged nacelles are just visible.

Above: Li-2V CCCP-H496 (c/n 18430801) came to grief at Ice Station Mirnyy in February 1958 when it stalled on take-off after becoming airborne prematurely.

CCCP H499 (*sic*; c/n 18430703), one more of the many Polar Aviation Li-2Ts; note that the registration is painted on with a space instead of a hyphen. It was later reregistered CCCP-04208.

King Baudouin. On 14th December the weather was favourable for the search. When approaching Mt. Sphinx at low altitude, the crew noticed a heap of things neatly arranged, but there were no people to be seen… Yet, in the course of a further flight along the mountain ridge the crew managed to notice the red-painted Auster.

A stretch of ice suitable for landing was discovered at a distance of some four kilometres (2.5 miles) from the place where the Belgian aircraft had crash-landed. It took the rescuers two hours to reach the crash site. When they opened the door of the wrecked aircraft, it was empty. From a letter left by the Belgian crew they learned that the crash had occurred on 5th December. On that day two members of the Belgian crew stayed near Mt. Sphinx, two others remained at the crash site waiting for help. On 10th December they grew tired of waiting and went towards the mountain to join their comrades. They had enough food to last until 16th December.

The Soviet crew went on flying and carefully scanning the area as long as the fuel supply lasted. To replenish the fuel, the Li-2 flew to King Baudouin again, whereupon the search was continued without even pausing for a meal. On 15th December the crew of the wrecked Belgian aircraft was finally discovered. In his report to the Chief Administration of the Northern Sea Route Viktor Perov wrote, among other things: 'From the moment of our departure from Mirnyy to the moment when the Belgians were saved we logged 38 hours in the air; of these, 25 hours were spent for the search'. Of course, the report failed to mention how many times within this period Perov's aircraft had suffered icing in the clouds, how often the pedantic navigator Boris Brodkin charting the aircraft's course had cursed the 'approximate' maps of the area; how many times flight engineers Vladimir Sergeyev and Yevgeniy Men'shikov had calculated the remaining amount of fuel in the aircraft's tanks over and over again. Nor did the report contain the strictly rectilinear tracks which were flown by the Li-2 at the hands of Perov and his co-pilot Vladimir Afonin who literally 'ploughed' the air, covering the snow expanse beneath with a network of headings in such a way that not a single square metre of the ice surface should fall out of their field of view.

Shortly after the flight that had ended in the rescuing of Belgian explorers the Soviet Li-2 crew was decorated with orders of the Kingdom of Belgium, and crew captain Viktor Perov was awarded the Order of King Leopold II – the highest award in Belgium.

It also happened that the Arctic pages of the Li-2's history carried the record of unexpectedly pleasant missions that fell to the lot of this aircraft. For example, by the end of

Above: Polar Aviation Li-2T CCCP-04219 in typical green finish, seen here in Antarctica in 1961. Oddly, many Polar Aviation Li-2s did not have high-visibility Polar colours, retaining the Air Force-style green finish with white trim at best. Note the astrodome on top of the flightdeck.

December 1972 the SP-21 research station was drifting at a distance of some 1,000 km (620 miles) from the Soviet mainland. On New Year's eve a Li-2 captained by A. Ya. Yevdokimov performed a special festive flight. After a 9-hour flight in adverse weather the aircraft, which was fitted with skis, landed on the ice floe, bringing New Year presents and letters from family and friends to the Polar researchers. But the main surprise for the polar explorers was a gorgeous Christmas tree which blazed with multi-coloured lights on New Year's Eve amid the icy wilderness.

Unfortunately, as a line from a song goes, 'accidents can happen, and they always do'. Several Polar Aviation Li-2s were lost in the course of Arctic and Antarctic support missions – fortunately with no loss of life. Thus, CCCP-H359 was damaged beyond repair at Ice Station SP-2 on 7th November 1950 when it struck ice hummocks with the port wingtip and crashed while attempting to take off. 7th November was a state holiday in the Soviet Union (the anniversary of the 1917 Revolution), and the reader might imagine that a 'present' of this kind was most unfortunate!

Li-2V CCCP-H502 was lost at Ice Station Mirnyy on 16th February 1958 when it ran off the end of the runway during taxying and sank (quite simply, the pilots had forgotten to unlock the tailskid, rendering the machine uncontrollable). Luckily the crew managed to jump to safety before the aircraft fell in. Another Li-2V, CCCP-H501, was written off in a crash landing in Antarctica – the pilots were so busy with small talk that they forgot to switch a fuel selector to a full tank in time.

Warbirds

The Soviet Li-2 did not become an 'everlasting' aircraft, as distinct from its American progenitor, the DC-3. This was largely due to

Centre and above: Two more aspects of Li-2T CCCP-04219 as the crew shovels snow, trying to clear the runway.

Above: Li-2T CCCP-04219 stands waiting as Soviet Polar researchers take samples of the Antarctic ice with the help of a special drill.

Here, a weather researcher launches a helium-filled balloon rigged with meteorological sensors.

the fact that it was overshadowed by the more popular IL-14 and An-2 aircraft which supplanted it in the niche of not-too-costly piston-engined aircraft. In consequence, in the 1970s/1980s it became difficult to find an airworthy Li-2.

However, a Soviet Air Force Li-2T coded '03 Yellow' (c/n 23441605) was a bit luckier than most of the others. Manufactured in Tashkent in 1952, shortly before the termination of series production, in the course of 20 years this machine was used by the Central Air Club named after Valeriy P. Chkalov (a DOSAAF institution) at Moscow-Tushino as a support aircraft of the Soviet National teams in aircraft, glider and parachute sports. In 1972, after the expiry of its 20-year designated calendar service life, the machine was struck off charge with 6,587 hours 37 minutes' total time and 3,000 cycles since new and five overhauls. For the 20 years that followed, the aircraft languished on the outskirts of Tushino airfield, gradually falling into disrepair.

In March 1992 a group of specialists from the Aviation Enthusiasts' Federation of Russia (FLA RF – *Fede**rah**tsiya lyu**bit**eley avi**ah**tsiï Ros**seey**skoy Fede**rah**tsii*) set to work restoring the Li-2 to airworthy condition. Between November 1992 and December 1993 the work performed on the aircraft was concerned with the systems, interior and exterior finish. The control surfaces were reskinned with new fabric, the aircraft was fitted with zero-lifed engines and reconditioned propellers, a standard set of flight instruments, an autopilot, modern navigation equipment and a modern radio. On 13th November 1992, defying superstition, the restored '03 Yellow' made the first post-restoration flight marking the beginning of its 'second life'. The check-up flight was performed by a crew comprising captain Merited Test Pilot Igor' P. Volk (FLA President), co-pilot Oleg Lyakishev and flight engineer Oleg Matveyev. This was the one and only airworthy Li-2 in Russia or anywhere else at the time.

Later, when the painting job had been completed (the original olive drab colour scheme with light blue undersides and Soviet Air Force insignia on the wings and tail was retained), the aircraft was placed on the FLA register as RA 01300 ФЛА РФ (that is, FLA RF; this prefix – or suffix – was almost invariably applied in Cyrillic). Since then the restored Li-2 became a regular participant of various airshows and demonstration flights – alas, usually bedecked in advertising stickers of various sponsors. (This is one of the downsides of operating a warbird. Sometimes you have a choice of either flying with some hideous ads plastered all over the aircraft or not flying at all!) By May 1994 the registration had been amended to 01300 ФЛА РФ (without the RA- prefix).

Above: The nose of a Li-2 sporting *Polyarnaya aviahtsiya* (Polar aviation) titles and one of the numerous versions of the Polar Aviation logo – a rampant Polar bear.

The Li-2 was demonstrated – both statically and in flight – at air events in Moscow, Lipetsk, Krasnodar, Orsk, Kubinka AB, St. Petersburg, at the MAKS airshows in Zhukovskiy, and at the 'Warbirds' exhibition of World War Two aircraft at Le Bourget. It performed flights in the Netherlands during the festivities dedicated to the 50th anniversary of operations dealing with the dropping of supplies, the landing of assault troops and the liberation of the Netherlands from Nazi occupation. The aircraft took part in the festivities on occasion of the Russian Navy's 300th anniversary in St. Petersburg in July 1996; it performed at an air show in Voronezh.

On 30th September 1998, for the first time in the history of Russian aviation, an FAI commission awarded the Phoenix diploma to the team that had restored the Li-2. The FAI President handed it over to FLA RF representatives during a solemn ceremony at a general conference of the FAI as a sign of international recognition of the legendary Li-2 aircraft's historical value.

On 9th-16th May 1999, 01300 ФЛА РФ made a circuitous flight from St. Petersburg to Moscow via Murmansk, Smolensk, Tula, Volgograd and Novorossiysk; all of these cities had earned glory in the great war. The mission was to deliver to the mayors of these cities an address containing an appeal for halting all wars on our planet. This flight received a blessing from Patriarch of Moscow and of All Russia Alexiy II and was performed with the support from the mayors of Russia's Hero Cities (a title awarded to several cities for their deeds during the Second World War), from Russia's Council of Veterans, the Ministry of Emergency Situations, the CIS Interstate Aviation Committee, the Federal Aviation Service (that was the then-current name of the Russian CAA), Aeroflot and several other organisations. In 2000, with the approval of Russian President Vladimir V. Putin and benediction from the Patriarch of Moscow and of All Russia Alexiy II the Li-2 performed a flight called 'In the footsteps of our fathers'; this flight, devoted to the memory of victims of the Great Patriotic War, followed the ALSIB (Alaska-Siberia) route used in 1942-45 to ferry Lend-Lease aircraft from the USA.

This PS-84 in minimalistic Aeroflot colours carries 'M–62ИР' (M-62IR) titles on the engine nacelles.

Above: СССР-Л4402, most probably a Li-2T, at a Soviet airport.

Waved off by an apron control officer, an Aeroflot Li-2 is about to taxi out for take-off.

Above: At a signal from the apron control officer a freshly arrived Li-2 brakes to a halt after taxying in, the propeller wash kicking up a dust cloud behind it.

Passengers board Li-2P СССР-Л4976 (flag-less, as usual) parked in front of the old control tower at Moscow-Vnukovo. The style of the registration digits on Aeroflot's Li-2's varied widely.

МОСКВА
ЮД - 70 - 79

Left: Li-2 CCCP-Л47…5 (the third digit is not visible because of the open entry door) is loaded with lots of the proverbial good things in small packages from a funny-looking fork lift truck. This aircraft is most probably not a Li-2T, otherwise it would have been more logical to use the wide port side cargo door.

Below left: A Li-2P registered CCCP-Л473… (the last digit may be 0, 6, 8, 9 or even 2) is loaded with mailbags from the truck bed of a GAZ-51A registered YuD-70-79 at Moscow-Vnukovo.

Right: As an airport porter waits, a member of the flight crew of Li-2P CCCP-Л1269 holds up a brown paper bag full of newspapers to check the packing list and make sure that the papers should go on this flight. This method of delivering newspapers from Moscow to other cities was soon abandoned because the slow piston-engined airliners took so long to reach faraway places that the papers were one day old when they got there, and who wants yesterday's news? Instead, print shops were set up in major cities, and print matrices were delivered there by fast IL-28P (IL-20) jet mailplanes so that the papers could be printed there on the day.

Below: Passengers board a Li-2P with the new-style registration CCCP-63902 on the soggy apron of a provincial airport. Note the ladder propped up against the wing.

Above: Li-2T CCCP-51146 has a non-standard circular window above the forward baggage door and may be a survey aircraft of some kind.

Li-2P CCCP-16197 is seen at a dirt airstrip, probably in the foothills of the Caucasus. Note the sister aircraft taking off in the background.

Above: Li-2P CCCP-06134 No.1, an industry-operated aircraft, is seen a few seconds before touchdown. The registration was later re-used for a Mi-8T helicopter.

CCCP-63888, a typical Aeroflot Li-2P.

Above: A worthy tribute to a legendary aircraft. This Li-2 was preserved at Cherskiy airport, Yakutian Autonomous SSR. The rally, however, is not on occasion of the monument being opened (by then it had been there for quite a while) but to commemorate the crossing of the North Pole by a team of Soviet sportsmen.

'Jingle bells, jingle bells'?! Here we have quite a curious scene with a Li-2P having its tanks topped up by a TZ-51A refuelling bowser based on the GAZ-51A... and the famous 'one-horse open sleigh' standing by as an airport taxi! Note the An-2 biplane in the background.

Above: The end of the road. Li-2T CCCP-13383 (c/n 23444209) operated by the Flight Research Institute sits derelict with shattered windows and a hole in the starboard elevator's skin.

Above: The stripped-out hulks of two Aeroflot Li-2s await disposal. Actually the way the detached outer wing panel is packed for shipping suggests that one of the aircraft is moving to a different location – possibly for preservation.

After sitting for 20 years at Moscow-Tushino and falling into dereliction, Li-2T '03 Yellow' (c/n 23441605) became a major restoration project in 1992. Here the aircraft is seen on 20th March 1993; all control surfaces have already been reskinned with new fabric. These were the days you could walk freely at Tushino...

Above: The forward fuselage of Li-2T '03 Yellow' (c/n 23441605) was adorned with a modern blade aerial and an anti-collision beacon aft of it. Note the camouflaged Yak-18T lightplane (RA ФЛА РФ 01112) bearing the signature of the then Vice-President of Russia Aleksandr V. Rutskoy on the cabin door.

Above: The handwritten placard on the tail of the Li-2 at Tushino bears the touching inscription: *Samolyot pros'ba ne lomat'* ('PLEASE do not damage the aircraft')!

The finished result. Bearing ads for Global Edge, Singer sewing machines and Dobrolyot (a Russian cargo airline), Li-2T 01300 ФЛА РФ is seen here in the static park of the MAKS-97 airshow at Zhukovskiy.

Sadly, this remarkable aircraft (re-registered RA-1300K in 2001 in conformity with the current standard for privately owned or home-built aircraft) was lost in an accident ten years after it had been restored. On 26th June 2004 it suffered engine trouble shortly after take-off from Myachkovo airfield near Moscow on a positioning flight to Kaluga-Grabtsevo. (Myachkovo is the seat of several air clubs and the home base for many FLA aircraft.) The machine crashed just 2.5 km (1.5 miles) from the airfield boundary, demolishing the roof of a country house in the village of Zaozyor'ye situated next to the airfield. Fortunately, there were no victims among the inhabitants of the house; there was no explosion and no fire, albeit the fuel from the aircraft was spilled over an area of 60 m^2 (645 sq ft). Of the five persons aboard, three were killed outright. These were crew captain Oleg Lyakishev (Vice-President of the Aviation Enthusiasts' Federation of Russia), co-pilot Valentin Chuykin and flight engineer Oleg Matveyev. A further two persons were hospitalised with heavy injuries (some reports mention also Yevgeniy Voloboyev, possibly navigator, among those killed in the crash). Oleg Lyakishev lost his life together with the aircraft of which he was immensely proud; he got no chance to put into effect his plans for making a round-the-world trip in this veteran aircraft.

The only consolation for warbird enthusiasts is that currently there is an airworthy Li-2 on the airshow circuit – the immaculately restored Li-2P HA-LIX (c/n 18433209) owned by the Gold Timer Foundation and based in Hungary.

Chapter 7

The Li-2 Abroad

In the post-war years the Soviet Union began deliveries of the Li-2 to foreign customers. Only Tashkent-built examples were exported; the type saw service with the airlines and air arms of ten nations – mostly Warsaw Pact members.

Bulgaria

The first two Li-2s were reportedly delivered to Bulgaria in September and October 1946; one of them was registered LZ-LIA. Apparently these aircraft were operated by the **Bulgarian government**.

Civil Li-2 operations in Bulgaria began in 1948 when **TABSO – Bulgarian Air Transport** (the acronym means *Trahnsportno aviatsionno bolgaro-sovetsko obschchestvo* – Bulgarian-Soviet Aviation Transport Co.) was established as a joint venture. Unfortunately little is known about the type's career with TABSO, but the airline took delivery of at least eleven Li-2s. Known examples were LZ-TUA, -TUB, -TUC, -TUD, -TUE, -TUF, -TUG, -TUH, -TUM, -TUO and -TUQ, and some of the intervening registrations may also have been used by Li-2s. Additionally, Li-2 LZ-LIO was also reported for TABSO, though in reality it was probably a government or Air Force aircraft.

It may be mentioned that much later, when TABSO had been renamed Balkan Bulgarian Airlines (this took place on 1st April 1968), the registrations of TABSO's long-gone Li-2s were re-used for civil and quasi-civil Tupolev Tu-134s of various versions.

The **Bulgarian Air Force** (BVVS – *Bolgarski voyenno vozdooshni seeli*) reportedly operated 12 Li-2 transports as late as 1969, and a few were still active in 1972; no serials are known. The aircraft served alongside the more advanced IL-14T transports.

China (People's Republic of China)

China was a major operator of the Li-2, some 100 being delivered in all. The first Li-2T transport arrived on 13th September 1949; this and a further aircraft delivered in October were followed in 1950 by six UchShLi-2 trainers and a further four Li-2Ts and Li-2Ps in 1951.

The first Li-2 operator in China was the **Sino-Soviet Civil Aviation Society** established in 1950 (known in Russian as **SKOGA** – *Sovet-sko-kitayskoye obshchestvo grazhdahnskoy aviahtsii*).

In March 1954 SKOGA merged with the China National Airways Cpn. (CNAC) to form the **Civil Aviation Administration of China** (CAAC). The latter operated 29 Li-2s with simple three-digit registration numbers running sequentially from 301 through 329 (the B-nationality prefix introduced in 1972 was never applied to these aircraft). The examples registered 301, 311 No.1 (c/n 18433701), 312, 315 (the very first example delivered) and 323 are confirmed as being Li-2Ts. (There is a further Li-2 wearing the registration 311 (c/n 18439703) in the PLAAF Museum in Changping, but the registration may be fake.)

The CAAC's Li-2s operated from Xian, Chengdu and Taiyuan, among other things. The type's career with CAAC proved to be exceptionally long – some examples, including 325 and 327, remained active until the mid-1980s! When the Li-2 was finally ousted by the IL-14 and the even more advanced An-24 turboprop airliner on CAAC's local services, most *Cabs* were broken up, although two examples (301 and 305) survived as ground instructional airframes at the airline's technical school in Tianjin.

The **People's Liberation Army Air Force** (PLAAF, or *Chung-kuo Shen Min Taie-Fang-Tsun Pu-tai*) reportedly had some 100 Li-2s delivered before 1965. 30 of these were reportedly still active in 1997. Known serials are '3018', '3019', '3028', '3029', '3049', '5011', '5021', '5031', '5070', '38043' and '38046'.

Above: LZ-TUD and LZ-TUE, two of the Li-2Ps operated by the Bulgarian-Soviet airline TABSO.

'327' (c/n 18440509), one of 29 Li-2s operated by CAAC, was a Li-2F photo survey aircraft.

Above: Smartly-painted Czechoslovak Air Force Li-2P 'Salon' '2108 Black' retained the colour scheme it wore when it served with the Czechoslovak government flight as OK-BYO.

The **People's Liberation Army Naval Air Force** (PLANAF) also had an unspecified number of Cabs delivered before 1960. Nine reportedly remained airworthy by 1997; no serials are known.

Cuba

Six Li-2s were delivered to **Empresa Consolidada Cubana de Aviación**, commonly known simply as Cubana. No details are known.

Czechoslovakia

The nation's flag carrier **ČSA Československé Aerolinie** (Czechoslovak Airlines), one of Europe's oldest air carriers, took delivery of eight late-production Li-2Ps (OK-GAA through -GAH) in 1952. OK-GAA was leased from the Czechoslovak Air Force until 1953 while the others were delivered directly. In Czechoslovakia the Li-2 bore the nickname *ličko* (pronounced '***lich**ko*').

Civil Li-2 operations in Czechoslovakia turned out to be rather brief; in 1956 the seven remaining aircraft were withdrawn from use and then transferred to the Czechoslovak Air Force in early 1957.

The **Czechoslovak Air Force** (CzAF, or ČVL – *Československé Vojenské Létectvo*) likewise introduced the Li-2 in 1952, operating a total of 19. The first ones, which were delivered directly, bore the alphanumeric serials D-29 through D-38 (the latter serial was used twice) under the system in use at the time; the letter was a code denoting the squadron to which the aircraft belonged. A different system was introduced in mid-1957, with four-digit serials matching the last four of the aircraft's c/n; the existing aircraft were reserialled and the ones transferred from ČSA received the new-style serials from the start. The new serials were '1801', '2105' through '2109', '2209', '2210', '2304', '2305', '2407', '2501', '2703', '2708', '2710', '2804', '2891', '2901' and '3002'.

Several versions were operated. Thus, D-29 (later '2105'), D-38 No.2 ('3002'), '2210' and '2501' were Li-2Ps; the ones serialled D-30 ('2106'), D-33 ('2107'), D-34 ('2109') and D-37 ('2108') were Li-2T transports; '1801', '2209' and '2804' were Li-2F photo survey aircraft, while D-35 ('2891', c/n 23442801), D-36 ('2901') and '2710' were Li-2D troopships. The other aircraft remain unidentified.

In the mid/late-1960s the CzAF phased out the Li-2, replacing it with the IL-14 and its licence-built version, the Avia 14. Li-2F '1801' was preserved near Prague-Ruzyne airport in ČSA colours with the fake registration OK-1962, becoming a bar, but was eventually consigned for fire rescue training and destroyed. Li-2P '2105 Black' had a happier fate: painted in fake Soviet Air Force markings as '20 Yellow', in 1969 it became an exhibit of the Slovak National Uprising Museum in Banská Bystrica, commemorating the Li-2's contribution to the liberation of Czechoslovakia from Nazi occupation in 1944. The colour scheme represents another Li-2 which actually took part in the shuttle flights during the uprising, carrying Slovak partisans. Two more Cabs were preserved elsewhere in Slovakia, and a further two ('2710' and '3002') reside in the Military Museum at Prague-Kbely.

The **Czech Federal Government Flight** (LOMV – *Letecký oddíl ministerstva vnitra*; also called LS FMV – *Letecká společnosť federalního ministerstva vnitra,* Airline of the Federal Ministry of the Interior) operated four Cabs. One of them (OK-BYP) was a Li-2T; OK-BYO and -BYQ were VIP-configured Li-2Ps, while the exact version of OK-BYA is unknown. (All of the LOMV's fixed-wing aircraft were registered in the BYx block; the B did not denote the year of registration but stood for [*Veřejná*] *bezpečnosť* – 'public security', that is, police.) The aircraft wore a natural metal finish with a deep blue cheatline.

LOMV withdrew the Li-2 when the IL-14S VIP aircraft became available. OK-BYO and -BYP had been leased from the CzAF in 1953, and to it they subsequently returned as '2105 Black' and '2108 Black' respectively.

Hungary

Hungary was one of the major export customers for the Li-2. The first of the type's Hungarian operators was the **Maszovlet** airline (*Magyar-Szovjet Polgari Légikforgalmi Tarsasag* – Hungarian-Soviet Air Transport Society) established in 1946 as the successor of the pre-war Malért. The 12 Li-2Ps delivered to Maszovlet were appropriately registered HA-LIA to HA-LII and HA-LIK to HA-LIM.

The airline's first services were flown by a Li-2 from Budapest-Budaörs to Debrecen and Szombathely on 15th October 1946. At first Maszovlet served only domestic destinations; on 19th June 1947 a new page was opened when a Li-2 performed the airline's first international service from Budapest to Prague.

Unfortunately Maszovlet's operations were not accident-free. HA-LIK crashed fatally on 19th September 1949 due to ATC error; HA-LIL was damaged beyond repair on 2nd October 1952.

The Li-2Ps of Malév, including HA-LIQ, largely retained the livery of the airline's precursor Maszovlet.

In 1954 Maszovlet was wound up and a new, entirely Hungarian airline – **Malév Hungarian Airlines** (*Magyar Légiközlekedesi Vallalat* – Hungarian Air Transport Co.) – established instead, taking over all the assets of Maszovlet on 1st October. Malév's fleet of Cabs was more than doubled in 1956 when 13 examples were transferred from the Hungarian Air Force (which see); continuing the existing series, they were registered HA-LIN through HA-LIZ. With the exception of HA-LIN, -LIO and -LIP, which were Li-2Ps, the 'new' aircraft were all Li-2T transports. Thus the number of Li-2s that had seen commercial service in Hungary reached 25.

Most of the aircraft bore Hungarian personal names which matched the last letter of the registration. These were HA-LIA *Aladár*, HA-LIB *Béla*, HA-LIC *Cecil*, HA-LID *Dénes*, HA-LIE *Elemér*, HA-LIF *Ferenc*, HA-LIG *Géza*, HA-LIH *Helén*, HA-LII *Ilona*, HA-LIM *Mária*, HA-LIN *Nándor*, HA-LIO *Olga*, HA-LIP *Péter*, HA-LIR *Robert*, HA-LIS *Sándor* (= Alexander), HA-LIT *Tamás* (= Thomas), HA-LIU *Ubul*, HA-LIV *Vilmos*, HA-LIW *Waldemár* and HA-LIZ *Zoltán*.

Attrition continued after the change of ownership. On 23rd December 1954 Malév lost two more of its original Li-2s; unbelievably, the two aircraft (HA-LIF and HA-LII) crash-landed at different locations but for the same reason – due to heavy icing. Two and a half years later, HA-LIM was damaged beyond repair on 9th June 1957.

Malév phased out the Li-2 in 1963. Of the 13 ex-military aircraft, four (HA-LIP, -LIQ, -LIU and -LIX) returned to the Air Force in 1964, regaining their former identities as '504', '206', '306' and '209' respectively. Furthermore, HA-LIY was transferred to the Hungarian Defence Association (the local equivalent of DOSAAF). The others were either preserved at various locations around the country (sometimes as eateries) or ignominiously burned for fire practice.

The Hungarian Air Force (MHRC – *Magyar Honvedseg Repülö Csapatai*) operated 19 Li-2s (14 Li-2Ts and five Li-2Ps used as VIP transports) since September 1949. The first four 'Ts were allocated the serials S101 through S104 but never wore them, receiving three-digit serials matching the last three of the c/n. The Li-2Ts were serialled '109' (ex-S101), '201' (ex-S102), '203' (ex-S103), '206', '209' No.1 (ex-S104, c/n 18433209), '209' No.2 (c/n 23441209), '210', '301', '303', '306' No.2 (c/n 18439306), '307', '310', '901' and '902'. Most were regular transports, but '203' was a navigator trainer – either an UchShLi-2 or a locally modified equivalent. The Li-2Ps were '306' No.1 (c/n 18436306), '503', '504', '505' and '803'.

In 1952 the Air Force lost two *Cabs* in accidents: Li-2T '210' crashed on 22nd August, and Li-2P '306' was wrecked on 12th December same year. However, the great devastation came in 1956. In late October an anti-Communist uprising started in Hungary; it was soon quashed by Warsaw Pact troops sent to restore 'revolutionary order'. In the aftermath of the rebellion the Soviet Union imposed strict limits on the amount of military hardware which Hungary was allowed to have, and in compliance with Soviet orders 13 of the surviving 17 Li-2s were transferred to Malév Hungarian Airlines. The aircraft serialled '203', '206', '209' No.1, '209' No.2, '301', '303', '306' No.2, '307', '310', '504', '505', '803' and '901' became HA-LIY, -LIQ, -LIX, -LIZ, -LIS, -LIR, -LIU, -LIW, -LIV, -LIP, -LIO, -LIN and -LIT respectively. Only in 1964 did a few of them return to military service because Malév did not want them anyway. Two Air Force examples were handed over to the Hungarian police, which used them for anti-terrorist commando training.

The **Hungarian Defence Association** received ex-Malév Li-2T HA-LIY in 1964. After conversion for photo survey duties the aircraft served on in this role until 1971 when it was finally retired.

Li-2T '209' No.1, which was retired in 1974, had a happier fate than most of its Hungarian sister ships. After a period of preservation at Szolnok it was acquired by the **Gold Timer Foundation** in 1997 and painstakingly restored to airworthy condition at Budapest-Budaörs

The aircraft made its first post-restoration flight on 21st September 2001 with the same registration HA-LIX it had worn during its years of airline service. Now it is painted in an attractive publicity scheme with Sunflower titles (the name of the restoration project's main sponsor). Inevitably some items (such as the passenger seats) are non-authentic.

A rare view of three North Korean Li-2s. The nearest and farthest ones are in the livery of the airline CAAK.

North Korea

The North Korean national airline **Chosonminhang** (Civil Aviation Administration of Korea – CAAK) operated two Li-2s registered 501 and 504. The aircraft were still operational in 1983 (in those days North Korean civil aircraft did not yet carry the P- country prefix). However, virtually all of North Korea's aviation is of a near-military (or very military) nature and some of the aircraft nominally owned by Chosonminhang (now renamed Air Koryo) are in fact operated by the **North Korean Air Force**, which had at least one camouflaged example.

Poland

Poland was the first foreign operator of the Li-2, affectionately known locally as *litka*. The type's Polish history began in August 1944, immediately after the liberation of Poland from the German troops. At that point the Soviet Union assigned the 2nd Independent Staff Squadron equipped with three Li-2s and six Polikarpov Po-2 liaison biplanes to the Command of the Polish Armed Forces (*Wojsko Polskie*). Although operated in the interests of the Poles, the unit was completely manned by Soviet personnel.

In early March 1945 the **Polish Air Force** (PWL – *Polskie Wojsko Lotnicze*) got the first Li-2 units of its own. The 6th Independent Special Mission Air Transport Squadron (6. *Samodzielna Lotnicza Eskadra Transportowa Specjalnego Przeznaczenia*) was established at Okęcie airfield near Warsaw (now the city's airport), making domestic and international flights in the interests of the Provisional Government and the top command of the Polish Armed Forces. It was equipped with five Li-2s and five C-47s. The co-located 7th Independent Air Transport Squadron (7. *Samodzielna Eskadra Lotnictwa Transportowego*) activated a month later was tasked with domestic communications flights, operating nine Li-2s. This unit was disbanded in December 1945, its aircraft being transferred to the civil register as a first step towards the revival of LOT Polish Airlines. This temporarily left the PWL with just four Li-2s.

During the war the Polish Li-2s were armed and wore Soviet insignia. After the end of the hostilities in Europe the armament was removed. On 14th July 1945 the Soviet red stars were replaced with the Polish *szachownicy* ('chequerboard') insignia. The following day the Polish Li-2s made a symbolic flypast over the fields of Grunwald to mark the 535th anniversary of a historic battle which had taken place there in 1410.

In 1947 the Officers' Flying School in Dęblin (OSL – *Oficerska Szkoła Lotnicza*) received three Li-2s, which allowed it to begin training Polish flight and ground crews for the type. Little by little the Soviet airmen flying the PWL Li-2s were replaced by Polish ones.

The PWL had a penchant for recoding its Li-2s from time to time; besides, the history of some ex-LOT Li-2Ts after their return to the Polish Air Force is unknown. Therefore no fleet details are given here.

Polish Air Force Li-2s fulfilled a multitude of tasks. Their first missions flown in the wartime days included delivery of spares for combat aircraft to airfields close to the front lines – a support practice that continued in the peacetime years. In April-July 1947 a Li-2 was used to support a military operation undertaken to wipe out the UPA guerrillas which were still wreaking havoc in the eastern regions of Poland. These were remnants of the so-called Ukrainian Insurgent Army (UPA – *Ookra**in**skaya pov**stahn**cheskaya **ar**miya*), an ultra-nationalist outfit led by Stepan Bandera which had Nazi affiliations and was known for its atrocities against Polish civilians. Later, PWL Li-2s were much used for paradropping commandos of the Polish Armed Force' 6th Airborne Division (known as the Red Berets).

Relief flights during natural disasters were an important aspect of the Polish military Li-2s' activities. For example, in the spring of 1947 the aircraft of the 6th Squadron and OSL delivered emergency supplies to the victims of a major flood, paradropping foodstuffs in special bags from an altitude of 500 m (1,640 ft) and dropping cattle fodder. Within two days (27th-28th March) the Li-2s delivered 5 tons (11,020 lb) of food and 4 tons (8,820 lb) of cattle fodder to areas cut off from regular supply routes by the rising water.

Several PWL Li-2s were converted for photo survey duties. Additionally, in 1947 OSL developed a navigator trainer version of the Li-2, followed in 1949 by a bomb-aimer training version.

The Li-2's military career in Poland lasted more than 20 years. Though the type was progressively replaced by the IL-14, three Li-2s were still operational in late 1973. The final aircraft, '027 White' (c/n 18439102), flew its last operational sortie on 5th February 1975 and was preserved at the Aerospace Museum in Kraków.

Starting in December 1945, **LOT Polish Airlines** (*Polskie Linie Lotnicze LOT*; 'lot' is the Polish word for 'flight') operated a total of 39 Li-2Ps and Li-2Ts (the latter were ex-PWL machines). Deliveries took place in several batches. The first 30 aircraft delivered in 1945-47 were registered SP-LAA through -LAH, SP-LAJ through -LAP, SP-LAR through -LAW and SP-LBA through -LBK. Later, in 1951-53, nine more aircraft registered SP-LKA through -LKI were delivered; additionally, Li-2T SP-LDA was briefly operated on lease from the PWL. Many of the aircraft had proper names: SP-LAA *Alina*, SP-LAB *Baska*, SP-LAC *Celina*, SP-LAD *Duska*, SP-LAE *Elka*, SP-LAF *Fela,* SP-LAG *Gabrysia*, SP-LAH *Hela*, SP-LAJ *Jasiek*, SP-LAK *Krysia*, SP-LAL *Lucynka*, SP-LAM *Maciek*, SP-LAN *Nelli*, SP-LAO *Olenka*, SP-LAP *Piotrus*, SP-LAR *Rena*, SP-LAS *Stasiek*, SP-LAT *Tomek*, SP-LAU *Urszulka*, SP-LAW *Wójciech*, SP-LBA *Antos*, SP-LKE *Ewa* and so on.

Some of the Li-2s had been built in the wartime years and lacked wing de-icers. Such machines were upgraded locally with a hot air de-icing system; concurrently an extra cabin window was added on each side and an extra row of seats installed, increasing the seating capacity to 24.

LOT lost several Li-2s in accidents. Thus, Li-2T SP-LBG was struck off charge after an accident on 16th December 1963; SP-LAH crashed on 19th March 1954 and SP-LAL on 15th August 1960, to name but three. SP-LAA had a narrow escape one day when she was directed by a negligent controller to land in such a way that the aircraft nearly ploughed through a parking area thick with CSS-13 (Polikarpov Po-2) utility aircraft. The pilots discovered the danger at the last moment and barely managed to make a go-around.

In addition to passenger and cargo carriage, LOT utilised the *litka* for a variety of other tasks. Three high-time Li-2Ps (SP-LAA, -LAB and -LAD) were converted into crop-dusters and used in 1952-54 for fighting pests

Above: Li-2P SP-LKE was used as a navaids calibration aircraft by the Polish CAA

Polish Air Force Li-2T '029 White' (c/n 23442701) was the last operational Li-2 in Poland.

in Opole province. SP-LAC was converted into a photo-survey aircraft by LOT's maintenance department in 1952.

LOT retired the Li-2 in 1969. Later, the registrations SP-LAA through -LAG and SP-LBA through -LBH were re-used for the airline's IL-62 and IL-62M long-haul turbofan airliners.

On 1st June 1963 Li-2P SP-LKE was transferred to **the Polish CAA** (ZRLiLK – *Zarząd Ruchu Lotniczego i Lotnisk Komunikacyjnych*) for use as a navaids calibration aircraft. The Cab served on in this capacity until 1970 when it was replaced by IL-14P SP-LNG. This was the final civil Li-2 to remain operational in Poland.

Romania

In common with most of the other Soviet Bloc nations, Romania's post-war civil aviation started as a joint venture with the Soviet Union. In July 1946 the airline **TARS** (*Transporturi Aeriene Româna-Sovietica* – Romanian-Soviet Air Transport) received the first of an eventual 26 Li-2Ps. The aircraft were registered YR-DAB, YR-DAC, YR-TAA through -TAP, YR-TAR through -TAT, YR-TAV through -TAX and YR-TAZ; the registrations YR-TAE and YR-TAO were used twice. It should be noted that YR-TAC, -TAE No.1, -TAH, -TAJ and -TAO No.1 were extremely short-lived, the aircraft being sold to Maszovlet in 1946 (the year they were delivered) as HA-LIA, -LIB, -LIC, -LID and -LIE respectively.

The aircraft saw service on domestic and international services alike. Over the years TARS lost three Li-2s in crashes: YR-TAA on 15th November 1950, YR-TAI on 21st November 1947 and YR-TAV on 13th August 1947.

In 1954 TARS ceased to exist and the aircraft were transferred to the new Romanian flag carrier **TAROM** (*Transporturile Aeriene Române* – Romanian Air Transport). The latter continued operating the type, gradually replacing it with the IL-14P and IL-14M. As they were displaced from first-line service, the aircraft found other uses; thus, YR-TAM was converted to a geological survey aircraft in 1963.

Two aircraft (YR-DAC and YR-TAN) crashed on 13th June 1964 and 11th August 1966 respectively. YR-TAS was transferred to the Agricultural High School in 1968. Between 1960 and 1968 eight of TAROM's Cabs were transferred to the Romanian Air Force. The airline retired its last Li-2 in 1970.

The **Romanian government flight** operated two VIP-configured Li-2Ps registered YR-PCB and YR-PCD (the PC stood for *Partia Comunista*). In 1954 both aircraft were transferred to the Romanian Air Force as '807' and '805' respectively.

'4506 Black' (c/n 23444506), a Romanian Air Force Li-2.

Two more civil-registered Li-2s, YR-MIG and YR MIR, were operated by government agencies until 1976; the former aircraft was operated for TAROM.

The **Romanian Air Force** (*Fortele Aeriene ale Republicii Socialiște Române*) operated at least 18 Li-2s, many of which were ex-airline aircraft. The Cabs were serialled '008'*, '102', '502'* (ex-YR-TAL), '505'* (ex-YR-TAP), '607', '702', '802'* (ex-YR-TAO No.2), '804'* (ex-YR-TAZ), '805'* (ex-YR-PCD), '807'* (ex-YR-PCB), '905'* (ex-YR-TAE), 1001* through '1004'*, '4506'* (ex-YR-TAW), '8002'* (ex-YR-TAG) and '8004'* (ex-YR-TAK). Aircraft marked * are Li-2Ps; '702' is confirmed as a Li-2T.

Yugoslavia

Twelve Li-2Ps registered YU-BAA through -BAJ, -BAP and -BAR were operated by the **JUSTA** joint-stock airline (*Jugoslovenska-Sovjet Transportna Aviacija*), the forerunner of JAT Yugoslav Airlines, since 1947. WIth the exception of one aircraft, which crashed on 27th November 1947, all of them were returned to the Soviet Union as early as September 1949. Incidentally, the crashed aircraft was registered YU-BAD and carried the fleet number 13 on its tail! Two wrongs don't make a right, as you see.

At least four other Li-2s serialled '7011', '7103', '7317' and '7318' saw service with the **Yugoslav Air Force** (JRV – *Jugoslovensko Ratno Vazduhoplovstvo*). The first of these aircraft was converted to the so-called Li-3 by retrofitting Pratt & Whitney R-1830 engines and American propellers.

Vietnam

The **North Vietnamese Air Force** (NVAF) operated an unknown number of Li-2s; only one aircraft – an apparently ex-Chinese machine serialled 198 – has been identified so far.

Yugoslav Air Force '011 Black' preserved in Belgrade id the so-called 'Li-3' – a Li-2T with P&W R-1830s.

The second prototype PS-84-K transport

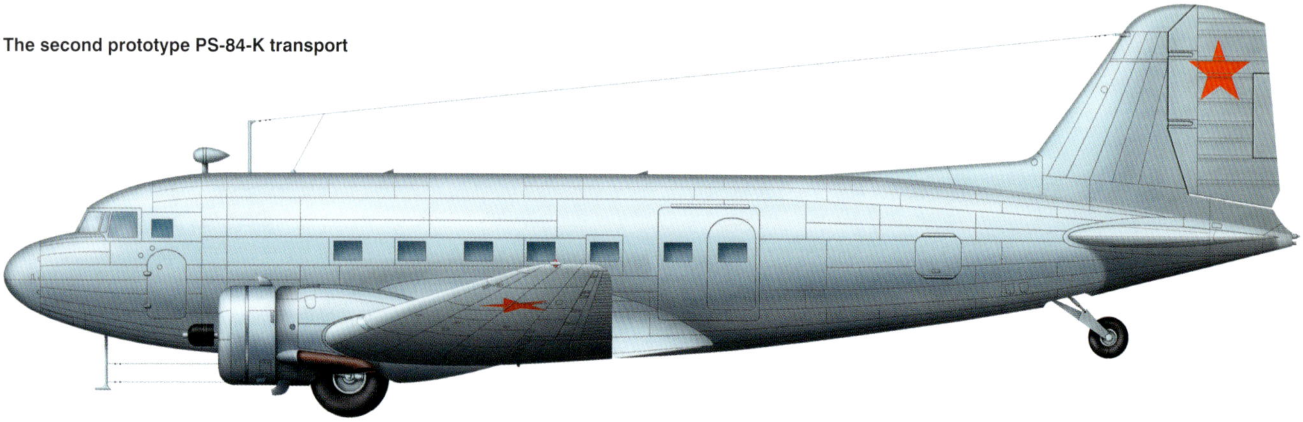

A PS-84 of the Special Northern Air Group operating into Leningrad from Khvoynoye airfield, October 1941

A Li-2NB of the 62nd Long-Range Bomber Division

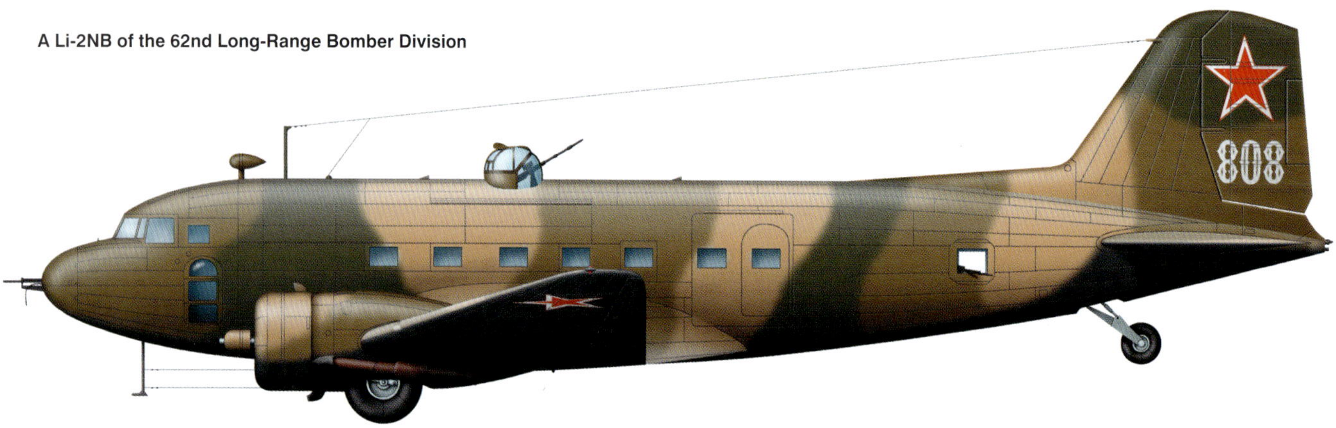

A Li-2 of the Black Sea Fleet Air Arm operating near Melitopol', the Ukraine, in 1943

A Li-2 bomber operated in May 1944

A Li-2T operated on the Far Eastern TO. Mukden, Manchuria, August 1945

A 1st Guards Long-Range Bomber Regiment/1st Squadron Li-2 captained by Deputy Squadron Commander Capt. M. V. Levin. Leningrad Front, 1944

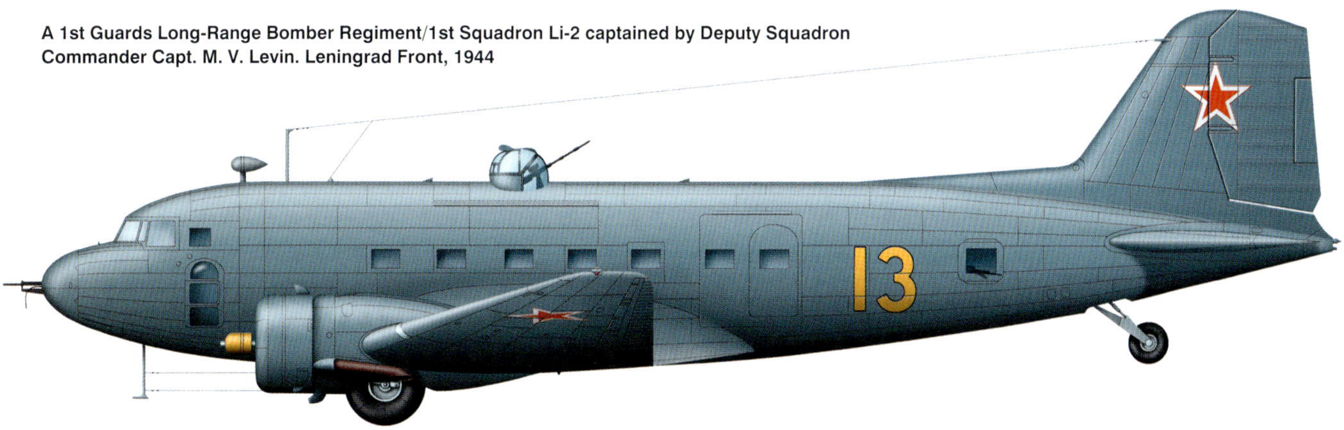

A Li-2T operated in 1946

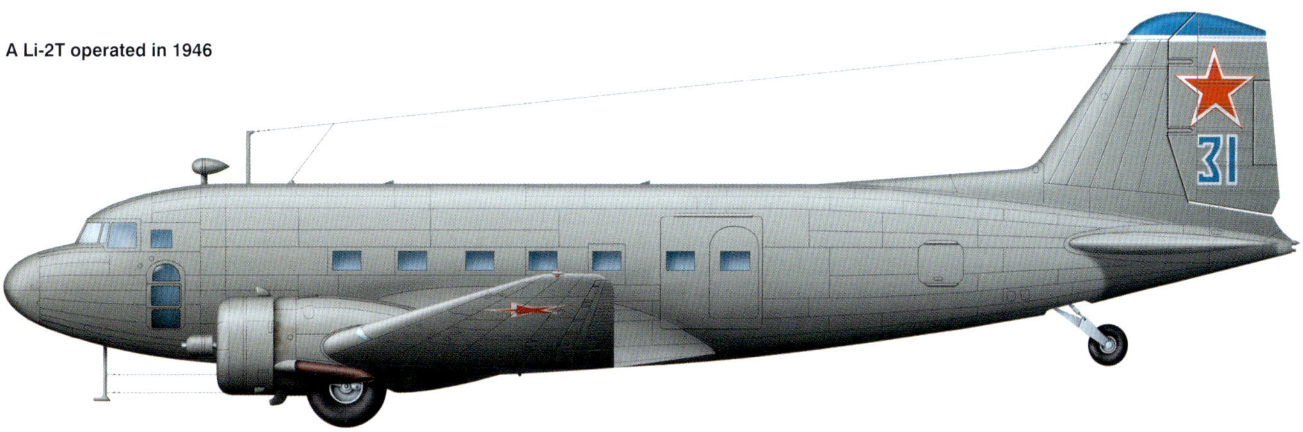

CCCP-H328 (SSSR-N328), an Aviaarktika (Polar Aviation) PS-84 with non-retractable skis

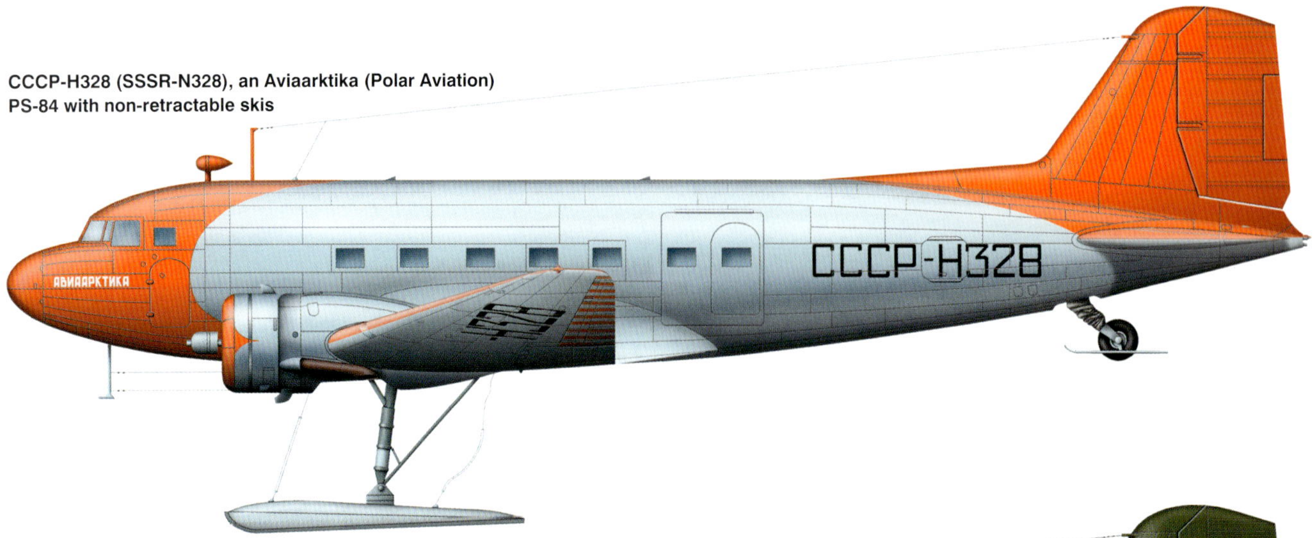

A North Korean Air Force Li-2T (1950)

This Polish Li-2T was the last Li-2 to fly in Poland (1974)

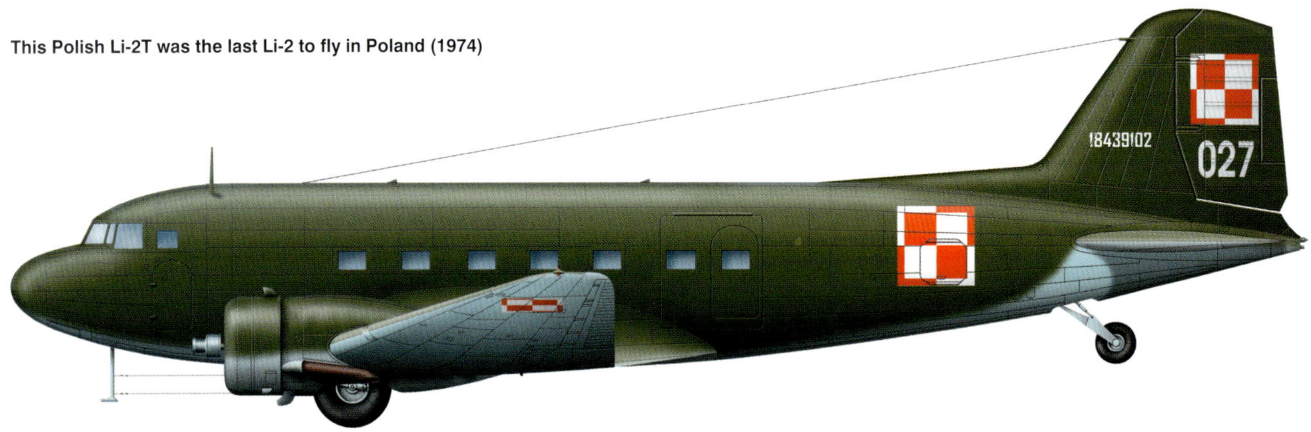

Li-2T CCCP-63885 operated by the Yakutian Civil Aviation Directorate/Salekhard United Air Detachment in 1964

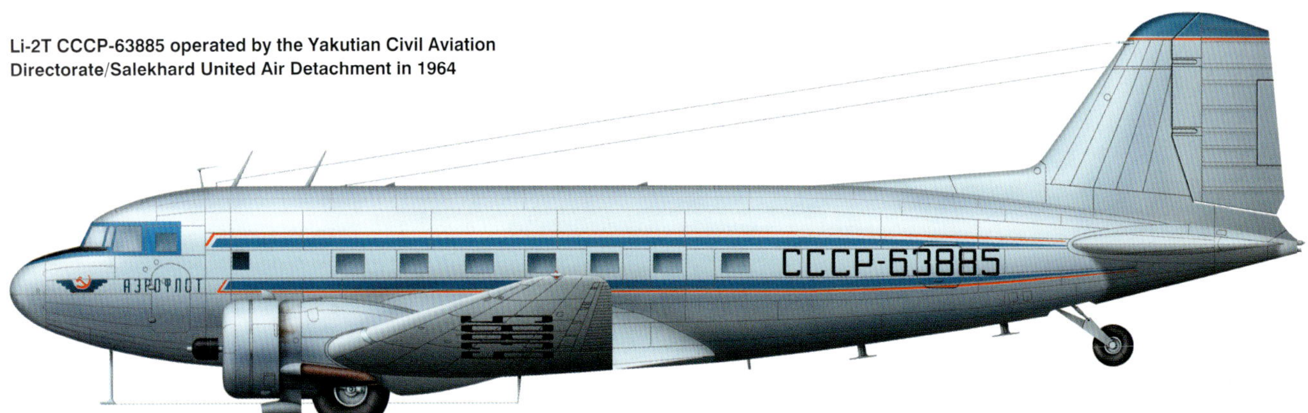

Above: A Soviet Air Force Li-2T coded '08 Yellow' (c/n 23443408). Note the white-painted rudder trim tab.

This Li-2T ('55 Yellow', c/n 23440706) adorned with the Guards badge and emblazoned *Za Rodinu!* (For Motherland!) is in the base museum of the Russian Air Force's 610th Combat & Conversion Training Centre, Ivonovo-Severnyy AB.

Above and below: This Li-2T resides in the Great Patriotic War Museum in Minsk, Belorussia.

Above and below: Li-2T CCCP-93914 No.1 (c/n 23440808), an MAP aircraft, was one of the exhibits at the Central Russian Air Force Museum in Monino south of Moscow. The registration later passed to an Antonov An-26.

Above: Li-2T RA 01300 ФЛА РФ (c/n 23441605) during the 'open house' at Kubinka AB on 29th May 1993. Note the Icarus badge on the nose and the 'Vnukovo, ARZ No.400 GA' (Civil Aviation Aircraft Repair Plant No.400) titles near the entry door.

The same aircraft at the MAKS-1997 airshow in company with IL-14P 02299 ФЛА РФ. The Li-2 is now registered 01300 ФЛА РФ (without the RA prefix) and bedecked in sponsors' logos.

Above and below: Li-2T 01300 ФЛА РФ at Moscow/Sheremet'yevo-1 in its penultimate colour scheme with large *Miru-Da!* (Yes to Peace!) titles.

At Sheremet'yevo, the Li-2 was parked on the grass. During airshows the crew also tried to operate from the grass if at all possible in order to ease the wear and tear on the tyres.

Above: Decline and fall. Li-2T '305' (c/n 18440206) in Civil Aviation Administration of China livery sits at the Tianjin Technical School beside an IL-12 and a Y-5 (licence-built An-2), all of them looking very decrepit. The IL-18 on the left is a bit better off.

'315' (c/n 18433101), a Li-2F photo survey aircraft operated by CAAC. The protective door of the camera port is barely discernible aft of the wings.

Above: Li-2 '311' is preserved at the People's Liberation Army Air Force Museum at Datang Shan AB, Changping, but the registration is a fake; this is not Li-2P c/n 18433707 but very probably an ex-PLAAF Li-2T (c/n 18439703)!

The Mystery Aircraft of North Korea. This North Korean Air Force Li-2 has an unidentified ventral appendage shaped like a cylinder and an observation blister to starboard, suggesting it is some sort of testbed or survey aircraft.

Above: Shown here in March 2000, this Li-2T in false Soviet Air Force markings is on display at the Great Patriotic War Museum at Poklonnaya Gora in Moscow. Earlier it was on show in an olive drab scheme as '01 Yellow'. In reality it is ex-CCCP-48986 (c/n 18438101).

This Li-2T in old-style Hungarian Air Force insignia is preserved in a park in Kecel, Hungary. The interior is accessible to visitors.

Above: The immaculately restored Li-2P HA-LIX (c/n 18433209) is now the sole airworthy Li-2 in the world. The Sunflower titles are those of the main sponsor.

One more view of HA-LIX in the static park at the ILA-2004 airshow at Berlin-Schönefeld.

We hope you enjoyed this book . . .

Midland Publishing titles are edited and designed by an experienced and enthusiastic team of specialists.

We always welcome ideas from authors or readers for books they would like to see published.

In addition, our associate, Midland Counties Publications, offers an exceptionally wide range of aviation, military, naval and transport books and videos for sale by mail-order worldwide.

For a copy of the appropriate catalogue, or to order further copies of this book, and any other Midland Publishing titles, please write, telephone, fax or e-mail to:

Midland Counties Publications
4 Watling Drive, Hinckley,
Leics, LE10 3EY, England
Tel: (+44) 01455 254 450
Fax: (+44) 01455 233 737
E-mail: midlandbooks@compuserve.com
www.midlandcountiessuperstore.com

US distribution by Specialty Press – see page 2.

Earlier titles in the series:

Vols 1 to 10 are still available
Vol.11: Myasishchev M-4 & 3M
Vol.12: Antonov's Turboprop Twins
Vol.13: Mikoyan's Piston-Engined Fighters
Vol.14: Mil Mi-8/Mi-17
Vol.15: Antonov An-2
Vol.16: Sukhoi Interceptors
Vol.17: Early Soviet Jet Bombers
Vol.18: Antonov's Heavy Transports
Vol.19: Soviet Heavy Interceptors

Red Star Volume 20
SOVIET/RUSSIAN UNMANNED AERIAL VEHICLES

Yefim Gordon

The Lavochkin OKB's La-17, produced in target drone and recce versions, was the first Soviet UAV to find large-scale use. The Tupolev OKB also developed a line of UAVs, including the Tu-123 Yastreb, Tu-141 Strizh, Tu-243 Reys and the latest Tu-300 recce/strike UAV. Yakovlev's unmanned aircraft are also covered including the Pchela (Bee) surveillance UAV. Mention is also made of UAVs and drones developed by such companies as Strela and the Moscow Aviation Institute.

Softback, 280 x 215 mm, 128 pages
143 b/w photos, 29pp of colour, plus line drawings
1 85780 193 8 **£18.99**

Red Star Volume 21
ANTONOV'S JET TWINS
The An-72/-74 Family

Yefim Gordon and Dmitriy Komissarov

The need to provide a state-of-the-art jet successor to the An-26 led Antonov to develop a twin-turbofan tactical airlifter, the An-72, with its signature high-mounted engines, employing the Coanda effect to dramatically improve wing lift and STOL capability.

The prototype flew in 1977 but it was not until the mid-1980s that production began. Comprehensive listings, both of An-72s and An-74s, detail registration/Bort number, c/n, f/n and operator.

Softback, 280 x 215 mm, 128 pages
125 colour, 90 b/w photographs, 4pp of line drawings
1 85780 199 7 **£19.99**

Red Star Volume 22
MIL'S HEAVYLIFT HELICOPTERS

Y Gordon, S & D Komissarov

The prototype Mil' Mi-6 heavy transport and assault helicopter first flew in 1957. In 1959 it served as the basis for the unconventional Mi-10. In 1967, Mil' amazed the world with the mighty V-12 capable of lifting a 25-ton payload; then in 1977 the OKB achieved success with the smaller but more advanced Mi-26, the world's largest production helicopter. The development history, design and civil and military use of all three types is described in detail.

Softback, 280 x 215 mm, 128 pages
174 b/w photographs, 21pp of colour, 10pp of line drawings
1 85780 206 3 **£19.99**

Red Star Volume 23
SOVIET/RUSSIAN AWACS AIRCRAFT

Yefim Gordon and Dmitriy Komissarov

The need for effective protection of Soviet airspace in areas lacking adequate cover by ground radars led to work on airborne early warning systems. The Tu-126 AEW aircraft, evolved from the Tu-114 airliner, entered service in 1961. It was replaced in the early 1980s by the Ilyushin/Beriyev A-50 AWACS based on the IL-76MD. The highly unorthodox An-71 with its tail-mounted rotodome and the Ka-31 AEW helicopter are also described plus other unbuilt projects.

Softback, 280 x 215 mm, 128 pages
144 colour, 70 b/w photographs, plus 5pp of line drawings
1 85780 215 2 **£19.99**

Red Star Volume 24
TUPOLEV Tu-144
Russia's Concorde

Yefim Gordon and Vladimir Rigmant

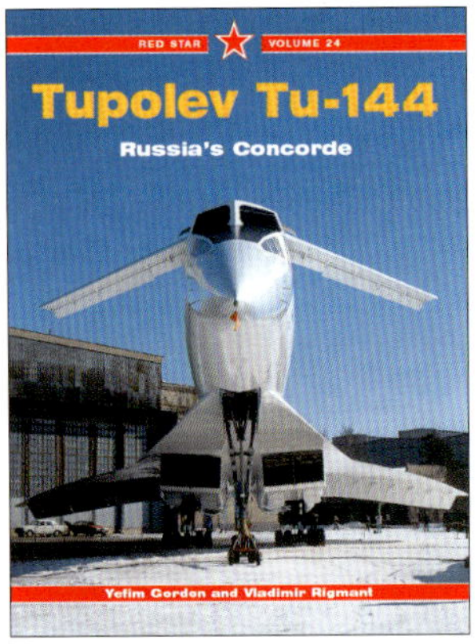

Tasked with creating a supersonic transport ahead of the West as a matter of national prestige, Andrey Tupolev met the target at the cost of a tremendous research and development effort. The Tu-144 took to the air in December 1968, ahead of the Anglo-French Concorde. This detailed account includes the reasons behind its premature withdrawal and a description of its recent use in a joint research programme with NASA.

Softback, 280 x 215 mm, 128 pages
151 b/w photos, 15 pages of colour plus drawings
1 85780 216 0 **£19.99**

Red Star Volume 25
ILYUSHIN IL-12 & IL-14
Successors to the Li-2

Yefim Gordon and Dmitry Komissarov

Designed to supersede the Li-2, the 29-seat IL-12 airliner entered Aeroflot service in 1948. Some 600 were built for Aeroflot and the Soviet armed forces. The improved IL-14 entered production in 1953, the type was exported to China, Bulgaria, Romania and Poland as well as being built by VEB in East Germany and Asia in Czechoslovakia. The total production of over 1,000 aircraft included 203 Avia 14s and Avia 14 Supers – the latter being a pressurised development.

Softback, 280 x 215 mm, 128 pages
180 b/w photos, 16 pages of colour plus 12 pages of drawings
1 85780 223 3 **£19.99**

Red Star Volume 26
RUSSIA'S MILITARY AIRCRAFT IN THE 21st CENTURY

Yefim Gordon

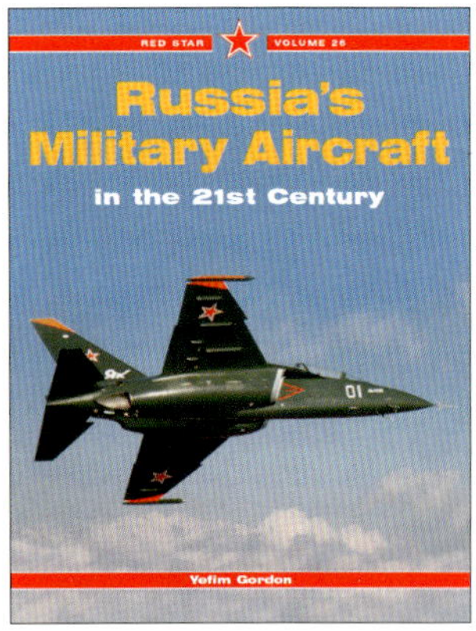

While the large new aircraft programmes of the Cold War era are a thing of the past, military aviation in Russia is not standing still. This volume looks at programmes like the new Mi-8MTKO and Mi-24PN night-capable helicopters, the latest Sukhoi upgrades such as the Su-24M2, Su-25SM and Su-27SM, new and more capable missiles for the Tu-95MS and Tu-160 bombers and the revamping of the training fleet with the Yak-130.

Softback, 280 x 215 mm, 128 pages
269 full colour photographs, plus line drawings
1 85780 224 1 **£19.99**